HYPERFORMANCE

HYPERFORMANCE

Using

COMPETITIVE INTELLIGENCE

for Better Strategy and Execution

T.J.WATERS

JOSSEY-BASS
A Wiley Imprint
www.josseybass.com

Published by Jossey-Bass
A Wiley Imprint
989 Market Street, San Francisco, CA 94103-1741—www.josseybass.com

Library of Congress Cataloging-in-Publication Data
Waters, T. J.
  Hyperformance : using competitive intelligence for better
strategy and execution / T.J. Waters. — 1st ed.
    p. cm.
  Includes bibliographical references and index.
  ISBN 978-0-470-53364-2 (cloth)
  1. Business intelligence. 2. Strategic planning. 3. Competition. I. Title.
  HD38.7.W38 2010
  658.4'72—dc22

                                            2009051936

Printed in the United States of America
FIRST EDITION
HB Printing   10 9 8 7 6 5 4 3 2 1

#435422399

Police, firefighters, medics, and soldiers make life-and-death decisions every day. The danger can be immediate, the surroundings chaotic, and the information incomplete, if not patently wrong. Yet they willingly lead where others fear to tread.

This book is dedicated to my brother, Staff Sergeant Robert C. "Doc" Waters, and first responders everywhere.

You make us proud.

Contents

HYPERFORMANCE

Introduction

A few years ago, a close friend asked me to meet with his company's senior leadership. A competitor was taking market share away from them as easily as a child serving himself an ever-larger piece of pie. And the competitor was so aware of what my friend's firm would do that the competitor's apparent reaction often slightly pre-empted my friend's company's initial action.

I attended a meeting of the C-level leaders of this medium-sized manufacturing firm. I listened to them talk about their corporate strategy, a broad outline of their plans for the coming year, and how this one competitor had already yanked the rug out from under them. It was obvious the competitor had a top-notch intelligence program. I offered what I thought was a compelling evaluation:

"They can win with a wooden sword."

The boardroom fell silent as a funeral, corporate pallbearers bowing their heads around a boardroom table coffin. I allowed them a moment of reflection, certain someone would speak up. Finally, the chief operating officer broke into a wry smile.

"Sun Tzu," he nodded gravely.

I shook my head, only now accepting the gravity of the situation. This guy's idea of a strategy session was reading fortune cookies.

"Never mind," I squeaked, wordlessly willing my friend to seek employment elsewhere.

In the intelligence field, I tend to hear a lot of military comparisons to competition. Smart companies use intelligence as the armed forces do: planning where and how to attack. Unfortunately that comparison is lost on many U.S. business leaders. They quote Sun Tzu's *Art of War* from cover to cover yet say that intelligence is "too military" for business purposes.

Most senior leaders haven't served a day in uniform since high school band camp, yet they bark orders to their "troops" without the benefit of in-depth intelligence. The result can be seen in the *Wall Street Journal*'s daily business obituaries: thousands of shuttered firms, millions of laid-off employees, and billions in lost market capitalization, and all because leaders don't consider a formal intelligence program to be good business.

But every now and again, a leader comes along who recognizes that intelligence is imperative to creating and maintaining a distinct advantage. He takes on and soundly defeats the competition because he understands victory is not about money, or equipment, or employees, but rather on how well the company manages uncertainty. Even if he doesn't believe that business is war, he acknowledges that beating a worthy opponent takes preparation. He can win with a wooden sword.

The wooden sword is a reference to the great Japanese swordsman and strategist Miyamoto Musashi. Born in 1584, he was one of the last great samurai. At the age of thirty, he was undefeated in over sixty individual contests, most ending with his opponent's macabre death. Around 1612 Musashi stopped using steel altogether in favor of wooden swords, individually crafting one for each engagement.

After accepting a challenge, Musashi would spend weeks searching for just the right local tree. On finding it, he would measure and consider each branch until he intuitively knew the right one to excise. Finally, he would reverently carve, shape, and finish a perfect new sword. He would learn the new sword, practicing feverishly, with hours stretching to days, before he was at last ready to receive his challenger.

He carried on like this for thirty more years. He remained undefeated and killed the majority of his opponents.

When Musashi retired in 1643, his victories were chronicled in villages throughout Japan. In the weeks before his death in 1645, he wrote *A Book of Five Rings,* one of the greatest treatises on strategy ever put into print. In fact, it is required reading in Japanese business schools and remains as timely for commerce today as it was to combat in the sixteenth century.

Far from being a tome on swordplay, Musashi told his readers to spend their time and energy learning about their competition. If you know how and where the competitor will strike, you will soundly defeat him every time, regardless of any technical advantage he might have. That was the power in a wooden sword. It didn't take weeks to find the right tree, the right branch, or the right carving techniques. A farmer's rake handle would have been more than sufficient.

Musashi spent those weeks learning everything he could about his opponent. Whom has he defeated? How did he go about doing so? What strategies did he follow based on clan, school, region, and experience? Through careful study and experimentation, he answered all of these questions and identified his opponent's weaknesses.

In the private familiarity sessions with his new sword, he would insert openings in his defense precisely designed to elicit his opponent's weakest techniques—the ones Musashi wanted to be assailed by. In the actual duel, he waited patiently until he recognized the aperture of his opponent's ill-chosen technique. Then, with the benefit of weeks of practiced muscle memory, Musashi unleashed his explosive countermove with lethal precision.

Most opponents never knew they'd been manipulated.

Clearly my friend's competitor knew how to do this as well. Their leaders picked battles carefully. They knew which products to promote and which to let slip quietly into obsolescence.

Can your firm do that? Can you learn to take advantage of your competition's weakest points? Would you know their weak points if you saw them? Most companies don't. As Musashi proved four hundred years ago, with information like that, a wooden sword is a lethal weapon.

In a fragile and uncertain business environment, shareholders are increasingly demanding that management keep up with the competitive Joneses. But it's not just the Joneses anymore. Now it's also Nagawa, and Jacquay, Madarov and Bolivas. Once a firm goes global, every one of its competitors has no choice but to do the same. With financial and communication technology worldwide over the Internet, everything is global.

It means uncertainty has increased by several orders of magnitude. Leaders who only a few years ago thought they could get everything they needed to know over the Internet are learning the reality of economist and Nobel Prize laureate Herbert Simon's words when he said, "A wealth of information creates a poverty of attention."[1] There's simply too much information out there.

Basic Google queries yield millions of hits. Rather than accepting that the information we seek is not available, we instead feel betrayed that the answer is right in front of us. But it is lost in the vast electronic forest of pages stacking useless returns on our screen. Leaders feel misled. Stupid. Trapped.

I hope this book helps change that. It is written for leaders like those at my friend's company. Though they may not like or subscribe to some of the concepts and methods I outline here, they will at least understand how their competitors are exploiting and manipulating them. Maybe they can explain it all to the executives who will be called in to replace them once shareholders have had enough.

There's something in here for practitioners as well: a few new techniques and some templates on my Web site that you can download (tjwaters .com/Hyperformance). But mostly there are ideas about how to serve leaders better. Don't wait for them to tell you what they want because in most cases, they have no idea. It's not that they're not intelligent and motivated people; rather, they just don't know what they don't know. And in fact, this can help you coax them into new areas, getting better clarity on your rivals, and causing those rivals all manner of fits in trying to figure you out. It will bring practitioner and leader closer together, each coming to rely more on the other than they have in the past.

I've been in the intelligence business for longer than I care to admit, moving from research to corporate director to consultant to government officer to military contractor. I've had the honor of working alongside the best and brightest, as well as the indignity of working with the inept and incompetent. Like any other profession, there's always room for improvement.

When intelligence works and makes a measurable impact on the daily activities and long-term success of an organization, it is intimately tied to leadership's overall strategy. That's what this book is about: tying intelligence and strategy together in a unique way. Little here is fundamentally new. Strategic thinkers like Miyamoto Musashi of feudal Japan, the late Colonel John Boyd of the U.S. Air Force, and the masterful Peter Drucker have done much of this many times before. But I hope my unique proposition of linking strategy to a functional intelligence discipline, where each feeds the other, causes leaders to think about competition and conflict in a whole new light.

Strategic planning was a popular corporate endeavor until a few years ago. When the business market was good and stock prices were rising quickly, competitive strategy was no longer considered necessary. The global economy was carrying every reasonably well-run business with it—the "rising tide lifts all boats" approach we read so much about back in the day. But as my father is fond of saying, time and tide wait for no one. Just as the global tide picked up these many firms, it also sent them crashing back down on the rocks. Welcome to 2008.

Corporate leaders, board members, institutional shareholders, executive directors, and a host of other decision makers find themselves in the unenvious position of having nobody left to blame. Now they have to make tough decisions on their own. Now *their* performance, or rather a lack of it, will be on display for everyone to see and judge. If they fail, they will join the statistical ranks of the global business meltdown. So what's a leader to do?

First, they should understand they have options. Second, they should know they can make a difference in the lives of their employees, customers, and shareholders. Third, they should learn they cannot just survive the current market ebb; they can emerge from it stronger and better prepared to take on any competitor foolish enough to challenge them. It's not easy and can be hard on the ego. But done right, the results are spectacular.

Nonprofit groups—religious, educational, cultural, and public service organizations—have many of the same competitive pressures in addition to several unique ones of their own. I've been involved with several large nonprofit groups over the years, and the conflict for resources, the strain to serve clients, and the pressures from stakeholders have never been higher. While profit is not their goal, neither is failure, and leaders' fiduciary responsibilities carry no less liability than any firm regulated by the Securities and Exchange Commission.

Small firms will find a few tools they wouldn't otherwise have time and resources to develop. I hope they help these companies grow and expand, feeding the job-creating economic beast that is the United States. Major corporations will find these templates are easily shared across a large organization by e-mail because they're all Microsoft Excel files. There's no software to download on corporate networks (I'm trying to make this as painless as possible).

All organizations are increasingly facing analytical rather than time-based competition. Companies that correctly analyze competitor, market, and customer information, and then act on it in a timely fashion, will gain a competitive advantage. Time itself offers no distinctive advantage. However, how companies deal with time—how they analyze information, adjust strategy, and maneuver their resources—creates competitive advantage. Fusing intelligence and strategy in order to make faster and more robust decisions with less information is the only means for long-term survival. That's the purpose of competitive intelligence.

Over a decade ago, futurists Alvin and Heidi Toffler characterized how companies were increasingly engaged in time-based competition, citing what they referred to as the hyperconnectivity of global business.[2] Leaders who want to survive must embrace this new reality and accept it is now the norm. It requires a new and unheard-of level of performance.

Hyperformance.

Part One: Understanding Intelligence and Strategy

The DNA of Competitive Advantage

O ne of my closest friends, a long-time partner in crime from our undergraduate days, is a now a professor in the very same Department of Biology where we once tormented instructors with our collegiate antics. Ethan's doctorate is in one of the most difficult, most fascinating, and now most contentious disciplines in the biological sciences: genetics.

James Watson and Francis Crick examined the x-ray studies of one of their contemporaries and first proposed the double helix orientation of the DNA molecule. Their 1953 paper, "Molecular Structure of Nucleic Acids: A Structure for Deoxyribose Nucleic Acid," identified the unusual orientation of the DNA strand and the base pairs of nucleotides that hold the two separated strands together.[1] Watson and Crick received the Nobel Prize for the discovery in 1962, and their names have been synonymous with genetics ever since.

So what could this possibly have to do competitive intelligence?

The purpose of DNA is storing and, over time, expressing information. By its own elegant structure, DNA is intended to be copied, moved, stored, altered, and improved for one purpose: to be passed on. To reproduce. To continue. To be as valuable tomorrow as it was today, or perhaps even more so. Businesses are just like biological organisms in that they wish to remain a going concern.

The areas of DNA with information for building an organism are called *genes*. Other DNA sequences have other sets of instructions, very similar in many respects to software codes (thus, malicious software is described as a virus), that are triggered by internal and external stimuli. This can be as basic as the passage of time or as complicated as a foreign chemical that is threatening the strand's existence and requires a defensive response.

By way of perspective, the largest human chromosome is over 220 million base pairs long. That's a single chromosome of the twenty-three pairs we pass on to our children. Overall there are 3 billion base pairs in each meter-long DNA strand. It's a lot of data packed into every one of our cells. The twisted orientation of DNA is the most efficient way to pack all of that information in as small a space as possible. So overall, the DNA strand is a pretty resilient little model for how business can approach the concept of actionable information.

Companies have similar internal and external triggers. They too pass information on to future generations. They have instructions for building, serving, delivering, and protecting something. Like the DNA strand, they are prepared to take defensive actions when a threat looms. A business also processes, stores, and manipulates important data to store its prior history, serve its current needs, and protect its future interests. Like the DNA strand, it has to accommodate environmental fluctuations that are not always favorable: it must adapt and evolve. As history has repeatedly shown, adaptation is not always an easy thing.

One uncontroversial aspect of Charles Darwin's seminal work on evolution is the criticality of adaptation to survival. All organisms—biological, national, corporate, or otherwise—wish to survive, preferably to thrive, so they store up needed energy and resources for periods when times are tougher. At one time or another, resources were available for all. Sunlight and water, shelter and food, or finance and talent were easily acquired without difficulty. In modern times, however, things have changed.

Resources are increasingly scarce, and this scarcity is now an accepted tenet of existence. As the supply of resources dwindles, the costs of the increasing demand rises. Soon everyone is no longer able to share the limited resources equally. It becomes a zero-sum transaction. For one entity to acquire the resource another entity is left wanting. Competition picks up and creates conflict everywhere. We no longer live together in harmony.

Restaurants covet street corner locations because the ease of entry brings more traffic; as a result, competing restaurants cause the prices of the locations to escalate. Technology companies ratchet up starting salaries for promising graduates most likely to develop the next must-have technology application. Small businesses pitch angel investors and venture capitalists who have less money to spread around than a decade ago. Conflict is not just *a* way of life; it's *the* only way of life.

The purpose of intelligence is to reduce uncertainty in conflict. That's it. That's the whole complicated mess of it. From Cain and Abel to the War on Terrorism, minimizing the uncertainty faced in conflict, combat, or competition has always been the sole purpose of intelligence. While the Bourne trilogy and a resurgent James Bond franchise may alight our imaginations as well as movie screens, in the end, the entire intelligence enterprise of every country or company on earth can be reduced to these four simple words.

But uncertainty is a daunting taskmaster.

Everyone who has ever had to make an important decision has stared into the cold, dark face of uncertainty and trembled. If there were no uncertainty, there would be no reason to consciously have to choose. The correct choice (however we might characterize it) would be immediately obvious. We could simply wave our hand and the problem would vanish. Then we'd have lunch.

But that's not the world in which we live. Every person on the planet must make decisions every day, most of the time with incomplete information. I call them UFOs: useless, false, or outdated. This generally describes what we most often have available to help us with decisions. That's the problem with information: by itself, it's not anything we can make a decision by. It's not actionable.

If it's not actionable, then it's not useful. Quite the contrary, in fact. It's keeping us from making decisions needed to move on with the day. It's slowing us down, making us second-guess ourselves, encouraging others to second-guess us as well, and generally making a mess out of everything. The delay causes other decisions, meetings, and phone calls to stack up. Our productivity drops and aggravation rises. We are less and less effective at our jobs. This is when the dinosaur reference shows up.

I'd love to claim credit for this biological comparison to business, but far smarter people than me began using this metaphor years ago. Comparing business paradigms to dinosaurs meant companies could not adapt to the changing pressures of business. The Internet was in its nascent stage, but the general pace of business, and of life itself, was picking up. Those who kept up with the increases in global communications and decreases in global trade barriers thrived. Those who didn't— dinosaurs who couldn't adapt to the Internet's devastatingly lethal Cretaceous period—fell by the wayside.

So how do organisms, companies, and nations survive such rapidly changing conditions? Is it random? Is it divine intervention? Or is there a plan hidden from outside view, a methodology to ensure, or at least prepare, for an enduring future? If so, what would such a plan look like? How would it work? And how can other organisms make their own similar plans?

These plans are called *strategies*. They've known a series of different definitions over the years depending on who is doing the explaining. From biology to business, from statesmanship to nuclear warfare, strategy is how leaders plan to achieve a specific goal that inevitably revolves around the assumptions of continued existence and growth.

This is an important point. It's not enough to simply survive. Poets and philosophers may beg to differ, but a benign strategy of live and let live, though popular over the centuries, has always failed. *Always.* The menace of conflict simply overwhelms the well-meaning altruistics, largely because it's almost never about only one thing. Conflict has the many heads of Homer's Hydra, the grip of Jules Verne's octopus, and the cunning of Cuba's Che Guevara.

This is what ultimately killed the dinosaurs. It wasn't just one thing, like a comet or a volcano. It was the complex interplay between a comet *and* a volcano. *And* the loss of food sources. *And* the increasing carbon dioxide in the atmosphere. The cooling of the planet. The rise in sea levels. Declining reproduction rates. Each became a force multiplier on the other, compounding like interest on a bad loan until ultimately the outstanding balance was more than the population could maintain. The dinosaurs, creature and corporate, became fossilized records of failing to adjust to a changing environment.

Strategy is a collection of ideas about how to win a conflict. In the best of times, they are written out and tested against available evidence. When that evidence is vague or unclear (remember the UFOs), leaders ask questions to gain additional clarity. As those questions are answered, they have fewer unresolved conflicts and greater confidence with the world and their collective place in it. They start thinking about other questions that were not as pressing until this recent boost of confidence. Now that the primary problems have been assuaged, they can concentrate on secondary concerns.

This is what a good intelligence capability can do: help craft the right questions, because many times leaders don't know what questions to ask, much less when and where to ask them. If we were to design a procedure for exactly how things are now, with a happy customer and a competitor firmly off balance, we'd have our conflict strategy (where we ask questions) firmly aligned with our intelligence capability (for minimizing uncertainty). They must be synchronized, adjusting to the relentless ebb and flow of business activity and information. This is where the DNA metaphor comes into play.

Firms that have learned to make this adaptation have figured out their intelligence operation must be as integral to their business as the strategy it supports. Each must mirror the other. Leaders have questions regarding strategy, and intelligence finds new information to explain the conflict. In other circumstances, intelligence raises the questions themselves, providing insight and opportunities leaders were otherwise unaware of.

Strategy and intelligence must be as tightly interlinked as the two strands of DNA wrapped in that double helix. DNA strands are held together by base pairs of four nucleotides. These base pairs are always in a specific orientation that works only when they're in the correct order. These four nucleotide pairings appear many millions of times throughout a completed DNA strand.

To create a similar bind between intelligence and strategy, we would use the oft-cited four components of the intelligence cycle: tasking, collecting, analyzing, and disseminating. Like the nucleotides in the DNA strand, the four components work only in the correct order.

Decision makers task the intelligence operation with their needs—the decisions they wrestle with, the questions they ask. Intelligence professionals collect the necessary information through computer databases, contracted research, outreach programs, and a thousand other methods for collecting raw data. Qualified professionals analyze the collected data, providing the necessary context for decision makers. Finally, the subject-specific perspective is disseminated to the decision makers, and the entire process begins again.

Like the DNA strand, a business has a great deal of things going on at once across its entire length. Questions arising in one area—finance, for instance—will be completely different from questions in the product development group in another area of the organization. But whatever information is tasked, collected, analyzed, or reported becomes part of the firm's intellectual memory.

This is where the analogy to a DNA strand is more than cosmetic; it explains why strategy and intelligence must be inextricably linked. The magnitude of competitive information moving in, on, and around a company is simply staggering. It occurs at every level of the firm, not simply in the executive suites, meaning that every part of the organization must be capable of conducting and applying it. The purpose of this activity, the management of uncertainty, must permeate the enterprise.

Fire in the Belly

With firms of every conceivable type—in product and services, big and small, publicly traded and family owned—the conversation always starts the same way: "We always seem to be putting out fires." The reason this phrase is so common is that it accurately reflects where most business leaders spend the majority of their time: trying to control, minimize, and correct the latest crisis. Most don't realize this catchphrase isn't just superficial; it's endemic to the fundamental problem of how they deal with uncertainty.

This comparison toward corporate combustion evolved because business leaders choose to have the same circumstances as those forced on a firefighter. Despite a highly skilled workforce with state-of-the-art communication equipment, firefighters have little specific preparation for each conflict. As a result, nothing really begins until someone yells, "Fire"!

Firefighters have no idea what kind of problem they're facing until they arrive on scene. En route, they might learn the fire is residential versus industrial. But that's after the clock is already ticking and they're entering harm's way. They know nothing about this specific location. Are dangerous chemicals inside? Is natural gas piped in nearby? Is anyone trapped inside?

The uncertainty firefighters face is hard for outsiders to grasp. Often they know absolutely nothing about the situation until they're literally walking through flames. As soon as the truck rolls to a stop and they start pulling on gear and getting access to a water source, they're observing the blaze and analyzing what they see. What's burning? How intensely? Is it growing? If so, how? They face massive uncertainty, risking their lives as they try to answer the most basic of questions to support their leadership's nascent strategy.

Firefighters are quick thinkers and highly trained. They have to be because their base strategies are standardized, awaiting real-time intelligence to confirm that certain conditions exist before they adjust to the circumstances at the scene. Once the type of fire, the conditions of the structure, and a host of other questions are answered, specific changes are communicated to customize their assault.

The basics of the fire triangle are drilled into rookies early in their training: fuel, heat, and oxygen are all a fire requires, and it must have all three. Take away any one, and the fire collapses and dies out. When firefighters arrive and begin their reconnoiter, the information they gain is radioed to a commander, who decides which dimension of the fire to attack and how. Skills and strategies follow standard operating procedures until leadership decides what to do.

But this takes time. The destruction is continuing and possibly growing, increasing uncertainty because the information initially communicated may no longer be accurate. It's why the initial period of firefighting is the most hectic and confused and when most accidents and injuries take place. This is when uncertainty is highest.

A four corners display (Figure 1.1) depicts the relative degree of uncertainty that firefighters face in four distinct dimensions. In each area, the shaded regions show uncertainty in the context of darkness and spread. There's little uncertainty in the areas of strategy or protagonists. They've relentlessly trained together, knowing each other's strengths and weaknesses. Leaders' basic strategic preferences are common knowledge to all. Firefighting skills are gained through repetitious training. Command strategies are developed through experience and classroom education. All of this has been worked out in the past. As a result, uncertainty is very low in both areas. It's the specifics of the *present* fire that are unknown.

The fire triangle still exists, of course, but how to attack it is impossible to determine until the firefighters arrive at the scene. The uncertainties caused by chaos, randomness, and pure chance are rampant in the antagonists quadrant. There is no preparation on the specifics of the fire

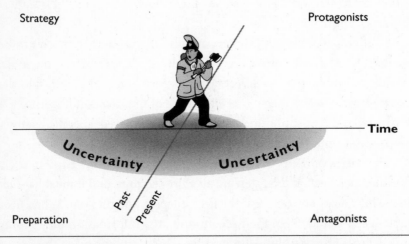

Figure 1.1 Firefighters have high uncertainty when it comes to preparation (they don't know where the next fire will be) and conflict (they don't know what random flammables might be present) when they arrive.

beforehand; the firefighters must gather all their own information as the conflict unfolds. Uncertainty is very high.

Once they've learned a bit about the site, leaders can formulate a strategy based on the skills of people available to combat the fire. They know firefighters have all the requisite skills; it's just a manner of communicating the specific scene circumstances based on the intelligence gathered at the scene. Leaders can choose to use retardants (reduce oxygen), back burns (consume fuel), or water deluge (reduce temperature) to bring a fire under control.

Unlike a fire, however, competition isn't always rational. Whereas fire is responsive to physics, people are highly unpredictable. Unconstrained by simple rules of physics, rivals can react in foolish ways. Fire has only three dimensions. Business has dozens, from industry type, to regional location, to financial structure, to many others. Uncertainty becomes exponential. Like the fire triangle, each dimension shapes the others (Figure 1.2). Devoid of preparation and forced to react to events as they occur is a good way to get burned.

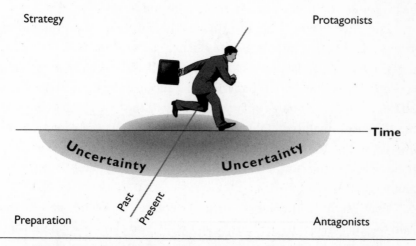

Figure 1.2 Businesses without a reliable intelligence function have a similar high uncertainty in preparation and antagonists. Hence, they are always "putting out fires."

Many leaders run their businesses the same way. Despite highly skilled employees and expensive communications infrastructure, there is virtually no preparation for the conflict they know is coming. Like firefighters, they walk in virtually blind, hastily designing reactive strategies with no specific preparation to minimize their uncertainty.

The Intelligence Cycle

The classic intelligence cycle is neat, easily displayed, and quickly understood. The problem is that it doesn't really work that way. It's too static, too rigid, with too much distance between leaders and intelligence professionals. It's too linear for the complex problems businesses face today. They no longer have the luxury of things simply being complicated.

There are myriad ways to explain complicated versus complex, but let's keep things simple and consider the nature of conflict in two popular sports. Baseball is a sport where (broadly speaking) a single player is sequentially active at a time. In football, twenty-two men are moving and altering each other's behavior in each play. Baseball is complicated. Football is complex. This distinction is often lost on people.

The pitcher winds up and throws the ball. And then the batter swings. And then if he misses, the catcher captures the ball. If he connects, a defending player tries to catch the ball and then throws it to the appropriate teammate. The batter, having successfully hit the ball, takes off for first base. The only concurrent activity is the base runner connecting the bases in a predictable order. His destination and direction are known, so the defending team simply has to throw the ball to the teammate closest to the runner in order to intercept him. There's little uncertainty here.

Contrast this with football. The eleven players on each team take the field together. When the ball snaps, all twenty-two players begin moving. Their actions are highly unpredictable. The routes taken vary widely from one play to the next, one quarter to the next, one game to the next. Each player's activity can have a compounding effect on the activity of the other twenty-one. It is dynamic and evolving, and it engages a number of stakeholders (players) simultaneously. It is, in a word, complex.

This is an unswerving contrast. Actions are often complicated—they can be formulated and standardized—while *inter*actions are always complex. *What* we do is complicated; *how* we do it is complex. This is due to the influence of chance. Random (chance) events are part of complex systems. Things we cannot anticipate, avoid, or control influence decision making in ways that cannot be predicted.

We adjust to random events not by stopping, as we would with a complicated problem, but rather by using these as feedback to adjust decisions on the fly based on prior planning. In other words, we adjust our strategy to work around these interruptive events and continue toward our intended goal. People continually incorporate feedback from everything they see and hear.

Every action we take creates a reaction, and that reaction is incorporated into our next action. This is a feedback loop. Feedback loops are how we control everything from reaching for a doorknob, to feeding ourselves, to waving at a friend we see on the street. Each action has a multitude of unexpected responses that we have to incorporate and adjust for. This is true in intelligence as well.

Managing Versus Leading

Decision makers, regardless of how smart or intuitive they may be, rarely make good decisions over long periods unless they have a support element to help them do it. Once leaders have outlined a strategy, they protect it as if it were their baby. Whatever can be created must be protected, and a competent intelligence function will follow the leader's strategy, filling in answers and making suggestions while abiding by the decision maker's lead.

But being a follower is not synonymous with being a doormat. Intelligence exists to answer questions, but it also exists to discretely challenge leadership when needed. Leaders should expect their intelligence staff to challenge them; certainly their external stakeholders will, and as my military clients like to say, "It is better to sweat the brief than bleed the battle."

Intelligence staff must (respectfully and professionally) challenge leaders' biases, assumptions, and the second-order effects of their decisions.

Senior leaders answer to someone: stockholders, customers, board members. There's never been a leader who was beyond reproach. If leaders are to survive the juggernaut of forces aligning figuratively and literally against them, they will need and should expect the complete support of a skilled intelligence staff.

To do that requires an uncharacteristic level of trust. Trust is the single most important factor between leaders and those who serve them. It's also the greatest metric followers use to evaluate their superiors. Having been given information not shared with others, how does the leader use it? Does she abuse her authority with it? It's happened many times before and likely always will, particularly if an honest initiative by the intelligence professional leads to a particularly tempting opportunity.

This level of commitment is not easy. It is not just acquiring and analyzing data. It is also managing the leader's expectations. Leaders outrank everyone else, but their staff has to manage them—their time, their priorities, and their access to information. Executive assistants set the schedule on a calendar, but the intelligence professional helps decide the priority of decisions. How much time to dedicate to each? Which decision must be made now and which can wait? It means understanding a leader maybe better than she understands herself. When you disagree, (and at times you certainly will), you must do so without being disagreeable. There will be days when the pressure seems overwhelming.

But knowing where the limits and comfort zones are can minimize these. A leader who prefers the big picture shouldn't be bogged down with details. If time is an issue, don't wait until the end of the meeting to bring up a problem; start with it to ensure it is addressed. Maximize the interaction between strategy and intelligence to ensure the leader is prepared for the next meeting with her superiors.

Leaders should expect intelligence professionals to ensure they are addressing the right problem. What may appear simple could actually be complex; what looks isolated may be endemic and growing. Leaders want all the facts required for a decision and want some options to work with. Even if intelligence professionals don't like the options (*especially* if they don't like them), they must ensure that leaders are aware of them. Challenge what is actually known from what is simply expected. What assumptions are leaders making? Why do they think that? How valid is the information?

Being a leader is about making difficult decisions with incomplete information. That will not change (if anything, it will only get worse). Intelligence professionals must prepare some thoughts on the problem being addressed and offer options, but be prepared to say, "I don't know," when they don't. They'll gain respect as a result, particularly after they go out and find the answers in a timely fashion.

Stages of Conflict

This intelligence-strategy linkage, which is never restricted to the C-level executive team, should be applied in all three stages of conflict: strategic, operational, and tactical. Everywhere along the business DNA strand, the four stages of the intelligence cycle support different decision makers' needs. A board member is briefed on a new corporate debt restructuring, an engineering chief collects data on a competitor's patent filing, and a field sales group is e-mailed an evaluation of a competitor's new product. All of these efforts minimize uncertainty on decisions made throughout the firm.

This chapter opened by noting how the DNA strand stores, transfers, and expresses information over time. That's worth revisiting. Derisively characterized as the fourth dimension (after height, width, and depth), time rarely gets its due attention. More often than not, however, it is the most important dimension.

Time is what differentiates discrete stages of a conflict. Strategic stages are long, over-the-horizon decisions that make take years, or longer in some instances, to discern if they were correct. Operational stages are often characterized as campaigns (referring to the life span of political campaigns) and measured in months. Tactical stages are local maneuvering efforts over or around a competitor's activities.

Like many other aspects of conflict, time is contextual and rarely translates well from one industry to another. Development times and costs for fashionable clothing lines are completely different from those for computer game software. The sunk capital costs and strategic risks of drug development can stretch into decades before a new medication is available at the drugstore. Alternatively, the latest movie tie-in toy for a child's fast food meal can be designed, produced, shipped, and delivered in a few weeks. Just as these strategic-level time lines vary wildly, their operational and tactical times are likewise dissimilar, with each industry operating with its own uniquely individual rhythm.

The size of competing firms, the depth and breadth of the market, and the expansion or contraction of that market also factor in for these time signatures. The size of the firm is generally a resource constraint: Microsoft can afford to spend big dollars sooner and faster than a small mom-and-pop business. But it is not automatic. Smaller companies often develop stronger ties to customers because they have fewer of them. Larger firms spread themselves around the market more, and sometimes too much. Customers may appreciate the smaller companies' perceived more attentive nature, especially if the customer is (or recently was) a small firm itself.

In either case, what the customer wants is *value*. Do you know your customer's values? As before, asking better questions results in better decisions. What are the dimensions of value for your customer's business? What are the dimensions of value for your competitor? Focus your time and attention on these critical values. Determining the dimensions of value identifies vulnerabilities to exploit. Design solutions for customers and complications for competitors. The common denominator between them is time.

What we see in all three dimensions is that decision makers have less time and less information in which to make decisions. This rush is largely driven by the speed of global communications, the hyperactive nature of competition, and the complexity of industry. Decision makers often must publicly respond to a crisis before they fully understand what has taken place, much less have time to rationally analyze it. Ironically, smaller firms may have an advantage in some respects. Their smaller geographical configuration means that information remains in a single time zone, a single language, and a single leadership culture, allowing faster decisions and allowing the small business Davids to craft better strategy than the corporate Goliaths.

But it still comes down to supporting individual decision makers across a firm. And across any organization, everyone's appreciation for, comfort with, and reaction to uncertainty and decision making will be individually unique. At the Pittsburgh Mind-Body Center at the University of Pittsburgh, Amhad Hariri is unlocking the complexities of decision making and how we can work around any genetic predispositions we might have that might work against us.[2]

Hariri's lab models genetics and MRI-derived brain scans to determine how individuals respond to different types of risk and reward. Some genetic variations reduce the fear of uncertainty in the brain. Others make individuals more aggressive in unskilled gambling situations. How and why the brain's reward system works, certainly an important aspect of strategy and intelligence, is an emerging science with important implications for business, government, and military decision making. Hariri's research has found that only about 20 percent of the variation for an individual's tolerance for managing risk (read: uncertainty) is genetically bound. The rest is a result of education, experience, upbringing, and training. So modeling the behavior of a specific person requires an elegant analysis of all these factors. The company a leader keeps can also drive decision making, including a negative impact. The 24/7 news cycle requires leaders to make faster decisions with less information. Only an integrated intelligence-strategy link can analyze an opportunity (or problem) with enough advance notice to determine a course of action and maneuver around the issue accordingly.

But speed itself is no panacea. Speedy decisions are useless if they are flawed, based on inaccurate or nonexistent information, and ultimately negatively affect the outcome of the conflict. Even small companies can be stuck in bureaucratic or technical lethargy with the wrong leadership. Initiative is a superb advantage if leaders give teams the freedom to storm the market when the time is right. A well-timed initiative can trump the economies of scale, capital, or political connections. But such time-centric advantages are fleeting. If successful, they'll be copied immediately and competitive advantage will be lost.

Rallying the Troops

Military planners spend an inordinate amount of time reading over intelligence assessments to decide how to engage an adversary. If the right skills and tools are not available, they don't execute the plan because they know it will fail. So they collect new information, develop new strategies, or use different skills and come up with a newer, better plan.

The four corners display for a soldier is radically different from that of a firefighter (Figure 1.3). With reliable intelligence about a target, planners can develop the best strategy for engaging it. They'll assemble whatever specific skills are needed for that specific target using a specific strategy as opposed to a standard off-the-shelf solution. Soldiers, with their skills and communication systems, respond to each other and with

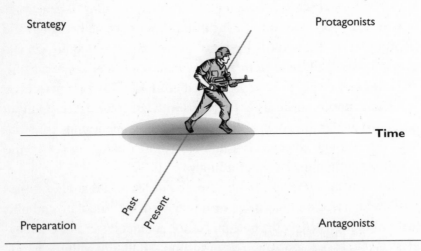

Figure 1.3 By comparison to firefighters and businesspeople, soldiers deal with much less uncertainty, using intelligence to plan their operations and applying a strategy to manipulate opponents to improve their likelihood of success.

How do I explain the successful insurgents in Iraq and Afghanistan? Quite simply: an insurgency is a radical change in conflict (Figure 1.4). It's not just a different battle but a completely different war. Insurgencies eliminate the line between protagonist and antagonist so soldiers cannot easily discern an enemy hiding among a civilian population. Uncertainty escalates rapidly and slows decision making because intelligence preparation focused on locations rather than populations. This creates operational delays through randomness and chaos, offsetting U.S. technological superiority, and turning the advantage to insurgent forces. Time becomes the insurgents' weapon as they outwill (outlast) the invading force. Companies facing the threat of disruptive technologies face equal uncertainties: they are unable to discern who their adversary is, what the adversary's technology is capable of, and how best to respond. Like an insurgency, the adversary does not fit into a nicely labeled category and therefore is a very dangerous opponent.

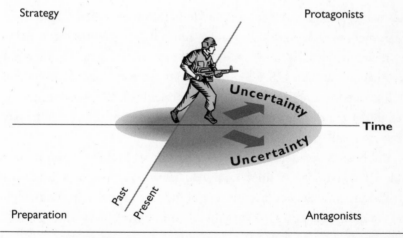

Figure 1.4 Insurgents change the conflict from territory to population, eliminating the line between protagonist and antagonist and increasing uncertainty by masking the identity of the enemy. Business leaders face a similar dilemma from so-called disruptive technologies, which radically change the environment.

the environment to carry out the strategy as quickly as possible. When planners have enough lead time, uncertainty is minimal.

The soldier's skills are as finely tuned as those of firefighters. Leaders are similarly experienced and have formally studied the combat arts. But unlike firefighters, they usually have advanced preparation before they enter a combat area. They're able to design strategies that allow them to affect their antagonists in the conflict dimension, shaping the battlefield as they fight on it in the present. Properly done, uncertainty is minimized.

This doesn't guarantee a positive outcome to the conflict. Far from it. By its very nature conflict is chaotic, the forces of random events affecting each other in unanticipated ways. But with proper preparation, leaders worry less about minimizing random events and focus more on how shaping the battlefield forces opponents to make mistakes, increasing the opponent's uncertainty.

Firefighters Copy the Suit-and-Tie Crowd

The success of alternative futures and forecasting in business has led the fire services to seek innovative ways to integrate intelligence methodologies for reducing uncertainties about the threats they face. The National Fire Academy and the U.S. Fire Administration are moving to incorporate intelligence training into their course curriculum. With over 1 million firefighters, paramedics, and emergency medical technicians nationwide, this is no small project.

But business leaders can also learn a lot from firefighters. Both must deal with a great deal of uncertainty. Business leaders are at a disadvantage because intelligence is rarely taught in U.S. business schools, though that is rapidly changing to catch up to a number of successful overseas programs that target American companies.

But there's a business unique to the United States that is the envy of the world for its worldwide brand recognition, maniacally dedicated customer base, and unparalleled financial success. A look into the team inside the team that makes the National Football League the most successful team sport on the planet is the focus of the next chapter.

Leadership's
New Benchmark

I f business is war and football is business, is football then war?

I mentioned in Chapter One the complexity of football. The common stereotype of professional football players as dumb jocks doesn't stand five minutes of scrutiny when you consider their typical schedule. Sure, there are workouts—weightlifting and practice scrimmages. But mostly there are meetings. Sometimes it's five guys around a conference room table; other times the entire team meets in an auditorium. Granted, the seats are plush leather in stadium-style arrangement, but it's still a meeting. You think you spend a lot of time in meetings? Consider the NFL team's typical weekly meeting schedule in Figure 2.1. What could they possibly be doing?

They're *preparing* for the competition. Only a fraction of the day is spent out on the field in practice. Over 75 percent of their time is spent in an auditorium, meeting room, classroom, or viewing theater. Football players already know how to play tough; what they want is to play smart. This is where intelligence supports strategy. Few other leaders have as insightful a grasp on the competitive environment as that of an NFL head coach.

Under the guidance of Tampa Bay Buccaneers director of player development Eric Vance, I received an extraordinary view inside the rarefied world of an NFL team. After a tour of the Buccaneers' new

Sunday	Monday	Tuesday	Wednesday	Thursday	Friday	Saturday
1	**2**	**3**	**4**	**5**	**6**	**7**
		Players Day Off	5:30-6:30 a.m.–Open Weight Room	5:30-6:30 a.m.–Open Weight Room	5:30-6:30 a.m.–Open Weight Room	7:00-9:00 a.m.–Breakfast
			7:00-9:00 a.m.–Breakfast	7:00-9:00 a.m.–Breakfast		7:00 a.m.–Treatment/Lift Group
		7:30-9:00 a.m.–Breakfast	7:00 a.m.–Treatment/Lift Group	7:00 a.m.–Treatment/Lift Group	7:00-9:00 a.m.–Breakfast	8:00 a.m.–S.T. Walk-Through
			7:30-8:00-401K Meeting	Players Weigh-In		8:15 a.m.–QB Meeting
		8:00-12:00 Run & Lift	8:00 a.m.-S.T. & QB Meetings	8:00 a.m.-S.T. & QB Meetings	8:00 a.m.–FG Pro Meeting	9:00 a.m.–Team Meeting
			8:45 a.m.–Team Meeting	8:45 a.m.–Team Meeting	8:15 a.m.-S.T. & QB Meetings	9:05-9:50 a.m.–Walk-Through
		9:00–Treatment	8:50-10:35-Unit Meetings	8:50-10:35-Unit Meetings	9:00 a.m.–Team Meeting	Pack Game Day Bag
			10:45-11:15 a.m.-Walk-Through	10:45-11:15 a.m.-Walk-Through		12:30 p.m. Security Briefing
		11:30-1:00 p.m.–Lunch	11:15-12:30 p.m. Lunch/Taping	11:15-12:30 p.m. Lunch/Taping	10:30-10:50 a.m. Walk-Through	1:30 p.m. Buses Depart Facility
			12:00-12:30 p.m. Position Meetings	12:00-12:30 p.m. Position Meetings	10:50-11:00 a.m. Stretch	2:00 p.m. Plane Departs
			12:40 p.m.–Special Teams on Field	12:40 p.m.–Special Teams on Field	11:00 a.m.-12:15 p.m. Practice	3:45 p.m.–Arrive in Boston
			12:55 p.m.–Pat & Go	12:50 p.m.–Pat & Go		**Night Before A Game Meetings**
			12:55 p.m.–Stretch	12:55 p.m.–Stretch	12:00-1:30 p.m. Lunch	7:00 p.m.–Chapel & Mass
			1:05-2:55 p.m.–Practice	1:05-2:55 p.m.–Practice		7:30 p.m.-S.T. & QB Meetings
			Post-Lift/Meetings	Post-Lift/Meetings		8:00 p.m.–Unit Meetings
			5:30 p.m.–Coaches Dinner	5:30 p.m.–Coaches Dinner		8:30 p.m.–Team Meeting
						8:45 p.m.–Snack
						11:00 p.m.–Curfew/Bedcheck
8	**9**	**10**	**11**			
Game Day	7:00-9:00 a.m.–Breakfast	Players Day Off	6:30-8:30 a.m.–Open Weight Room			
Game #5			7:00-9:00 a.m.–Breakfast			
@Dallas Cowboys	9:00 a.m.–Treatment	7:00-9:00 a.m.–Breakfast	7:00 a.m.–Treatment/Lift Group			
12:00 p.m. Kick Off			7:30-8:00-401K Meeting			
	10:00-12:00-Run & Lift	8:00-12:00-Run & Lift	8:00 a.m.-S.T. & QB Meetings			
7:00 a.m.–Wake Up Call			8:45 a.m.–Team Meeting			
	8:00 a.m.-S.T. & QB Meetings	9:00 a.m.–Treatment	8:50-10:35-Unit Meetings			
7:00-9:00 a.m.–Pregame Meal			10:45-11:15 a.m.-Walk-Through			
Mandatory Check In	Meeting Schedule	11:30-1:00 p.m.–Lunch	11:15-12:30 p.m. Lunch/Taping			
	12:15 p.m.-S.T. & QB Meetings		12:00-12:30 p.m. Position Meetings			
8:00 a.m.–Early Bus Departs	1:15 p.m. Team Meeting		12:40 p.m.–Special Teams on Field			
9:30 a.m.–Last Bus Departs	Position Meetings		12:50 p.m.–Pat & Go			
12:00 p.m.–Kickoff	(Film Review)		12:55 p.m.–Stretch			
5:00 p.m.–Depart Dallas			1:05-2:55 p.m.–Practice			
8:30 p.m.–Arrive in Tampa			Post-Lift/Meetings			
			5:30 p.m.–Coaches Dinner			

Figure 2.1 A typical weekly meeting schedule for an NFL team in midseason.

state-of-the-art office and workout facility known as One Buc Place, Eric introduced me to some of the Buccaneers brain trust.

Dave Levy is the director of video operations. A twelve-year veteran of the team, Levy is responsible for collecting game film from the previous week for analysis, as well as film from the following week's competitor, and making it available on the Buccaneers' private computer network. The NFL tightly controls game film and how it's used. At each game are two NFL-regulated cameras: one in an end zone and one in the press box at the fifty-yard line. With each camera crew are representatives from that day's opposing team and the next two teams in the schedule to ensure there's no funny business during taping.

Actually *taping* is a misnomer. All game film is digital now, and Levy's production lab is the most advanced in the NFL. Team owner Malcolm Glazer gave Levy a blank slate for designing the best video lab in sports. Game film is forensic. The action is too fast and chaotic to analyze during the game itself, and the NFL forbids video or computer analysis while a game is in progress.

Levy's department, once crammed into a back office at the old Buccaneers facility, now has some of the best Hollywood-quality studio electronics available. In addition to the stored video is a computer system to slice and dice the data into individual plays. A bank of computer servers is filled with cutouts of the games, cross-referenced in a file structure unlike anything else in sports.

Every play is meta-tagged to make it easily called out by coaches, staff, and players. Each first down is compiled in a file. So is every kickoff return. Every passing play is filed separately, as is every draw play. This multidimensional cataloging makes reviewing specific plays easier.

Levy's staff prepares individual video montages for each player every week of the season, showing who will be lining up against him for the next game. The video shows the opposing player's two most recent games and how he played against the Buccaneers the last time the teams squared off. Players use various handheld video devices so they can study at home.

But simply collecting videos and cutting them up into individual vignettes is not enough. Sure, players gain insight into their opponents' moves by watching film, but somebody must still analyze the information before it is of any real value. If Levy's staff of video technicians represents the science of collection, then the quality control coaches and scouts provide the art of analysis.

Every NFL team has a professional staff of scouts and coaches whose job is to analyze game video and live practice sessions of opposing teams. They write reports, assemble various plays into instructional vignettes, and chart opposing team strategies on whiteboards for players and coaches. Many are former players. Shelton Quarles is one such player turned analyst.

A native of Nashville, Tennessee, Quarles played for Vanderbilt University before going professional and spending ten years as a linebacker for the Buccaneers. He was a member of the 2002 Buccaneer Super Bowl Championship team and holds the record for the team's longest play: a ninety-eight-yard interception for a touchdown against the Green Bay Packers in 2001. When his playing career ended in 2007, the Buccaneers front office chose to leverage Quarles's experience and brought him back as a scout. They have not been disappointed.

On the day we spoke, Quarles was reviewing game video and furiously scribbling notes from the previous week's Detroit Lions game. He was a game film addict as a player and quickly took to the role of scout. Game film is very revealing when properly used. Like a military battle, it's only afterwards, in the quiet calm away from the action, that events can be isolated, judged, and evaluated for leadership.

"Timing," he said. "I was always working on timing when I played. How did he fake, trying to make me hesitate? What's his preferred first contact?"

Quarles backs up a video clip to explain. "See this? It's so subtle you wouldn't notice it in real time. He's trying to compel the defender to overcommit, using his own weight and momentum against him."

"Like judo?" I ask.

"Exactly," Quarles nods. "The guy next to him does something completely different. It's a ploy causing hesitation. Look at that—almost two seconds. He's got plenty of time to see where the play is going and move in that direction, forcing the lineman to readjust."

Quarles and the other scouts spend countless hours dissecting plays, scribbling notes, talking with each other and the team's quality control coaches. They are responsible for figuring out the competing team's most likely strategies based on previous patterns. They brief the offensive and defensive coordinators, who have notes from their own analysis of the game.

The coaches and staff then meet with the players. There are breakout sessions for defense and offense, as well as full team meetings throughout the week. Quarterbacks have their own coach and forensic film assessments. Special teams, which handle things like extra points and punts, have been the deciding factor for several Super Bowl champions in recent years, and they similarly meet to discuss game film, play charts, and biographies of opposing players. That's when the real homework begins.

In addition to the game film provided by Dave Levy, every player receives a two-inch-thick binder every week. In it are Shelton Quarles's scouting reports, analysis by quality control coaches, and play charts diagramming the opposing team's preferred plays. As if memorizing their own six-hundred-page playbook at the beginning of the season wasn't taxing enough, every player gets a new custom-tailored report (in essence, an intelligence product) every week of the season.

With this product they do homework on their own, debate with teammates and coaches, and watch *more* game film. Whereas fans watch the ball, players are watching the competition, trying to discern the opposing team's technical skills, psychological tricks, physical capabilities, and tactical decision making. This is important because during the game it is the *players* on the field, not the leadership on the sidelines, who make the majority of individual decisions. Like a field sales organization, this is when boardroom strategy bangs heads with the stark reality of competition.

Managed Learning

This type of organizational learning was the mantra of legendary management consultant W. Edwards Deming. No stranger to conflict, Deming was a key assistant to General Douglas MacArthur during World War II. He advised the general on numerous aspects for rebuilding Japan's shattered economy after 1947. In 1950 Deming returned to Japan, sharing his theories on manufacturing and management, playing a significant role in positioning Japan as a world leader in what became the globalization movement. Deming is widely regarded as one of the most prominent Westerners in modern Japanese history, and in 1960 he was granted the Order of the Sacred Treasure medal, a civilian award given at the discretion of the emperor.

Deming was featured in a 1980 NBC television special, "*If Japan Can . . . Why Can't We?*" that profiled the island nation's unparalleled resurrection as a manufacturing behemoth, with Deming credited for much of the success. In 1982 MIT's Center for Advanced Engineering published Deming's *Quality, Productivity, and Competitive Position,* which was later republished as *Out of the Crisis.*[1] Far from engineering geek-speak, Deming's work focused on what he considered the real problem of business: leadership or, more correctly, the lack of it.

Deming points out how failure to prepare brings about market loss, which then brings about job loss. He believed company leaders should be judged not just on quarterly dividends but also on their innovative plans to stay in business, protect company investments, and provide jobs through new products and services. He urged a long-term commitment to what he referred to as *new learning* and how such a philosophy must be forced on organizations if they are to grow and survive. (Note again how survival hinges on growth.)

In the mid-1980s, Deming's expertise was finally recognized in the United States, and he began a long association in rebuilding America's automobile industry, whose market share losses to Japan (using Deming's techniques) could no longer be ignored. In 1986 Ford rolled out what would become the wildly successful Ford Taurus/Mercury Sable. For the first time in over sixty years Ford's earnings exceeded those of cross-town rival General Motors. In a letter to *Autoweek* magazine, Ford chairman Donald Peterson wrote, "The changes that have been taking place here have their roots directly in Dr. Deming's teachings."[2]

Deming's enduring work are the fourteen points for management that he set out. The first of these key principles is, "Create consistency of purpose toward improvement of product and service with the aim to *become competitive and stay in business.*"[3] The American business establishment pigeonholed Deming as a manufacturing expert, but in fact his focus was leadership. Without effective leadership, a company will not survive. Deming didn't so much make a transition from conflict (war) to competition (business) as he proved their enduring similarities, that is, how much the two parallel each other.

In doing so, he quickly went from military consultant for the victor of World War II to business consultant for a defeated nation looking to reestablish its leadership. He was as successful in the latter as he'd been with the former because conflict and competition are flip sides of the same coin. Each requires a desire to minimize leadership uncertainty (through intelligence) so they can develop a series of well-planned decisions to achieve a specific goal (their strategy).

Deming posited two key leadership ideas. The first is that *experience by itself teaches nothing.* Everyone has experience, but not everyone can apply it. Second, *there is no substitute for knowledge.* As previously noted, the world is drowning in information but starving for knowledge. These are powerful statements on their own merit; combined, they demonstrate why intelligence and strategy must be linked to be successful. The Japanese, having few natural resources as an island nation and even fewer as a conquered people, took Deming at his word and began a massive effort to assimilate knowledge from around the world.

These two key dimensions transcend business, politics, and combat. But by themselves, they are not enough to offer a reasonable expectation for success. It's not enough to simply gather the data. Information is useless unless it is analyzed and disseminated to leaders who can (and will) *act* on it. So we might broadly restate Deming's contribution to the intelligence and strategy matrix as *preparation* and *communication.*

These relatively simple characteristics have derailed more insightful, sincere, and intelligent leaders than all of their character flaws and criminal intentions combined. They are one brilliant man's interpretation for the concepts for adoption and adaptation. And they prove why professional football is the preeminent expression of integrating intelligence and strategy in business.

Huddle Up

Why do football players huddle in a circle to get their instructions? Can't the quarterback take a few steps away from the line of scrimmage, turn his back toward the opponents, and talk to his linemen before they step up?

Of course he could, and at one time this was the common practice. The modern football huddle was created by players at Gallaudet University.[4] Deaf players using American Sign Language (ASL) communicated on the field just as they did elsewhere. But the opposing sideline could intercept the quarterback's signs to the squad. So teammates huddled around where they could see the quarterback's hands and face (a crucial aspect of ASL) while blocking the line of sight to anyone else. This distinctive orientation for leadership's transfer of information remains to this day.

The transfer of information is largely a visual enterprise. When books and magazines are read, or television and computer screens are watched, information is filed away using means that cognitive psychologists are still figuring out. It is generally a one-way street, with information moving in a single direction. Technology has exploited this ease. Although information is often expensive to create, it is simple to copy at little additional expense. Hence we see online newspapers, sports listings, classified advertising, and a subculture of one-to-many technologies such as Facebook.

Contrast this with the act of communication, which is *exchanging* information. We listen and talk, a two-way exchange that is largely an auditory endeavor. Can we absorb information just by listening? Of course; we recall school lectures and telephone conversations years later. But the preferred means of long-term retention of information is visual. We are programmed for visual learning. Why are e-mail messages so easily misread? It's because text, for all its popularity, lacks the contextual nuances of body language and voice inflection. This forced the creation of emoticons (graphic displays of emotion) and textual shortcuts (like *LOL* for laugh out loud).

The professional application of the football huddle for protecting visual communications under extreme circumstances demonstrates the criticality of this exchange. While we can communicate by e-mail or text messaging, it's generally not optimal. But many of us have adopted it for a number of reasons.

Adopting is the act of finding and accepting something created by another to take by choice into a relationship. *Adapting* is a modification of current activity according to changing circumstances. Appreciating the difference between the two terms is crucial to leaders' applying them successfully. Adoption means identifying the advantages of another organization. Adaptation is applying those advantages to your own organization.

It's not simply identifying a new method or tactic and transferring it over like some plug-and-play application. It must be adjusted to fit the new organization. Tailoring adopted methods, techniques, tactics, maneuvers, or skills requires organizational leaders to create circumstances where adaptation is required, not just encouraged.

Organizational inertia will create a slow death to any adaptation attempt that is not fully backed (read: forced) by the highest levels. I argue that leadership must be the force behind the adaptation. If it is left to the trenches, it will receive superficial attention at best, awaiting a future time when nobody is looking to be pitched aside to join all the previous flavor-of-the-month ideas that died after initial leadership interest.

Adopting and adapting require leaders to foster an environment that may appear to border on anarchy to an outside observer. This is not the place or time for quiet, established, and time-tested standard operating procedures. They are too rigid for the pace of business today. Leaders must identify what needs their attention the most at any given time. These are the areas where they must concentrate their limited time.

Time is the assassin targeting many potential leaders. Plenty of people have leadership potential, but they cannot effectively manage the limited time available to prove themselves to colleagues and stakeholders. They don't spend the time to identify what requires their time. No, that's not an oxymoron. It's an unfortunate fact.

In the hurried pace of phone calls, visitors, meetings, and deadlines, many leaders fail to optimize the time required to do their jobs. This most precious resource requires leaders to quickly and succinctly assess what most needs their attention and what can be delegated to others.

Why Aggressive Type A Personalities Accept Direction

A key measure of an NFL head coach's leadership is the implicit communication among his players, unit coaches, and staff. During a game, communication is extremely difficult due to the noise, the time pressures, and the knowledge that someone is always watching. The act of being watched affects the outcome. In the sciences this is known as Heisenberg's uncertainty principle.

Werner Heisenberg was a German physicist who postulated that although it is possible to measure a particle's location or movement, it is impossible to measure both at the same time because both affect the other: determining the location affects the movement, and measuring movement changes location. Heisenberg's theory led to an important tenet: observation changes an outcome despite whatever care is taken to make the observation. We are uncertain as to any observable act's ultimate outcome because we have changed it just by watching. This uncertainty places Heisenberg's theory squarely at the feet of business leaders everywhere. And as leaders watch the changing pace of their business, they are changing the outcome.

Certainly mass and movement are worthy pursuits for an NFL head coach. But twenty-two players on over six thousand square yards of playing field is too complex to evaluate individually. Head coaches must entrust this responsibility to their staff and give them the freedom necessary to do the job. How many successful head coaches are micromanagers? None. They have to allow the staff to work without interference. Management, yes, but not interference. Keeping all the coaches, staff, and players oriented in the same direction is a leader's foremost role.

This is the reason weekly practices are interspersed among numerous team and subunit meetings. Although each player watches film on his own to learn his specific opponent's movements, game film must also be evaluated as a group. This is where implicit communication is solidified before a conflict begins. Football players are often cast as gridiron warriors because of this similarity to elite military units.

It is vital that the team, like a commando unit, communicate based on a shared agreement of the strategic plan. Whatever one player (or unit) knows, the rest must know as well. Communication and preparation consume coaches, players, and staff during the week. In practice sessions, players apply the knowledge they gained from Shelton Quarles and other team analysts in order to figure out how to counter the opponent team's advantages and exploit its weaknesses.

As the week progresses outdoor activities move from individual player tactics (specific blocks and feints) to unit operations (zone and area control) to team strategies (play combinations and counters). As the team studies and practices (preparation) together, adjustments (information transfer) move through the team and staff faster and with less prompting. Simulating plays and counters on the practice field allow players and staff to visualize what the game will look like. They see what works, what needs adjusting, or what strategies need to be abandoned completely and started fresh.

Subject matter experts like Quarles demonstrate how the analytical competition is every bit as important as the competition of muscle and hustle—and perhaps more so. The preparation before and communication during an NFL game is what keeps fans engaged. The teams are so well prepared and their critical uncertainties so reduced that they can offer the best they have in the contest.

As the game progresses, both teams evaluate each other in real time, honing and tweaking their strategies. Dave Levy is monitoring the recorded game video with a learned eye for additional context to be captured. Shelton Quarles is in the press box calling down ideas to coaches on the sidelines.

Intelligence and strategy evolve in unique and different ways depending on how the game is going and the time left for play. With all other parameters being equal, strategies for the closing quarter are often night and day different from the opening quarter depending on the score. Like Musashi foretold, spending the time necessary to learn about the opponent includes anything that players can gain during the actual contest.

Buccaneers head coach Raheem Morris began his career with the team as a quality control coach for the defense in 2002, the year the Bucs won the Super Bowl. He was recently promoted to the top job, at thirty-two one of the youngest head coaches in the NFL. That someone so young can order about older, more experienced coaches and staff is high praise for Morris. The Buccaneers are confident in what he can do because he, better than others, understands this conceptual duet of leadership.

Preparation before and communication during the conflict, abiding by the strategy outlined by leadership, minimizes uncertainty to the fullest extent possible. This is leadership at its highest caliber: having the poise and confidence to push decision making as far down the organizational hierarchy as possible. When competition is at its fiercest, there is no time to passively tender information to a central point for an official decision.

Having set up an organization that abides by his direction, with an analytical cadre preparing his troops and using fast-moving implicit communications, an NFL head coach is a textbook example of the symbiosis between intelligence and strategy. Because decision making has been pushed down to as close to the source of conflict as possible, the leader has time to prepare players to make the best decisions when face-to-face with their opponent.

This decentralized structure succeeds because coaches understand that their adversaries are intentionally being vague and the uncertainty about the adversary's actions is real. It is in each team's interest to remain as difficult to analyze as possible. Smart leaders allow their staff the flexibility to take analytical leaps when needed, proposing innovative (risky) solutions worked by the entire team to determine if the solution is (first) feasible and (second) advisable.

Decentralized decision making means faster choices, partly because raw information and finished analysis move through the organization faster and partly because it takes advantage of a wider spectrum of expert opinion than simply forwarding everything to a single point. Leaders who can comfortably work in these environments find themselves with less annoying minutia and more time for longer-term strategic planning.

While a head coach leads with the overall strategy, it is the line coaches (defense, offense, and special teams) who champion it. The units within an NFL team are largely autonomous, yet all are organized around the same strategic plan. With a network of professional staff in support, the head coach works the competition, developing a plan of action he knows will be carried out without second-guessing or micromanaging those who report to him.

Certainly there are few other jobs as complex as that of an NFL head coach. Club owners hire and fire coaches based on a myriad of individual metrics. It's not just the number of championships or their win-loss ratio. There are also the total points of each game. The annual team revenue from tickets and merchandise. There are also intangible metrics: the goodwill of the team's reputation, how they're doing in the draft, the media opinion of the franchise, and relations with the NFL. Like the loss of the dinosaurs, failure is not the result of a single pressure but rather the force multipliers of many interrelated pressures. This is business. Football is a game, but the NFL is a business.

In his 2006 bestseller, *The Blind Side: Evolution of a Game,* author Michael Lewis wrote that "a football field is a tightly strung economy."[5] This exceptional leadership structure is why the NFL is the most fanatically and financially successful team sport in the world. The action on the field defeats the technologies used to monitor and analyze it. It is a lesson military and political leaders have learned the hard way: tools don't solve leaders' problems; dedicated support staff like Shelton Quarles and Dave Levy do.

The modern game of football is faster than it has ever been, matched only by the skill with which teams reduce their competitive uncertainty while trying to force mistakes by their opponents. In the 2008 season, teams scored an average of 22.3 points per game, and the combined scores of all thirty-two teams broke the previous league record of 11,279. During this same season, randomness and chaos were reduced to their lowest points too: turnovers averaged 3.09 per game and offensive lines allowed only 4.04 sacks per game. Both figures are the lowest in NFL history.[6]

The intrigue of high-tech collection can be distracting, but there's no substitute for a creative and professional staff to prepare and organize leaders for future conflicts. As the brilliant French microbiologist Louis Pasteur once wrote, "Chance favors the prepared mind." As Pasteur was founding the discipline of microbiology and discovered a vaccine for rabies and other diseases, a similarly socially conscious mind across the English Channel was preparing something else.

One Hundred Years of Preparation

In the 1880s a young man named Robert Baden-Powell was serving with the British Army among the Zulu tribesmen of South Africa. His field skills impressed his superiors to a point where his successes were shared in his commander's dispatches home. This led to his subsequent transfer to the British Secret Service. Baden-Powell served as an intelligence officer in Malta for three years, often disguising himself as a butterfly collector as he weaved plans of local military installations into his drawings of butterfly wings.

A few years after a particularly successful military campaign in Africa, Baden-Powell wrote a summary of training lectures he had given young recruits on reconnaissance and military tactics. He hoped not simply to train young charges but, more important, encourage them to think independently, take some initiative, and survive on their own. Baden-Powell was a prolific author, and several of the books he wrote were popular among young British boys.

Baden-Powell organized a camping trip to Britain's Brownsea Island where he perfected his plans for applying these ideas to young men in their formative years. He wrote a book specifically for this younger generation, published in 1908,[7] which was the fourth-largest selling book of the twentieth century, behind the Bible, the Koran, and Mao Tse-tung's *Little Red Book.*

A year later an American businessman lost in London's disorienting fog was approached by a young British boy who promptly led him back to his hotel. The lad refused the businessman's offer of a reward, as it was against the ethos of Scouting. The businessman quickly tracked down Baden-Powell to see what this Scouting business was all about. When he returned home, William Boyce wasted no time setting up what we now know as the Boy Scouts of America.

Baden-Powell's lessons are as relevant today as when he penned them one hundred years ago. He felt strongly about initiative, group experiences, and executing a shared strategy. Baden-Powell intended his fledgling program to prepare boys for leadership roles.

These preparatory attributes for aspiring young leaders parallel the attributes of NFL professionals. Game film sessions involve individual study followed by group learning, something right out of Baden-Powell's military handbook. Professional football players seize the initiative on the field when random events or an opponent's forced mistake present opportunities. And their shared practice experiences give them an implicit communication advantage that few outsiders could ever attain. As a result, they are always prepared.

W. Edwards Deming would have made a great NFL coach. Preparation and communication, manifestations of his primary interests, are crucial to how a head coach prepares for each week's Sunday afternoon competition. One of Deming's pivotal leadership points is equally poignant for Boy Scouts, NFL coaches, and business managers everywhere, because without it, winning is impossible: "Long-term commitment to new learning and new philosophy is required of any management that seeks transformation. The timid and the fainthearted, and the people that expect quick results, are doomed to disappointment."[8]

Learning to Learn

This chapter makes clear that a large part of the NFL's success is a willingness (necessity) by leaders to quickly abandon strategies that aren't working and adopt new ideas. If ego interferes in learning, a losing record can easily lead to a change in leadership.

Adapting those ideas to the specifics of the organization, under considerable time duress, means that internal communications channels must be optimum. Silence is golden except when you're in a leadership position. If nature abhors a vacuum, human nature truly despises it, and a communications vacuum is one of the best ways in the world to increase uncertainty. Defeat, failure, and loss will be right around the corner.

Leaders cannot be successful on their own. The pace of business, globalization, and a twenty-four-hour-a-day news cycle are sizable foes to any leader looking to go it alone. That such a leader will lose is inevitable. Leaders are not successful based on their power; they're successful based on their networks. And those networks are not just their professional or social contacts. As you'll see in the next chapter, networks form the basis of companies, competitors, and customers. The question is whether you can employ them to your competitive advantage before your competitor does.

It's All About Networks

A
t the University of Essex in Great Britain, robotics expert Huosheng Hu is leading a project under a grant from the European Union to produce a school of robotic fish. The north Spanish port of Gijon was selected to host the school after the city's managers expressed interest in the technology. Hu's robotic swarm will monitor port oxygen levels, where officials hope it will eventually help them track oil spills or leaking sewage pipes that can lead to ecological disasters or disease outbreaks.[1]

The five-foot-long fish are autonomic—that is, they don't require a centralized decision maker. The robots communicate with each other in real time underwater, occasionally surfacing to allow a radio uplink to pass the information on to a central computer. But only the collected environmental data are sent to the central computer. The activity, movements, and direction of the fish will be completely decided by the robots themselves while they are at sea.

Using a number of tools and techniques to avert rocks, pilings, and other stationary objects, the fish "learn" the port's topography and navigate around random activities, like the comings and goings of port traffic, that are impossible to predict. This level of autonomy has never before been achieved in a field-deployed project like this, and it has caught the attention of scientists, engineers, and port authorities nationwide.

Swarm technology, linking multiple devices to a shared common control mechanism, has been around for several years. When one fish's sonar system detects an object in the water, the entire school will avoid it and make a "mental" note of where it was, how large it was, and the direction taken around it. The data are shared among all the fish in the network; each one does not have to "see" the obstacle from its own sonar to be aware. Instead, it learns this information. Swarm technology is a software engineering equivalent of W. Edwards Deming's learning organization.

Oil slicks and sewage do not seek to intentionally avoid robotic patrols. But what if they did? Suppose the oil or sewage was as smart as these robotic fish and could avoid them? What happens when the opposing force is intelligent and equally networked? How can we analyze their capabilities to find a way to defeat them?

The first thing is to accept that a network adversary is unlike a singular opponent. It's not the same fight. It's not even the same type of fight. One on one, an adversary might outmuscle, outsmart, or just outlast an opponent. But a network has an additional advantage that can be very taxing: resiliency.

Hu cites robustness as a primary characteristic of his robotic fish. They are robust in that the loss of a single robot—to a mechanical problem or a failed electronic component, for example—will not result in the collapse of the entire school. They are resilient in that they will continue to function. Whatever loss there is to overall effectiveness will be corrected by assigning the broken robot's role to another elsewhere in the school (network). This means temporarily working within another route schema until a correction can be made by repair or permanent replacement of the unit.

Resiliency means the network will continue on as planned, possibly not even measurably slowing down at all, as this type of failure is expected. Complex networks have failures, often many of them at various points, but they're rarely catastrophic. What will happen depends on the type of failure and where it happens within the network. What are the second- and third-order effects? And what happens afterward as a result of the failure?

"Failure Is Not an Option"

In late April 2009 a graduate school chum of mine at the National Aeronautics and Space Administration (NASA) called and asked if I could take a day off at the last minute, but he wouldn't say why. Since Robert and his wife, Tracy, are my children's godparents I implicitly trust him and didn't question his motives. I simply said yes, and he promptly hung up. A few days later, Robert told me to keep the following Monday free.

Monday afternoon I was standing on truly hallowed ground. Shaking ground actually, as I watched the space shuttle *Atlantis* (SST#125) lift off from the Kennedy Space Center on the fifth and final mission to upgrade the Hubble space telescope. It was an experience that, even after some time to reflect, is difficult to put into words. We had a behind-the-scenes tour that was similarly out of this world. One particular site on the sprawling Kennedy Space Center campus stuck with me, partly because it was a network that came to the rescue and partly because Hollywood came to tell the story.

A NASA official showed us the launch pad where *Apollo 1* fatally caught fire in January 1967 with astronauts Virgil "Gus" Grissom, Ed White, and Roger Chaffee still aboard. Forty-two years after the incident occurred, he still gets choked up telling us the story. As we walked around the abandoned launch pad, now a memorial to the three men, he told us about the many structural changes *Apollo 1* had forced on NASA. But he said the biggest change was among NASA staff members themselves.

When *Apollo 1* caught fire, there was literally nothing that could be done to save the astronauts. NASA was unprepared physically as well as mentally. But after that, he said, NASA changed. There were still accidents, of course; complex systems like spacecraft always will have them. It's an inherent problem of complexity: random chance can throw things wildly off course. But when another random chance occurred to a NASA spacecraft three years later, NASA's response was nothing short of heroic. Despite a few hardware improvements, the changes had nothing to do with the spacecraft itself. What changed was how NASA dealt with uncertainty in fixing a problem.

In 1970, *Apollo 13* was the third attempt at a manned space mission to the moon. Two days into the mission, the crew experienced a catastrophic (random) failure when an oxygen cylinder exploded, venting the precious gas out into space. The Ron Howard film of the same name chronicles the myriad problems NASA and other organizations had in getting the three stranded astronauts home alive.

Apollo 13 had three separate spacecraft aboard one rocket: a command module for launch and recovery, a service module to house the astronauts, and a lunar module for landing on the Fra Mauro highlands on the moon. Each spacecraft was designed for a separate purpose as a stand-alone entity.

Perhaps unintentionally, NASA's solution to the problem was to cobble the three spacecraft together and leverage the benefit of resilience that came from networking the disparate systems together. It was only by examining and connecting the command, service, and lunar modules together that NASA succeeded in returning the three astronauts hurtling through space back to earth. The three spacecraft were not designed to share power, propulsion, waste disposal, or oxygen together. That the astronauts were able to successfully link the three with virtually no tools, receiving instructions over a static-filled radio and in the bone-chilling cold of space, makes their successful return all the more astonishing.

Analyzing a network begins by understanding what it is as opposed to simply an assembly of similar things. Networks have three interrelated and distinctive characteristics.

First, a network has *nodes*. Nodes can be anything: people, buildings, companies, computers. On *Apollo 13* the three spacecraft were turned into nodes. Nodes are discrete entities linked by a common conduit. Nothing stands alone; they are all connected but not always in obvious cause-and-effect ways. The nodes may not appear to have any apparent similarities, but this can be misleading because some nodes play discrete roles in a network and their effects can be compounded.

Each node performs a role in the theater of a network. This *purpose* is the second characteristic. Purpose, in fact, is the signature function in understanding a node. If it serves no purpose, there's no reason for it to be linked, no reason to be part of the network. In addition to being good acquirers of information, networks are good at identifying nodes that are superfluous. Think about some of your coworkers. Is every one of them crucial to your firm, your section, or your group's work output? Assuming for a moment you need them all, are they interchangeable? Can you switch Susan for Bill if the need arose? Can he do the job as well as she can? If Karen calls in sick, can Pat take over without any interruption to services? Depending on the network, of course, certified public accountants (CPAs) in one office should certainly be able to do each other's work. But once they are outside a very general framework, the situation changes.

Outside, each node's immediate purpose in the network is less interchangeable. Functionalities may be interchangeable, but people generally are not. For this reason, many parts of a network that might otherwise appear identical are actually quite dissimilar. Their nodes are separate for a reason. The reasons could be functionality (CPA versus attorney, for instance) or it could be the abilities of workers within the same role.

Every firm has star performers as well as laggards. Everyone in the office knows Jim does less than half the work of Priya, that Cleveland files its reports only after Atlanta does, or that finance always messes up its PowerPoint slides. The manifestation of purpose in every node is individually unique. Finding and understanding that purpose can be challenging.

Typically the purposes of different nodes have to do with the movement of information or materials in the production of some value. Something must be delivered, then passed through to another node, to continue through the production process. So the node's purpose is likely to be processing based on criteria germane to its specialty. Perhaps it's accounting, or R&D, or marketing, but something has to happen to the product or service being created at this node in the network. At a minimum, a decision had to be made.

A decision was made to pass the information or material to this node. A decision must be made about when to pass it on to the next node. Somewhere between those two decisions are likely other necessary decisions.

Understanding what decisions are made at each node, by whom and how, reveals a lot about a network (competitor). What are the design parameters for its product? How does it provide its service? What are the costs? What are the utility characteristics? What is the business doing to exceed customer expectations that someone else could do as well? It's vital to understand this information to the fullest extent possible.

What is the behavior of the network at this location, this node? What happens to it when it leaves here? This is the third and final characteristic of a network: the *order* of the purposes or decisions. The decisions made by the nodes are important, but they have to be made in a certain order. Sure, there's lots of wiggle room in many decisions, but plenty of important ones work correctly only when they are accomplished in a distinct order. Raw materials cannot be ordered until after inventories have fallen under a certain threshold. Magazine ads cannot be created until after pictures have been taken of the new model for the automobile trade publications. Building a new manufacturing plant takes place before production line crew are hired.

Order is important. Understanding the specifics of how decisions are made and why they are in a particular order is the difference between understanding a network and merely observing it. These are the decisions we're most interested in because they often are responsible for the unbelievable triumphs and the catastrophic failures.

This is what made NASA's response to the *Apollo 13* disaster so successful. It wasn't just networking the different systems of the spacecrafts together. That would be a complicated problem but certainly possible. What made it challenging and really got the team down to the wire was the order in turning everything back on aboard their networked spacecraft *after* the three astronauts linked it together.

When the problem on the spacecraft was discovered, Ken Mattingly, who had been replaced as *Apollo 13*'s mission pilot at the last minute, spent hours in a simulator recreating the newly assembled network at a NASA facility in Houston. Ken and his team recreated the scenario aboard the crippled spacecraft to the fullest extent possible: temperature, lighting, equipment on hand—everything to replicate what the three astronauts were facing as they sped toward earth. Ken's job was to find the right order for turning everything aboard the spacecraft back on.

The astronauts powered down the three modules to preserve their batteries. After three days in subzero temperatures, nobody was quite certain how the integrated systems would respond to being turned back on. What if they missed something? What if there was a stray circuit somewhere? They didn't know it at the time, but in fact a short circuit had triggered the explosion in the first place. What would prevent the same thing from happening again?

More immediately, there was a finite amount of power available for the spacecraft. Spikes in start-up power limited how much amperage each system had available to it. Once under way, the system would settle down to its normal power consumption, but the compounding addition of each power-up meant subsequent systems had less amperage available for these spikes. Getting the order correct was crucial; otherwise the networked system would fail, and the spacecraft would burn up in the atmosphere or bounce off into space.

This crisis happened long before personal computers were available to model an optimal sequence quickly and accurately. A good Excel programmer could now write something to fix this problem in a couple of hours at most, including the time needed to test and retest the model. But in 1970, Ken Mattingly and the NASA team was doing it through trial and error. Near the point of exhaustion, they finally figured out a sequence to power up each system aboard *Apollo 13* and quickly scribbled it down to radio to the three astronauts. The rest, as they say, is history. But had they not gotten a working order together in time, the three astronauts themselves would have been history.

The Skill of Synthesis

A network is an inherently complex organism. It's not enough to just dissect the parts; you must also be able to reassemble them not just to their original state but to create something wholly new—like turning three separate spacecraft into a flying life preserver, for instance.

Live or inanimate, networks have little formalized hierarchy and (unlike the merely complicated) are generally nonlinear. They have multiple feedback loops across multiple dimensions, giving them a rapid capability to adapt or, alternatively, freeze up completely under extreme conditions.

Individual nodes can switch from being a consumer of information to a producer, then switch back again. Then switch again. Whether they are producing or consuming is dependent on what is happening around and within the network. It evolves almost continually: adopting, then adapting, repeated over and over in a continual state of flux that can teeter on anarchy. Yet most of the time, it emerges from the unexpected stimuli stronger than before.

It also means that networks are difficult to analyze, especially over long periods—and that is the only way to analyze networks: over time, and a long time at that—continually, in fact. Complex networks require near constant monitoring. Otherwise they evolve into an organization with capabilities a rival cannot match. The rival is weakened while the evolving network thrives. In thriving, it consumes more, leaving fewer resources for the disadvantaged rival. Unless the rival quickly recovers and reconstitutes itself, it may not survive. Biology or economics, the rules of survival are the same.

So how do you scrutinize a network over a long period?

First, you have to accept that flashing lights and buzzers will not mark the signals you're watching for. This is a chaotic world where small changes in activity are often difficult to detect. But one characteristic of networks is that small changes can radically affect outcomes, and sometimes in unexpected ways. You have to be vigilant in monitoring competing groups; if they detect a potential new opportunity, you cannot allow them to hoard it. This vigilance takes place throughout the competitor's value stream and is shared equally with all stakeholders in your own network. The information will be fragmented and incomplete, but by assembling the disparate pieces, you will begin to see a full picture emerge.

This is an important point. Analysis is taking something apart to figure out how it works. As a boy, I loved taking things apart: the lawn mower, my parents' record player, even my first tape recorder. Putting these back together in working order was always much harder, and things haven't changed since then. It still remains harder to put pieces back together than to take them apart, and it is made all the more difficult when you're not sure what pieces you have, don't know how they fit together (if they do at all), and are unclear about what the completed item is supposed to look like. That is synthesis.

If that wasn't enough of a challenge, add the fact that the environment is evolving and changing, so the parts you assemble into a working product or service may bear little resemblance to what you started with. This is what innovation is all about: learning from what has been done in the past and creating something new with the parts picked up along the way.

To go about this difficult process, start off relatively simply and delve down into the various layers of the network as time, resources, and information allow. Begin with a basic understanding of a competitor (or customer) business model, and then ascertain more about the individual pieces. It's not quick, easy, or inexpensive. But done properly, incorporating feedback from management as appropriate along the way, the results can lead you down pathways to new business ventures you would otherwise have never dreamed of.

Even under ideal circumstances, the data you can find about a competing network will be incomplete. But detailed granularity is often unnecessary. This is not a laboratory experiment; we can and should sacrifice precision in favor of accuracy. The entire point of characterizing a network is to develop a strategy to defeat it. Precision will be far more important in your own networks than in someone else's.

So you start small, diagramming the competitor in the starkest of terms, and gradually build. Build each data layer on individual pieces of your newly characterized network, and don't be concerned when different sources give different descriptions of the data. This insight can come from former employees, customers, suppliers, Wall Street analysts, media experts, and even other competitors. Just keep in mind they're all human, and humans can be lousy sources of information.

Ask any metropolitan police officer what she most dislikes about her job, and one of the top gripes will be accident reports—not the blood and the guts, though that can be traumatic, but rather the endless uncertainty of trying to document what happened. Five people can be standing on a street corner when one vehicle slams into another. These five people have a front-row view, but their stories about what happened are distinctly different. There are several reasons for this.

People have a hard time separating fact from truth. Fault is an issue of truth, and truth is highly subjective. My truth is not necessarily your truth. In any neighborhood in America, you will find multiple truths about any subject on which you care to ask. That's why officers try to interview witnesses quickly but separately. Left to discuss what they saw, the individuals' stories begin to change as they talk among themselves. This *network effect* can lead to arguments among the witnesses (the last thing an investigating officer wants to deal with), further blurring the information's veracity. The officer needs to document what each person saw, but she's primarily interested in teasing the facts out of each witness's truths. Unlike truth, facts are universal. My fact should be your fact.

So returning to the car accident, the fact is that a blue Ford Taurus ran into a stationary red Chevy Tahoe. But who is at fault could fill five different accident reports. In fact, it will fill more than that: those of the five witnesses and the drivers of the two vehicles (and perhaps passengers in the vehicles). There will be at least seven distinct versions of the truth, all convinced theirs is the only real version. Veteran police officers can cite example after example after example. It's why Joe Friday had his famous line on the television show *Dragnet*—"Just the facts, Ma'am." In other words, don't interpret for me; just recall exactly what you saw.

So should we only collect and analyze facts and not truth? Absolutely not. Gather it all and note it all, but then separate it all. Make it clear to anyone who might not know anything about car accidents exactly what this one entailed. What did it look like? Sound like? Then add in the contextual subjectivity of each version of "truth." This is where analytical competition becomes frighteningly clear: when analysts with widely divergent opinions on a topic are suddenly confronted with a fact that is unambiguous in its clarity, importance, and shock.

The Impossible Occurs

May 1, 2009, is a date business historians will write about for years. The Chrysler Corporation, bellwether of the American and world economies, filed for bankruptcy protection. Despite repeated government bailouts in the billions of dollars and weeks of political posturing, in the end poor decision making in an increasingly complex competitive environment brought the huge corporation down. Exactly one month later, before everyone could absorb that punch to national pride, GM followed. Two of the big three U.S. automakers were now in bankruptcy protection.

The second- and third-order effects on individual suppliers and their company towns will take years to recover from. Right now, as I write this only a few days afterward, the nation is trying to grasp what happened. Surely networks as large, as powerful, as resilient as Chrysler and GM would be able to survive. Right?

Apparently not.

Like the dinosaurs, Chrysler was befallen by a multitude of factors. Some were not its fault. Others were the result of poor industry leadership, bad decision making by management, and a disturbing lack of customer focus. This should be a warning call to companies worldwide that it can happen to them too. If Chrysler and GM failed to adopt and adapt, maybe every firm should carve out time to consider what this means for them. Forget the fact they're not in the automobile business. These are two of the largest network operations in the world, with access to virtually unlimited resources. Yet despite all they had, it was not enough to keep creditors at bay.

Inaction is the death knell for leaders. Intelligence professionals can provide all the analytical insight one could ever want, but if difficult decisions are not made, the competition will soon pass you by. Detroit's faltering sales have been noted for years. A particularly stark realization came in 2007 when Toyota finally surpassed GM in annual unit sales. GM's response was to stick its head in the sand. Those heads (executives and board members) rolled as the government took over and cleaned house.

Once a validated model of a network has been constructed, specific pieces can be assessed for stand-alone analysis and characterization. What makes up that single node, and how can we determine more about it? What's the value of this specific node? What can it tell us about the rest of the network? What purpose does it serve? What external drivers might affect this node? Things like exchange rates, outside temperature, interest rates, suppliers' inventory levels, and a host of other potential data sources could mean the difference between profits and loss. Only by asking the right questions will decision makers get the answers they need.

These are the roles of each specific node being analyzed. How does it complete its function? What happens if it is interrupted, interfered with, or simply removed? How long to replace it? What will replace it, and how? These are all relevant questions when building out a network model. When you can begin characterizing this type of information about a network, you're starting to know something about it.

But that alone is not enough. GM and Chrysler knew a lot about their competitors in manufacturing and finance, but it wasn't enough. There's a reason it's called competit*ive* rather than competit*or* intelligence. You have to know what's happening out in the world, and certainly with your customers. Hidebound, high-cost car manufacturers might learn something from an activist retailer about analyzing and synthesizing customer information.

The Network That Changed Music

By 2007, less than one-tenth of 1 percent of retail music sales were in the audiocassette format. Cassette tapes are a dying medium, as vinyl was before them and eight-track tape before that. Long popular on road trips, cassette tapes are now available on less than 5 percent of domestically produced automobiles. Even audiobooks, one of the last holdouts for the audiocassette industry, are succumbing. CDs are showing early signs of trouble too, though it's a bit early to call any mortal threats on them just yet. What's killing them all is digital delivery, and the grand dame of digital is a scrappy little project called iTunes.

iTunes is an interesting success in that its position as a cash cow for Apple Computer was an afterthought. iTunes launched in January 2001 as an application for Apple's Macintosh computer platform. Apple designed upgraded versions that worked on its new digital music player, the iPod, which rolled out just a month after the 9/11 attacks. While a nation mourned and girded up for war, Apple unintentionally created an outlet for everyone to hide right out in the open. With ear buds in, the entire world could be pushed aside temporarily. People could simply escape into their music.

The iPod phenomenon was born out of Apple's research into the burgeoning digital consumer products market for cameras, camcorders, and music players. Many of the popular music devices of the time were big, clunky, and difficult to operate without interrupting the music and, more important, the experience. Steve Jobs, Apple's enigmatic CEO, ordered company engineers to design something better, with Jobs himself directing the user interface team of Apple engineers and outside partners. What they did was reinvent the music *experience* and create an entirely new mobile digital platform.

Apple began by studying consumer behavior. How did consumers go about getting the music they listened to, as well as when, where, and how they listened to it? It then set out to build a service (iTunes) and a product (iPod) around that behavior. Apple is in the products business, so the vision at the time was that the iPod would be the big winner.

Oh, to be that wrong more often.

With every upgrade, iTunes continues to exceed Apple's wildest expectations. Yes, iPods were enigmatic and sold like wildfire, but iTunes was available to those without iPods. When the iTunes store debuted in April 2003, soon followed by a version that could run on rival PC platforms, the iTunes phenomenon took off. Music was just the beginning. This free download is now the most profitable part of Apple.

iTunes expanded to include videos, games, applications, and television shows and spawned the every-man broadcasting service of podcasting in audio and video formats. Apple users have always been a tightly knit group, and early iTunes and iPod customers were no exception. But nobody could have predicted how devoted customers would be to a product and how strongly they desired to participate in the service experience. iTunes would wreak on digital content communities.

Networks sprang up virtually overnight, linking hundreds of thousands of like-minded users across many dimensions, encompassing any area of common interest a group of people could have. Although they all could comfortably do it from the confines of their desks, running either Apple or Windows platform computers, more and more continued to take their network of new friends mobile. Networks are the new metrics of market segmentation. They are dynamic, nonlinear, and in a constant state of evolution. They are *communities*.

As a result, Apple developed a host of new portable digital devices, including iTouch, iShuffle, iNano, and the cellular game changer iPhone. It's rare that a company makes such a radical departure from its core business line like this. In just a few years Apple moved from underdog competitor against Microsoft's Windows platform to literally owning the digital media distribution industry. For years Wal-Mart's product distribution infrastructure was considered the best in the world. Apple blew it away on April 3, 2008, surpassing the Arkansas behemoth in digital music sales.[2]

Apple has maintained its leadership position through several key strategies that filter down to every rank-and-file employee throughout Apple and its partner affiliates. First, understand customer demands. What do consumers want from their products and services? Apple then looks at how it might elicit the next evolution. What can it bring to the market that doesn't now exist?

Some liken this to the Honda strategy. What business is Honda in? Cars? All-terrain vehicles? Motorcycles? Generators? Jet engines? The answer is, "None of the above." Honda is in the small engine business, and each of the products is an individual market Honda sells into. Keeping that sort of orientation ("minding your knitting," as some call it) has served both Apple and Honda well. Both are considered market leaders and a frequent target of their competitors' wrath as a result.

Apple and Honda are also relentless innovators with their in-house R&D laboratories and external partners. Neither firm shoves innovation down customers' throats with a lot of heavy talk about what makes their products better or stronger or faster. They merely provide a platform on which other innovators are invited to develop the next consumer must-have product. Apple's consumer research is predicated on its unique ability to determine what network (customer) activity can Apple improve on.

Customers are communities: friends, family, colleagues, poker buddies and book groups. What Apple offered was a way for these consumers to share interests with those already close to them: their personal networks. A network's value is predicated on the number of people in it: the bigger the network, the better it is. A network of one is useless; a network in the thousands is incredible. Each time word of mouth brought another one of these network members into iTunes, the service became that much more valuable.

As Apple expanded iTunes to distribute new digital content (video and podcasting, for example), these networks branched in new directions and created markets of new customers far beyond Apple's original computer-based consumer. By solving a consumer problem (improving the mobile music experience), Apple exceeded customer expectations. In the midst of a crushing recession and an uncertain political turnover, it reported its most profitable nonholiday quarter ever at the opening of 2009, when the rest of the economy was tanking. Most of that revenue was built on the iPhone, iTunes, and the iTunes spin-off App Store.

When a company exploits its network of employees, suppliers, and customers, it can find opportunities to alter the nodes within many different networks. Changing those nodes, those purposes (decisions) alters how the networks and systems perform. By offering a better product or service (or both), a company can rake in profits as its competitors stagnate, merge, sell out, or simply shut down.

It's coldly ironic that a counterculture technology firm prospers while stalwart cornerstones of American business file for bankruptcy. Many will rightly point accusatory fingers at the automakers' insular style and poor customer service. Those are fair indictments. GM and Chrysler each had millions of one-time customers, whereas Apple has millions of repeat customers across several market segments. Yes, cars are a once-a-decade investment and music is frivolous luxury, but the profit margins for each are time-weighted equally against their competitors. By any reasonable measure, it should be Apple filing for bankruptcy and Chrysler and GM raking in millions.

Apple's obsessive attention to competitor and customer networks is vindication that centralized, top-down decision making is dead. There can still be only one person in charge, and Steve Jobs's style is the subject of numerous analytical journal articles. But his decentralized leadership and customer focus have taken Apple far beyond what anyone ever thought it could achieve. Like an NFL coach, Jobs passionately pursues winning by ensuring his team has all the preparation it needs to make that happen. And this is why the enigmatic CEO sits atop one of the most profitable and fiercely loyal networks in business.

A Purpose-Driven Company

Nodes, purpose, and chronology are key to understanding a network. Of these, purpose is the most important. That's the forward-looking nature of the network: the *value* created by the nodes operating in this chronological order. That value is the competitive advantage created by these actions.

This book is a synthesis and an analysis. I have incorporated others' work, taking it apart (analysis) and reassembling select parts (synthesis) for the purpose of telling this story. This is common for any information-based profession, be it intelligence, medicine, finance, or law.

Although resiliency is an important characteristic of networks, it is their evolution into communities that offers forward-thinking firms a competitive advantage. Traditional market research provides little insight into communities. They defy common segmentation labels, evolving continually through the multiplicity of communications channels and defying national borders.

Communities describe every firm's future competitors, customers, and collaborators. As the next chapter reveals, understanding their networks can be accomplished with the latest technology or through good old-fashioned field research.

Part Two: Fieldwork

4

Collecting Data
New School and Old School

Jeff Welgan's homework had never attracted this much attention before. Public attention. *International* attention. In 2009, the Mercyhurst College graduate student was finishing his master's degree in intelligence studies in Kristan Wheaton's advanced analytical methods class. The students study several methodologies for analyzing competitive information and discuss applications in class. They finish by selecting one technique each and putting it into practice, briefing the rest of the class on what they found.

Jeff chose search engine optimization (SEO) as his individual studies project. SEO is a method for improving the way Web sites, blogs, and other Internet resources are found by popular search engines such as Google, Yahoo, and Ask.com. Jeff examined the number of tools available and thought they might have intelligence potential. Why monitor your own Web traffic if you could monitor a competitor's to determine differences in customer preference and behavior?

He theorized that the methodology of online searching might be important and could even have an impact on long-term company strategies. Every firm is promoting social media experiences through its Web sites. He wondered if it was possible to slice and dice Web site traffic data akin to how television audience data are parsed by various demographics. He believed that understanding how potential customers interacted by, with, and through these sites might be vital to future positioning strategies.

Jeff knew Web site behavior was based on content, just as search engine behavior was based on mathematic algorithms. Although he already understood the technical applications of such tools, he was now more interested in applications for competitive intelligence. Being a connoisseur of caffeination, he chose to compare and contrast internationally recognized Starbucks with the smaller, emerging competitor of Caribou Coffee. He hoped to identify differences in marketing and visitor demographics based solely on Web site traffic. Would this be of intelligence value for marketing and brand management leaders?

Jeff's study followed the classic scientific method process, keeping the two research targets similar in every way except for the area of study. Both companies serve similar types of coffee and other foods, both have similar customer experience models, and both generally pursue similar sociocultural customer characteristics. Although Starbucks is much larger than Caribou in revenue and locations, the positioning of the two firms in the marketplace is quite similar—perfect for the sort of analysis Jeff was trying.

Jeff used free services provided by SEO Web sites to run his models. He chose to collect and analyze page rank, site background data, sites linked in from elsewhere, visitor demographic data, and visitor behavior tracking. Keep in mind that Jeff doesn't work for either company, and neither firm was in any way involved with his study. This is an analysis that can be run by anyone on virtually any Web site they choose.

The analysis revealed much about Starbuck's brand value, as might be expected, but it also demonstrated the value of this new type of analysis. The free software tools Jeff employed give any company the ability to discern how and why customers select one firm, brand, or activity over another. Jeff's results tell a great deal about Starbucks and Caribou Coffee customers and their interests based on online consumer behavior patterns. He was able to visually display these data using Google's Insights for Search application, a free analytical tool.

Caribou Coffee visitors tend to be predominantly female (56 percent), middle-aged (36 percent between ages thirty-five and forty-nine),

Caucasian (91 percent), college educated (48 percent, with 17 percent of these with graduate degrees), childless (65 percent), and relatively affluent (33 percent make $60,000 to $100,000). Starbucks visitors reflected only minor differences, attracting more young adults (42 percent between the ages of eighteen and thirty-four), with a slightly more diverse population, including an above-average number of Asian customers. Starbucks visitors were to some extent more affluent: 31 percent make more than $100,000 annually.

Social networking sites were paying big dividends for Starbucks's advertising budget and would likely be a smart move for Caribou Coffee. Facebook refers 3.9 percent of traffic to the Starbucks Web site, yet did not show up as a top referral device for Caribou Coffee. A new Caribou Coffee ad campaign on AOL.com was bringing in traffic, something it may want to expand on given the more than 500 percent increase in referrals from February to May 2009. The same is true for Yahoo, where referrals to Caribou Coffee are rising at a greater rate than for Starbucks (more than 91 percent versus more than 3.3 percent).

Visitor behavior was similarly revealing. Caribou Coffee visitors have strong correlations to sites for schools, insurance, toys, pharmacy, and health care. There were also strong relationships to news agencies (particularly in the Minneapolis/St. Paul area, where Caribou is based), airline travel, and workforce-related sites. Starbucks visitors had strong linkages to commerce/food, fragrances/cosmetics, jewelry/luxury goods, women, and pharmacies. Visitors also clicked on sites related to other restaurants, shopping, and printing/graphics locations online.

Jeff's analysis notes the importance of finding the commonalities across various dimensions of customer sets. Search engine optimization can help assess the best route to direct a particular customer segment from one part of the Internet to a specific company's site. If you know what kinds of visitors a site attracts, you can find what other content those visitors enjoy and design integrated advertising campaigns to exploit their interests.

By knowing which keywords are preferred by your target market, segment leaders can invest in catchphrases, taglines, and other off-line marketing techniques that will resonate with that portion of their market. They can similarly analyze competitors' keywords to identify their customers.

By characterizing other sites that refer the preferred customer traffic, it's possible to focus on keywords from those sites. The analysis is complex, but one that can be done over time to reflect changing subdemographics in current customers, ways of finding new customer sets based on changes to your product or service, and how to develop preferred partnerships with other firms you think your customers might want to be referred to. This type of network analysis is not a one-time event. It requires ongoing monitoring because, as Jeff has shown, others will be trolling for the same data, pulling your customers away to their product or service.

What was also startling was the international aspect of Jeff's study. Both Starbucks and Caribou Coffee were receiving hits from overseas. But once people began talking about his study and it started picking up interest from e-mails, blogs, Twitter feeds, and other electronic media, overseas hits to Jeff's Web site picked up as well. Google's analytical software showed the geographical origination of visitors, indicated what semantic strings (search phrases) were used, and showed links to other locations they'd visited recently.

It was soon obvious this methodology had other applications, though they were not part of the original study. It could be used for funneling campaigns to drive traffic directly to the transaction page of Web sites to close the deal before surfers took their business elsewhere. By tracking messages from referrals, a campaign planner could identify key demographics based on age, gender, income, language, and location for optimal customer sets.

The marketing implications are staggering. Jeff has demonstrated a way to analyze thousands of individual consumer behaviors for specific patterns across multiple dimensions and visually display them in a way leaders can immediately apply to decision making. He could start a business tomorrow offering this service to marketing departments, public relations firms, lawyers, press agents, journalists, and political campaign managers across the nation.

Competitive intelligence is not the same as market research, which looks at broad groups of customers across an entire market. Most market research is very dry, utilitarian information that can be difficult for leaders without a statistics background to grasp. Jeff's analysis is not only aesthetically pleasing; it's focused on specific opportunities that should be acted on. *That's* intelligence.

As Apple had done, Jeff determined what customers were doing with regard to an experience they wanted to have: a cup of coffee. Apple had to conduct much of its research the old-fashioned way, taking more time at greater expense for fewer data. Jeff's method was done entirely online, incorporated a larger number of customers, over a greater geographical area, and with much faster results. Like Apple, he found how customers affected and were affected by other customers interacting with a product or service. He then identified ways both Starbucks and Caribou Coffee could reach those customers through the lowest cost possible.

He got an A in the course.

Old School Information

Jeff's digital dexterity is impressive. But there are many other information sources that cannot as yet be accessed over the Internet. They require good old-fashioned legwork: going to an office, library, or archive in person or by mail to access thousands of pages of documents, never really quite sure what you'll find. Fortunately, the U.S. government stepped in a few years ago and made this relatively easy.

In 1966 the Freedom of Information Act (FOIA) was passed into law. FOIA was intended to return government oversight of information to the hands of everyday citizens without interfering in the day-to-day operations of governance. All federal agencies are required to participate and must answer a request within a timely fashion, and the right of access is enforceable in court. There are exclusions to the act, but they are the exception rather than the rule.

FOIA includes records on individuals, commercial operations, non-governmental organizations, trade associations, and just about anything else on which the government would have a legitimate reason to collect information. This includes situations when the government collects information about particular events like the Olympic Park bombing during the 1996 Summer Olympics in Atlanta, Georgia; public demonstrations like the battle of Seattle over the World Trade Organization in 1999; or the Tylenol poisonings in Chicago in 1982. If the federal government had to respond or in some way get involved, there's a file on it.

For all its potential, FOIA costs for competitive intelligence purposes are remarkably low. Personal records are free up to a two-hour search in federal offices and up to one hundred pages in length. For commercial records, "it depends" is the best descriptor of costs based on time, copying expenses, the size of the file, and similar administrative issues. When costs are involved, they're usually less than fifty dollars—a pretty good deal considering what you can get.

But like any other government activity, one size does not fit all. Each entity has its own interpretation of useful information and timely access. The best thing to do is find out the particulars of a specific office before you need to make a request and then ensure it will have the information you want before you ask. Some can be real sticklers for accuracy: if the form is not filled out correctly or completely, the clerk can ship it back to you and turn to the next one in the stack to work on. The request must state succinctly what is desired ("send everything" is typically rejected). Assuming the paperwork is in order, agencies must respond within ten days.

The exceptions to the FOIA regulations make a lot of sense if we consider the various tasks that government completes every day. Safeguarding nuclear weapons, protecting the president, the names of undercover officers, and evidence in federal prosecutions are the sort of thing that should not be in the public domain. Fortunately the nine exclusions, which follow, do not pertain to any information regarding most individuals or commercial enterprises and should not interfere with any competitive intelligence probe:

1. Classified national defense and foreign relations information
2. Internal agency rules and practices

3. Information prohibited from disclosure by another law
4. Trade secrets and other confidential business information
5. Inter- and intra-agency communications protected by legal privilege
6. Information involving matters of personal privacy
7. Select information compiled for law enforcement purposes
8. Information regarding the supervision of financial institutions
9. Geological information on wells

Why Me?

So why would the federal government have data on individuals? It depends on who they are, where they've been, and what they did. People don't really think about how often they show up on the radar screens of different government agencies, but you'd be surprised. Even if it is not you that takes an action (or commits a crime), you can be referenced on someone else's record. Among the reasons the government will have a file on an individual are these:

- Investigated for criminal intent
- Filed civil suit against the government
- Associated with anyone convicted of a crime
- Indicted for a crime
- Codefendant of any convicted felon
- Jailed for any duration of time
- Armed forces veteran
- Internal Revenue Service prosecution
- Relative of a person incarcerated, indicted, or imprisoned
- Members of antigovernment groups
- Federal weapons license

With that much information on file, what can you find out about an individual? Plenty. You just have to know where to look. Why does a person take a particular position, release a product, or engage in a fight? Because that person has the will to take a risk, to do what is necessary, to not do something the way it's always been done. Companies compete based on the psychology, training, and experience of their people, so it is quite useful to know as much about their backgrounds as is legally and ethically possible. The rules about this information vary by agency, so my suggestion is just try a few out as practice. Military records are a good start.

The National Personnel Records Center, Military Personnel Records (NPRC-MPR) is the federal government's archive of personnel, health, and medical records for discharged or deceased military service members. Information from the records is made available on written request (with signature and date) to the extent allowed by law. If you are a veteran, you can order a copy of your records through vetrecs.archives.gov (the next of kin to a deceased veteran can do this too). For others, it is best to use Federal Standard Form 180, which includes the instructions for filling out the required data fields. All requests should be signed and mailed to:

National Personnel Records Center
Military Personnel Records
9700 Page Avenue
St. Louis, MO 63132-5100

But FOIA has limits. An agency can refuse a request if it is "a clearly unwarranted invasion of personal privacy." This can include medical, financial, and many personnel records. Exemption 7 provides protection for law enforcement records. The key decision factor is the balance between personal privacy against the public interest that is served by disclosure.

What About the Firm?

Why would the government have information on a competitor? It could be mandated competitive bidding for federal contracts. It might be a minority or disadvantaged business with federal contracts. Or perhaps one of its products hurt someone. If a product is recalled as a safety hazard, the Consumer Products Safety Commission's investigation, evidence, and analysis would be very useful to a competitor.

All of that investigation, including reams of experimental data the government would create during testing, is available for the asking. This can be invaluable for reverse engineering a competitor's product. If you don't have or cannot afford laboratory testing equipment and staff, the government is giving it to you for free. It could get you started in the right direction.

For some industries, product testing is one of the largest single expenses of development. Food and Drug Administration analysis of a new or previously approved drug that allegedly caused illness or death might be used to determine if your new drug needs a similar screening prior to release.

Drug manufacturers are always looking for ways to prove the efficacy of a new formulation without the expense of additional testing. If examination of a competitor's government evaluation can head off repeated testing of a product (or forewarn the company of testing that it should conduct), you've just saved millions of dollars in development costs. You've also probably avoided a public relations disaster and an equally expensive legal problem.

Subscription satellite imagery provides updated images as often as weekly on any point on the globe a company might want monitored. If you think a competitor's recent purchase of one hundred acres in Costa Rica might be for a new manufacturing plant, order up some satellite imagery on a regular basis to keep an eye on it. Past imagery on sites in the United States can be obtained through the Environmental Protection Agency or U.S. Geological Survey. The Drug Enforcement Agency has satellite photos of foreign agriculture sites that it uses to look for drug labs, but the photos are equally useful for tracking foreign agriculture production of corn, beans, coffee, and other staples.

When you read press reports about a competitor that is being investigated, it should immediately ring mental alarms that information is available for the taking. The Federal Trade Commission conducted an analysis of BP Amoco's West Coast prices after its proposed buyout of Atlantic Richfield Company for $26.8 billion. The entire study was obtained through a FOIA request by the *Oregonian* newspaper.

BP's competitors could look at price models (analyzed at taxpayer expense) and use them for their own purposes. The American Civil Liberties Union similarly used FOIA to gain information about the FBI's Carnivore System, which was intended to monitor e-mail and other electronic communication. The FBI shut Carnivore down in 2001 after extensive public outcry. The *Tampa Tribune* used FOIA to gain access to U.S. Navy and Coast Guard intelligence on drug smuggling out of Ecuador, which had valuable information on Latin American shipping, key leaders, and other data.

FOIA is also a great tool for innovation that equals the playing field between a small company and a large one. But that doesn't mean a large one can't use it as well. When Japanese engineers used FOIA to learn the braking designs of the U.S. Navy F-14 Phantom fighter jets, few people thought the same taxpayer-funded technology would be reapplied in the braking system of the thousands of sedans Japan was shipping to the United States at that time. Why reinvent the wheel? If a company in another industry has the technical know-how you require, find an office where it is on file and make a request. Again, millions of dollars have been saved by not having to repeat another's mistakes (only their successes).

The Federal Bureau of Investigation is without question the most packrat-focused agency of the national government. Any piece of paper or electronic correspondence, any evidence used in federal court, is on file somewhere. The downside of being the largest means it is also usually the slowest. The FBI collects and archives information (evidence usually, but not exclusively) in which the United States is an interested party (missing persons, fingerprints, stolen property, and product tampering, for example).

State FOIA claims are where I've found highly useful information over the years. It's high enough on a company's radar to warrant attention by leaders but local enough to be very specific with the data it provides. States have broad powers over companies and require a breathtaking amount of information. They also conduct inspections and investigations, and because their constituents are a lot closer to the action, they are thorough. Call reports, meetings, and paperwork records are all on file and available for review. Each state has its own rules, and there is wide variability in what states have and how helpful they are when sharing it.

Some examples of state records kept throughout the country are:

- Building diagrams
- Equipment specifications, component types and specifications, and Occupational Safety and Health Administration (OSHA) inspector reports
- Line speeds, process flowcharts, site diagrams, personnel specifics, capacity on day of inspection, morale, safety problems, health concerns, hazardous materials permits
- Raw materials
- Air, water, waste disposal permits, testing, periodic reports

An Example of How to Use This Information

Almost every county in the nation has record keeping that is at least as granular as at the state level. You might not think sorting through a competitor's local regulatory filing was worthwhile, but don't dismiss it. To show you how powerful yet easy this is, I'm going to outline one from start to finish.

This is a project I did a few years ago when I was with Celotex Corporation. Celotex was in the manufacturing business: ceiling tiles, gypsum wallboard, roofing tiles, and fiberboard. One of its biggest competitors was a firm I'll call Meyer Corporation. Meyer had around 40 percent of the market in the tile business and was a formidable competitor.

One day the senior vice president for marketing came in and closed my office door. Lance was my boss, one of my favorites over the years, and hardly ever closed the door when we spoke, so I knew something was up.

"I'm hearing some things from the boys in the field that Meyer's got a secret project going on," he said.

I put away what I was working on to give him my full attention.

"What kind of secret project?" I asked.

"Nobody knows. Real hush-hush. Some customers told the guys about it. They thought it was BS. Then Meyer's paint supplier mentioned the same thing," he said.

"Could be misdirection," I suggested.

"Could be a lot of things. I just want to know one thing," he retorted.

"The one thing it is," I nodded, pulling out a pad and pen. "Got it. Who can I call?"

He provided me the name of our regional sales manager for that area, and I was dialing before Lance was out of my office.

I knew Meyer Corporation had a good competitive intelligence department. This could simply be a denial and deception campaign (coming up in Chapter Six) to lead us down the wrong path and make us waste our time and resources, tying up staff when there was nothing to find. But the regional manager didn't think so. He'd dealt with Meyer far longer than I had, and he'd never seen anything quite like this. Weird, he called it. The whole thing was weird. It was so weird it brought the senior vice president to my office. I hung up with the regional manager and looked over the notes I scribbled as he spoke.

Meyer was spending large amounts of unplanned capital on its Macon, Georgia, plant. There had been no press releases for this expenditure. Nor were there any investor relations notices or Securities and Exchange Commission filings of unusual spending. There had been high turnover in Meyer's executive offices this year. I didn't have a lot of data to go on, but that's not unusual. If the solution was clear, it wouldn't need an intelligence shop to figure it out.

So I jotted down some clarification points. We needed to find out if the rumor of a lot of capital spending was true. If so, to what extent? What triggered this action? Why was it so confidential? How much was being spent? What changes could this mean to the company, product line, marketing, or production process, or cost structure?

Meyer Corporation's stock had been sinking for over a year. The CEO and CFO had recently been sacked, an action we had predicted six weeks before it happened. I resisted the urge to gloat when the *Wall Street Journal* carried the story afterward. Lance had pointed a finger in my direction and just smiled. He was pleased—surprised and more than a little suspicious but pleased. Now we had to do it again.

With Meyer Corporation's stock in the toilet and nobody steadying the helm, it would be tough to spend a lot of capital expenditure money.

Who would authorize it, release it, or explain it to investors? Assuming for the moment we were not looking at a misdirection project, what could this be? We came up with three scenarios.

First, this could be an employee safety issue. Maybe someone dropped an anonymous dime to the local OSHA office and an inspector came out to find serious problems. Second, there could be an active environmental nongovernmental organization (NGO) in the area. NGOs are increasingly flexing their political muscle, especially against manufacturers they believe aren't doing enough to clean up the environment. Finally, it could be a regulatory problem: one of the agencies holding the plant's operating permits had suddenly gotten involved for some reason.

I had nondisclosure agreements with a couple of outside research services. I'd used Global Information Research and Retrieval (GIRR) in Greensboro, North Carolina, several times and was always pleased with the results. Its researchers typically overdelivered what they promised and did it in a timely fashion. I gave them a call and told owner Donna Fryer what I thought I needed.

Two huge boxes were delivered to my office a few days later. We began with Meyer's local and state regulatory filings: everything the company had filed for air, water, waste disposal, and hazardous materials reports for the past two years. It took three of us several days to cull through two years of quarterly and annual reports. There were dozens of folded blueprints of the plant and accompanying office complex and also testing of their raw materials and waste disposal before shipment. There was a lot of information, much of it extremely technical and out of our area of expertise. We were not engineers, and that was what I most desperately needed. Several in fact.

I cannot read a blueprint to save my life and make no pretense about it. Others might not do this, thinking they could interpret the Indiana Jones cryptology of the pages' tiny characters. Same for the complicated chemical formulations, engineering schema, and other specialized data we were reading.

One problem companies have is knowing when to stop collecting data and when to start analyzing what they have. Another is knowing when to call in the experts, a problem mirrored in many ways in the medical field, from whom intelligence professionals are increasingly copying techniques and procedures. Dr. Jerome Groopman's book *How Doctors Think* is an especially good overview of how the medical community manages (and sometimes mismanages) uncertainty.[1]

I called Celotex's technical center and spoke with the R&D manager, with whom I had a cordial relationship. I needed help, I told him, and quickly. I asked if he and five of his staff could come up to the office and interpret a few things for us. Nothing fancy, I said, just point us in a direction, and we'll move out on it. He assured me he'd be there first thing tomorrow. I commandeered the conference room for 8:00 A.M.

Fueled by unlimited coffee and two boxes of Krispy Kreme doughnuts, the engineering staff were having so much fun an outside observer might have thought they were visiting Disneyland. Lance had an off-site meeting and didn't come into the office until nearly ten. By then, his conference room looked like a tornado had ripped through. His double-take as he walked by nearly twisted his head off. He slowly stepped into the room and motioned me over.

"I don't want to know what's going on in here, do I?" he asked.

Having seen some of the early results of this sugar- and caffeine-powered investigation, I was in high spirits.

"No, you don't. Wait until I've got a story for you," I begged.

Lance sauntered off to his office chuckling under his breath. Two days later, I briefed him and the senior staff. Beginning with a plant diagram of Meyer Corporation's manufacturing site, I described what we and the engineering staff believe had happened.

A Georgia Department of Environmental Protection (GDEP) engineer had sent his boss a memo through interoffice mail (Figure 4.1). I handed Lance a copy of the memo. In it, the engineer noted that Meyer had not made a quarterly filing. Thinking it was a clerical error, he pulled the file to see if he'd misplaced it. Still not finding it, he searched to locate a contact number for Meyer's safety, health, and ecology manager intending to simply give him a call with a friendly reminder. Nothing more.

Georgia Department of Natural Resources
Environmental Protection Division, Air Protection Branch
4244 International Parkway, Suite 120, Atlanta, Georgia 30354
Telephone: (404) 363-7000; Fax (404) 363-7100
Lonice C. Barrett, Commissioner
Harold F. Reheis, Director

MEMORANDUM

To: Mr. Joe Smith
From: Doug Waldren
Date: October 12, 1999
Subject: Inspection Report, Meyer Corporation, Inc.
Macon, Georgia (Bibb County)

INTRODUCTION

On September 29, 1999, I conducted an announounced air quality inspect located at 4523 Broadway. The facility is classified as an "A" source in t 021-00030) and is currently operating under Air Quality Permit No. 32 construction and operation of an acoustical ceiling tile manufacturing p

I was assisted by Ms. Terry Dane, Engineering and Maintenance Coord Environmental Consulting, Inc.

PROCESS DESCRIPTION

The facility manufactures mineral and cellulose-based ceiling tiles. Ra perlite, mineral wool, recycled newspaper, and tile scraps. Perlite is exp tile, while the mineral wool enhances the acoustic properties of the tile. slurry using water. Tile scraps and scrubber water are recycled into the

Large sheets of ceiling tile are shaped in a rotating vacuum drum. The sheets, and finished. Finishing can include sanding, trimming, shaping or painting.

The perlite expanders, boardmill dryers, paint line dryers, and tile dryers, embossers, with propane backup. Fourteen of scrubbers and eight baghouses

All paints used at the facility are water based, but some forms the back coat. The back coat is applied to prevent bowing the paint spray booths are controlled by water curtains and fiberglass filters.

The facility also has some wood burners that are no longer usable but a These should be removed from the permit when the Title V permit is is

H:\DWWW\SOURCES\MEYER\J09900NS-REP.WPG

Process	Source Code	Limit on Days of Operation	Actual Days of Operation (9/98 – 8/99)
No. 2 Boardmill Dryer	172	330	286
No. 3 Boardmill Dryer	173	340	286
MPIF	270	340	261
No. 2 Board Paint Line	212	340	253
No. 3 Board Paint Line	213	281	254
Paint Mixing	290	365	Not recorded
No. 4 Board Paint Line	214	310	307
MIT Line	280	73	59

Figure 4.1 The Georgia Department of Environmental Protection memo from an engineer to his supervisor that started the trouble for Meyer Corporation.

Instead, he noticed a number of omissions in Meyer's recent filings. As an engineer, a few inconsistencies on the page caught his eye, so he sat down with a calculator to figure them out. Several of Meyer's calculations were gravely wrong—not simply a rounding error, but incorrect math that was difficult to imagine an engineer committing.

GDEP sent Meyer a letter asking for clarification of the problems the engineer had identified (Figure 4.2). Meyer quickly replied, citing that the safety, health, and ecology manager had been fired and a new one would be forthcoming with the information as quickly as possible. Yet nearly three months later, still no records had arrived. The quarterly filing was now more than ninety days overdue, the fourth quarter filing was late, and so was the annual report. GDEP informed Meyer that three noncompliances on the permits kicked in financial penalties.

Meyer's corporate office sprang into high gear and replied to GDEP with what it planned to do (Figure 4.3). Several line processes would be upgraded with new wet scrubbers to replace outdated environmental control machinery called bag houses. New holding tanks would be installed, with everything up and running as quickly as an installation contractor could get it done. The capital costs of the equipment would easily exceed $2 million (not including installation or delays), and Meyer was racing to get internal approvals completed and the funds authorized.

The newly hired safety, health, and ecology manager was apparently not up to the job and summarily dismissed. A new executive position was created to oversee the problem as a capital construction project and to conduct some handholding with the GDEP. The new Meyer corporate executive temporarily moved from headquarters to Georgia, and his first order of business was to meet GDEP officials in person to discuss the problems, the solution, and the way forward.

Meyer Corporation filed numerous engineering overviews on upgrades to the plant. Process design changes, manufacturing recipe changes, and waste disposal changes were outlined in exceptional detail (Figure 4.4). All of it was now sitting in front of the leaders of Celotex Corporation, several of whom had engineering backgrounds. They were all smiles.

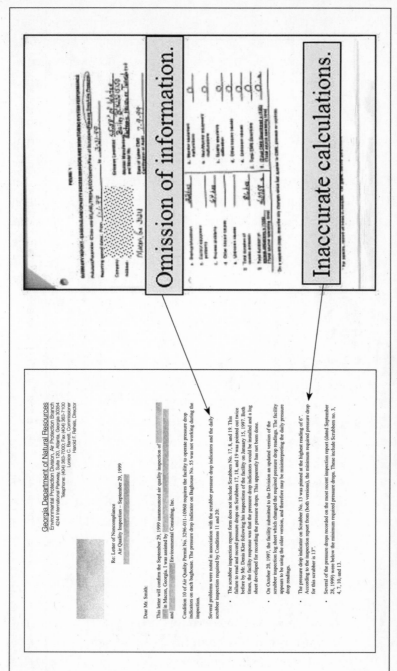

Figure 4.2 The Georgia Department of Environmental Protection asking for clarification on the problem, citing Meyer Corporation's own quarterly records.

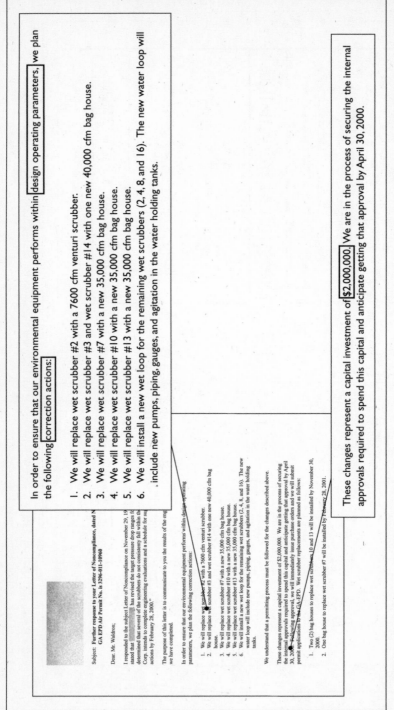

In order to ensure that our environmental equipment performs within design operating parameters, we plan the following correction actions:

1. We will replace wet scrubber #2 with a 7600 cfm venturi scrubber.
2. We will replace wet scrubber #3 and wet scrubber #14 with one new 40,000 cfm bag house.
3. We will replace wet scrubber #7 with a new 35,000 cfm bag house.
4. We will replace wet scrubber #10 with a new 35,000 cfm bag house.
5. We will replace wet scrubber #13 with a new 35,000 cfm bag house.
6. We will install a new wet loop for the remaining wet scrubbers (2, 4, 8, and 16). The new water loop will include new pumps, piping, gauges, and agitation in the water holding tanks.

These changes represent a capital investment of $2,000,000. We are in the process of securing the internal approvals required to spend this capital and anticipate getting that approval by April 30, 2000.

Figure 4.3 Meyer Corporation screams "mea culpa," promising over $2 million in capital expenditure improvements and citing exactly which systems it will upgrade or replace.

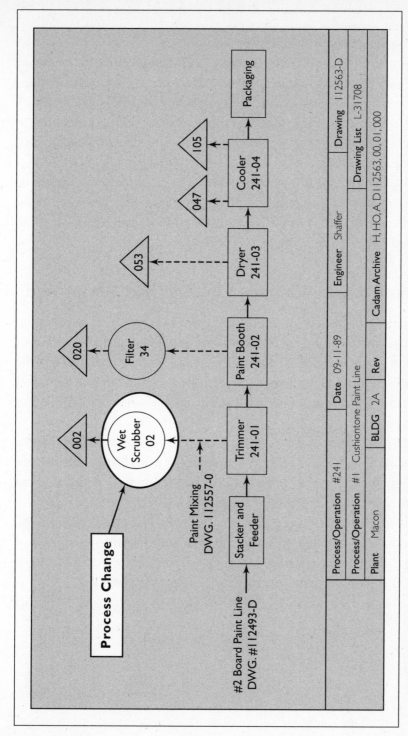

Figure 4.4 Meyer Corporation manufacturing process changes in its own documentation, which should not be in a publicly accessible file.

We concluded that honest calculation errors were compounded by sloppiness and inattention to detail. GDEP had given Meyer plenty of time and autonomy to iron out the problem on its own. Penalties were now pending, as was the tacit threat of publicity at a time when Meyer's stock could ill afford any external shocks. Meyer had no choice but to comply with GDEP requirements as quickly as possible to avoid negative exposure.

We exploited this information with our customers and suppliers, stunning Meyer's field sales staff. Our sales personnel knew more about was happening in Macon than their people did, and it gave us some needed sway on several important initiatives.

Know What Information Is Out There About You!

Search engine optimization exploits technology to collect information on a competitor's customers. Their behaviors leave a great deal of information lying around for rivals to pick up and analyze. In addition to the information put out by companies themselves, FOIA can be used to collect from a rival's customers, suppliers, partners, and a host of other sources.

The two radically different procedures demonstrate the importance of securing loose company information. Nondisclosure and secrecy agreements are every bit as vital as locks on the building's doors. Without them, companies are essentially giving away their business.

And this threat exists right out in the open. Placing competitors and customers in an enclosed space, ratcheting up the time pressure, and creating a dynamic audience experience can modestly recreate Michael Lewis's "tightly strung economy," as you'll see in Chapter Five.

5

All the World's a Trade Show Stage

J ohn Hill is the president and CEO of the consulting company that bears his name. He lives, works, and breathes trade shows in the largest trade show market in the world: New York City. John has consulted for some of the world's largest global corporations yet still counts small businesses among his favorite clients. When it comes to trade shows, he literally wrote the book.

John's *Tips and Tales from the Booth: Avoiding Trade Show Mistakes* is the bible for sales and marketing, public affairs, general counsel, R&D, and technical services staff of any trade show exhibiting company.[1] He is widely regarded as one of the top minds in trade show strategy and tactics. One of his favorite citations on the criticality of trade shows comes from *Exhibitor Magazine,* which notes of survey respondents that "72% regularly spy on their competition at trade shows."[2]

That's quite a figure considering how many of the remaining 28 percent were likely stretching the truth just a bit. Many might dismiss this as part of doing business, but that's because they simply don't know what to do about it. Hill is uniquely qualified to advise in this endeavor. Not only does he have thirty years of business consulting and trade show experience, he also had a few years of military special operations intelligence gathering prior to that.

John is a former U.S. Navy SEAL, a plank holder from the original under-water demolition teams (UDT) that evolved into the modern SEAL team. In addition to their more lethal kinetic responsibilities, UDT/SEAL oper-ators are also masterful collectors of information. They are a preferred tool in the Department of Defense's arsenal for intelligence operations in areas hostile to an official U.S. presence. The skills John practiced then give him a keen eye for reconnaissance on the battlefields of business.

"One thing we all try to do is identify what's changed with a firm's booth from one year to the next," John tells me. "How has the booth layout changed? What's new in their brochures?"

Brochures, marketing briefs, and press releases are available in bulk volume at trade shows. In addition to the materials at individual booths, many exhibitors also leave a stack in the convention center press office, which often has longer hours than the actual trade show floor, to accom-modate journalists arriving in off-hours. John has seen representatives from one company come in and remove all of a competing firm's bro-chures from the press office, leaving a pile of their own instead. That's why press offices now often have a young intern to act as a babysitter, keeping rivals from sabotaging each other's marketing material.

Scouting Redux

Jeff Lumetta was walking marathons at the Consumer Electronics Show (CES) in Las Vegas in 2009. As vice president for research and develop-ment for global electronics giant Jabil Circuit, there is plenty that he wants to see and lots more he anticipates he'll want to see but just doesn't know about yet. Unlike other industrial giants, Jabil doesn't have a booth at CES.

"It just doesn't make sense for us," he told me. "Consumers don't know who we are. Manufacturers do. Suppliers do. Folks in the logistics chain do. But not consumers. There's no reason for us to set up a display."

Jabil prefers to meet with customers at large shows like CES in pri-vate, renting a suite at a nearby hotel or within the convention center itself rather than going to the time and financial expense of maintaining a booth. "We take the time to target specific customers—that doesn't suffer. But rather than talking with them at the booth, we find more productive uses for our time," Jeff said.

By not having a booth, Jeff has more time to work his way around the show, often in parallel with Jabil customers. Jabil is a big believer in partnering, and not just from the R&D side of the house. Other Jabil staff from sales and marketing are doing the same, but for Jeff and other techies, CES is all about the technology.

"We're walking around with customers looking at what's on display, particularly your smaller technology firms. They're entrepreneurs, they've got an idea that's new, and they want to partner with someone. We, and the partners we represent, are looking for the same."

Jeff never once calls them customers, only partners, and he spends a lot of time with them at CES through dinners, meet-and-greets, and external functions where they not only talk about technology but also theorize on how they can help each other's business. It's reminiscent of the Buccaneers' ethos of watching game film together—the advantage of common strategies and implicit communications gained by evaluating the competitive environment together.

"Competitors are after some of our partners. I know it, and they know it. It's a kind of game. We'll see a competitor approach a partner to discuss undercutting us in price by 5 or 10 percent, and the partners just smile at them," Jeff said. That kind of relationship, where customers (my word) view suppliers as trusted agents for their business, is important to Jabil, says Jeff: "Everyone is trying to compete on cost. We compete on value. We know we can't compete with some of our overseas rivals on costs. So we concentrate on how to make our partner's business better. When we see technology outside the electronics industry we think would be useful to them, we'll call or stop by to discuss it. It creates a robustness that transcends cost. They appreciate a supplier who stops by with an idea rather than an invoice book looking to make one more sale."

There comes that concept of robustness again. Jeff's relationship with partners appears more like a network of trusted interlocutors than companies simply buying and selling from each other. Jeff sees the current market conditions, which shrank the attendees to CES in 2009, as an opportune time to look for quality employees, many of whom will also be scouting around at CES.

"These guys are not unemployed," he said. "They're underemployed. They're still working, but the company's not funding new projects, so they're cooling their heels waiting on the economy to recover. Maybe the firm gave them a lot of stock options as an incentive to stay. But given the market conditions, the options aren't worth the paper they're printed on. Smaller firms are looking to get acquired by a larger firm. Many will forgo a cash purchase just to get into a larger company that can open doors for them. We look for that, and we talk with our customers when we see something we think they would like too."

Jeff also tracks where different parts of the technology industry are moving. He gave me an example of a company that makes laser printers. While circuit boards for printers are a pretty straightforward technology, Jabil looks at where printers are going for their partners. What documents are *their* customers printing? What other devices do they want to hook up to those printers? Hardwired or wireless? Point-to-point or one-to-many? Knowing industry trends means Jabil can help its partners shape their industry rather than simply react to it.

So when Jeff is walking around a trade show, he's scouting (analogous to Baden-Powell's work for the British Secret Service a century earlier). What's happening? How is the industry evolving? What can Jabil do next year for its customers better than they did this year? Again, adoption and adaptation make a significant impact because they are occurring at the highest levels of a firm.

Is he looking at his competition? Of course. But he's also watching the entire competitive space—the "ecosystem of a [product] segment," he called it, figuring out what can be done better than before. That's the premiere value of a large trade show like CES. As Jabil's R&D chief, he wants to know what technology investments to make over the next year and how to make those investments the right way.

Smile for the Camera

Video and audio recording laws can vary from state to state, but at a minimum most convention centers post signs stating still photography is not allowed. That doesn't always stop the practice, however. John Hill has seen a lot of technical collection in trade shows overseas where laws are considerably different than in the United States.

"In Germany they will throw you out for snooping," he told me. "You are to stay at your booth unless it is obviously clear you are socializing with someone from another booth and they are willingly allowing you to do so."

John said that guards at a trade show in Florence, Italy, walked around with automatic weapons. The show was in a state-owned museum where a ban on photography was aggressively enforced. A different show in Bologna, however, featured a large number of Chinese personnel walking around and chatting with everyone. All of them also seemed to have a small camera in their breast pocket. Once engaged in conversation, they would trigger the camera to record video and audio of every person they spoke to.

Even where photography was banned, John said he would often see people with cameras and long lenses shooting over the top of the trade show floor to a booth far away. This gives photographers cover for action (they're not "in" the area), and they can always claim they were photographing the trade show layout rather than an individual company's booth. What companies really want to know is whom competitor leaders are talking to, walking with, drinking with, and interested in.

The bigger problem John sees is that leaders responsible for the booths aren't thinking about these issues. He has worked several by doing freelance photography for local news outlets. He can walk around with press credentials and ask permission to shoot a booth. Yet nobody asks what happens to the photographs. Some will obviously be used by the news outlet, but nobody asks if he might try to sell the others to potential competitors. He doesn't, but plenty of others will.

Technical gadgetry aside, intelligence professionals' insight into human psychology and behavior is often the most valuable asset they bring to information collection at a trade show. On many occasions, they can recruit and maintain impressive human source networks despite extremely hostile conditions, gathering information without paying a dime for it.

It is not at all unusual to see someone walk up to a booth and make idle chitchat as an entry to collect information. I've done this myself many times. At an industry trade show years ago, I had a standard trade show uniform: a 1980s era Metallica T-shirt, blue jeans, and dirty white-top sneakers. I'd visit competitors' booths during slow periods when meals were being served or a popular speaker was in the main auditorium. Booths are generally vacant at these times or staffed by the third string: the young, the new, or the socially clumsy. Most senior management are hobnobbing elsewhere, leaving the booths ripe for a competitor to pick clean.

My custom was to saunter up, pick up a brochure, and flip through it until someone behind the table responded. At that point, one of my colleagues would walk up behind me. "David" was always quite good at this. He would be decked out in a three-piece suit with all the trimmings. He oozed his blue-blood background; you could almost smell money on him. He had an M.B.A. and a law degree and knew how to put on airs when the time came. But right now he simply walked up and stopped.

Without acknowledging David at all, much less indicating that I worked with him, I'd make a remark about the product or service in the brochure and how much better a competitor's product was at a booth nearby. Then I would turn, deadpanned, to David. He would glance quickly at the stunned staffer, who always rushed in to fill the deafening silence.

This is an elicitation tactic, and a fairly reliable one. Elicitation is a powerful means of collecting information without using direct questions. In this case, a simple look was all that was needed for an untrained booth jockey to leap to his company's defense in front of a potential client. Junior people want opportunities for advancement too, and reeling in a big customer would guarantee they wouldn't be working the graveyard shift at a trade show anymore.

As soon as they started yammering, I would saunter on off around the corner to set it up again with another staff member working the show. David would eventually break away when he got what we were after, and we'd set it up again over and over. We never lied about who we were or what we were doing. I employed powerful psychological tools to exploit the biases of the people in the booth. Based on my attire, they assumed I was a roadie—someone working the trade show in setting up the booths, then waiting around to pack them up and load them onto trucks.

The booth jockeys assumed I was not a threat. I didn't look like it, act like it, or sound like it. I was playing to an inherent American bias that assumes everyone is what he or she appears to be. But assuming is foolish. You never assume anything in an environment where 72 percent of the people present admit to spying on you! On the extremely rare occasion when someone asked who I was and what I was doing, I freely gave my name and company. I was always properly badged as an attendee and never attempted any subterfuge. Given the nondisclosure agreements that are so typically part of any business transaction, now I had a simple and defendable means for deflecting the question. I wouldn't lie because I didn't need to, and it wasn't worth the hassle it would create.

Some will read this and think I'm spoiling the stew here. I'm revealing key methodologies used at a trade show. That anyone can read this and know everything they need to know about how to stop a rival from collecting information is flattering, but flawed. It doesn't work that way because it's not that simple. It reminds me of a similar accusation many years ago.

When I was young, I loved magic. Doug Henning, Harry Anderson, and two eccentric characters named Penn and Teller. For over thirty years, Penn and Teller have taken their unique craft from street corners, to Broadway, to a five-year engagement at the Rio Hotel and Casino in Las Vegas. One of their shticks when they were first breaking out was "revealing" how magic tricks were done. This created quite a stir (which was the whole point).

Magicians have a code of silence as sacrosanct as that of a priest or physician. Secrets are supposed to follow a magician to the grave. Yet here were these two upstarts revealing how many of the most popular stage illusions of the day were done. The magic world was beside itself, and the media were eating it up.

An intrepid journalist at this time interviewed Harry Blackstone Jr., one of the most accomplished and professional magicians of his time, a revered sage of the profession. The journalist caught up with Harry somewhere and breathlessly asked if this was the end of magic as an entertainment profession. Harry just smiled, patted the journalist gently on the arm, and assured him everything would be okay. "A good magician," he explained, "can show you how the trick is done and then do it again right in front of you, and you'll never see a thing."

Intelligence is the same. Though we know most of the techniques, tactics, and procedures used for collecting information, we remain blissfully ignorant of protecting ourselves from them. Sometimes we need a helping hand, a convenient "authority" to politely stop interlocutors from taking things from us. Note I did not say *steal*. You can't scream, "Thief!" if you give something away, and increasingly businesses allow the entire world to take any intellectual property they want.

Everything's Bigger in Texas

At a pork producers show at the Dallas Convention Center a few years ago, the place was crawling with swine songs. Just about all types of pork-related product you could think of, and likely a few you would never believe, were represented there. The place was awash in barbecue sauce and ten-gallon hats. Everyone was having a grand time, which is part of the attraction.

Trade shows often craft a carnival atmosphere. It gets everyone in a good mood, which keeps the attendees happy, which keeps the exhibitors happy, which keeps the festival organizers happy. The only thing that makes people unhappy is when festivals get out of hand and the crass realities of competition interfere with the experiential nature of direct marketing masked as entertainment.

You've likely noticed a few signs prominently displayed in convention centers around the country reading "No Photography Allowed." The signs are often followed by the same text in Spanish. But in Dallas, Atlanta, New York, and other major cities, the signs are often also written in Japanese.

Japan has one of the oldest and most advanced government-sponsored competitive intelligence operations in the world. Called the Japan External Trade Organization (JETRO), it is the gold standard in state-sponsored business intelligence and has offices throughout the United States. JETRO officers are known for attending a wide variety of conventions and trade shows and for taking an enormous number of pictures while there.

Look through the listing of exhibitors in your next major trade show, and you'll likely find a JETRO booth tucked away in some inconspicuous, low-traffic corner of the exhibit room floor. You'll also likely find a cadre of highly trained intelligence personnel diligently collecting brochures, taking photographs, and shooting video throughout the area. Is this legal? Yes, depending on local statutes. Is it ethical? Absolutely. The Japanese recognize they have the right, indeed the responsibility, to know as much about their competition as is legally possible. They just do a better job of it than we do.

So you will see them everywhere, even at a pork producers convention, collecting information and sending it to Tokyo, where it will be shared among several Japanese companies. Japanese vendors purchase American pork products, and they, like anyone else, want to minimize uncertainty in future business transactions. What new products are being introduced? What are breeders saying about current stocks? What do pork commodities look like right now from an investment standpoint? What volumes are producers expecting one, three, or five months out? All of this information and more is efficiently collected and sent back to Japan for analysis.

A few years ago, JETRO officers were so aggressive with their cameras that convention center officials, tired of complaints from exhibitors, began posting their "no photography" signs in Japanese to prevent claims from attendees that they couldn't read English. Virtually every high school graduate in Japan can read and write English, so the likelihood of sending someone who can't speak the language to an American trade show is rather outlandish. But business leaders should take a moment to reflect on the bigger picture.

Competitive intelligence is so important, so crucial to Japanese interests that they have created a government agency whose main role is to collect information from companies overseas and funnel it back to Japan. More to the point, Japan is not the exception. Most foreign intelligence services are allowed to collect information on American companies to share with their corporations. American business leaders must understand that national allies are still business rivals competing for the same finite international markets. Japan, Israel, France, Germany, and China do not hesitate to put the full capabilities of their intelligence services to use against American firms, placing us at a distinct disadvantage.[3]

Paradise by the Dashboard (Devices) Light

Mike Murphy truly loves his car. His friends love their cars too. Classics. Convertibles. Specialty cars. If it's got four wheels, it's Mike's kind of thing. He and his buddies also share another passion: media. Movies. Music. You name it. How does one combine a love affair with both definitions of heavy metal? Create a company that designs and builds mobile computing platforms. So that's just what he did.

It began as a hobby. One guy designed a computer platform with electronics that could handle the vibrations of an automobile. Another stripped down the Windows XP operating platform so it didn't have all the extraneous stuff they didn't need. They played with it for a couple of years, each tinkering with and building on the success of the others and developing new ways to enjoy media in an automobile.

Hardware issues like buttons and switches weren't a problem because there weren't any. Knowing they would customize each unit to their own preferences, they didn't concern themselves with ugly controls that took away from the aesthetics of the car. They used a seven-inch touch screen. Each interface can be user customized for specific applications, as can the controls for those applications—even the ones they haven't thought of yet.

They added plug-in capability for the Internet and backup cameras. Nobody planned to get into the safety features on the cars, but it didn't take long for one person to design plug-ins that monitor and visually display car sensor data.

After a couple of years, Mike and his friends realized that what they were doing was more than a hobby. More and more people were interested in the product they inadvertently developed: a media-centric mobile computing platform that was as individual as the people who built them. Dashboard Devices was born.

"If someone could think of it, we tried it," Mike told me. "Integrated cell phones? Got it. Internet access? Got it. We've done all sorts of stuff. Sometimes we did it just to see if it would work. We even integrated a hands-free microphone so you can answer e-mail with an audio file rather than typing!"

Rather than build up inventory and pitch wares in a growing recession, Mike decided to preempt their marketing, announcing at the 2009 Consumer Electronics Show that their first product would be available in six to eight months. By demonstrating the real product rather than a prototype, Dashboard Devices had the luxury of feedback from a knowledgeable cadre of potential customers. These feedback loops were invaluable as Mike and his partners talked to consumers, original equipment manufacturer buyers, and commercial application developers.

"It's made all the difference in the world. We could adjust on the fly as people came to us with new ideas. That integrated feedback made us a better company and made a lot of folks interested in working with us who wouldn't have been otherwise."

When I asked how, he rattled off a litany of ideas people had shared: "Documents, relational databases, even photograph uploads from cars to a central facility for small- to medium-sized companies. We can do all of that; it's just not been our focus. We're looking at the consumer market for our kick-off. But the commercial implications are huge. As we ship larger volumes, the per unit costs drop for everyone."

Dashboard Devices has only one real competitor, though there's not much competition from it right now. "They announced a product three years ago," Mike said. "Nobody's seen it yet. Yet there we were in the largest electronics show in the world. It was really cool!"

Not that there wasn't some competitive probing at CES. He watched a major automotive manufacturer's employee photograph nearly every square foot of Dashboard Device's booth. "But," Mike told me, "he won't get anything. Other than the touch screen on the front of the unit, there's nothing to be gained from the external view of the box that anyone can copy or exploit from a photograph. Maybe he'll send me a few of his pictures."

Mike was so busy working the booth he didn't get to enjoy the rest of the show. He isn't too worried about the intrepid photographer and actually took the man's interest as a compliment: "Those guys know cars. They know technology. For us to be of that much interest, we must be doing something right."

When I asked about the effects of the expanding market for hand-held media devices like the BlackBerry and iPhone, Mike said they still had a vocal band of car enthusiasts who want something better. They want centralized media in a mobile platform that doesn't just follow them around; it interacts with them. "We've got a dual zone setup that's incredible. Think about the car commercials you see now with the kids watching a video in the back seat. How are they controlling it? Are mom and dad crawling over the seats to get to it? How's that supposed to work? We've got a system where the driver has total control of what's happening in the rear seats, yet if somebody sitting in back is working the GPS system, they can send the results to the front of the car for the driver to see."

It's the *interaction* with the media, pushing front to back, back to front, or running multiple applications from a single computer, that sets Dashboard Devices apart.

"Apple positioned iPod as a take-it-or-leave-it product. That's not what people want if they have a choice. Right now they don't, so they plug the iPod into the car. But imagine what they would do if they had a choice." Mike chuckled before he continued: "Look at FM radio. It was the pinnacle for decades. Now you've got automakers installing MP3 players in the dash and calling it cutting edge. That technology is already several years old. They'll never keep up with cutting-edge applications because their project lead times are entirely too long. They will always feature last year's technology."

The real deal breaker to Mike and his target market is having someone else's technology package forced on them when they buy a car: "Look at Sirius and XM radio. How many cars come with that now whether you like it or not? A free ninety-day trial; then you had to pay for the subscription separately."

He was right: my 2007 Chevy came with XM satellite radio.

"You didn't keep the subscription past the free ninety days, did you?" Mike asked.

I hadn't. I didn't like paying for the privilege of listening to commercials when those advertisers paid for me to listen on FM for free. Apparently I was not alone. XM and Sirius merged in 2007 when neither company was able to find a tenable business model on its own. But their combined fortunes have not improved either. In February 2009 the *New York Times* reported that the combined company was exploring a possible bankruptcy filing, having been "unsuccessful in connecting with younger listeners" and citing "competition from other sources."[4]

Dashboard Devices may be on to something.

I'm a Small Business, and I'm Here to Help

As Mike Murphy proves, small businesses aren't at a disadvantage at trade shows or conventions. In fact, one of the most cost-effective ways for a smaller firm to leverage its participation in a trade show or convention is to sign on as a volunteer for the event.

Many industry organizations offer speaking opportunities for opinion makers, thought leaders, emerging companies, and other movers and shakers to make a formal presentation. A panel of industry volunteers evaluates the proposals submitted by willing members and decides which ones to invite for a full speaking engagement (usually providing them free room and board) and which to offer a poster session (where they must pay their own way). But this is not as benevolent as it might appear.

I know of a medium-sized chemical company that considered it a rite of passage for its up-and-coming research staff to volunteer for such a role every year. The young chemist or engineer would receive a stack of presentation proposals. The thing about these proposals was that many of them were from other up-and-coming professionals at rival firms.

Research scientists love to talk about their work. They're generally detail-oriented people and talk about those details in their presentations and supporting material. This firm's engineer would evaluate all of its rivals' emerging research and product development by learning what their scientists were doing often before their own companies were aware of it. Many scientists are totally disengaged from the business side of their work; they see only the freedom of science rather than the revenue of exclusivity. They happily share their most recent cutting-edge research with an industry panel with which they have no secrecy or nondisclosure agreements. For some reason, they share the most granular information in their proposals. Naysayers wave off concerns in this area, saying they are "only sharing the failures, what didn't work." This in fact is often the most valuable information of all.

If a company can avoid expensive research activity by concentrating on other endeavors with a significantly higher likelihood of success, they will be more than happy to pony up fifty to one hundred hours of a young protégé's time to evaluate the competitor's new product development or R&D efforts. Who bothers with late-night garbage can raids when it's perfectly acceptable to share information in such an open and collegial forum? It happens every day, and most leaders have no idea how their employees are giving away the farm.

Many times the young volunteer researcher will help compile the list of who will be invited to present and who will be turned down or offered only to provide a poster on the convention floor. This is the corporate equivalent of only placing at the high school science fair. You get to attend, but nobody is really interested in your work. Once again it's fairly simple for someone (from the presentation evaluation committee or elsewhere) to offer sage advice to the disappointed young researcher.

"I really liked your work," says the volunteer, "but I'm only one guy, and I got voted down by the others. I thought it was actually one of the best proposals we got. I'd love to hear more about it."

"Really?" perks up the downtrodden researcher/product manager.

"Oh yeah. I thought it was cutting edge."

"Thanks! I appreciate that. Not everyone at my company seems to listen to me. I'm the new/outside/young/geeky person in the department."

"That's too bad. Now when you were first isolating the crystals from the bath, that probably took about an hour right? How'd you prevent them from sticking to the glass?"

"Oh, that was pretty cool. I just . . ."

And the two new best friends step over for a cup of coffee, the researcher providing all the details NOT in the original proposal that are likely all the rival volunteer needs to recreate the same experiment in her own laboratory. The pair might later meet for dinner or drinks. Somehow (you know how these things are) the conversation invariably returns to work. And once more, the excited young wannabe, happy to have a willing ear that seems truly interested, says far more than his leadership would ever willfully allow.

Less than a year later, this company will be stunned when a competing group beats it to the marketplace with a nearly identical product. Technical schematics, cost models, revenue forecasts, market segmentation analysis, and customer contact sheets have been shared with competitors through simple, cheap, and effective ruses like this one.

This is all perfectly legal. There's not a general counsel in the country who doesn't stay up at night worrying about this sort of thing because it's happening every day in every industry in which there is more than one significant competitor.

Business as Theater

Where there is value, there is a profit margin. Where there is a profit, there will be competition. Trade shows and conventions shatter the comparative calm of genteel rivalry because this is where the gloves always come off. Walk customers around and be a partner, not just a supplier. They'll thank you by continuing to buy from you.

Be wary of invitations that appear out of the blue. Someone may have some interest in your latest widget design. Make sure nothing is public for the first time. If you don't want your booth or personnel to be photographed, by all means confront the photographers.

Werner Heisenberg said that watching affects the outcome. Knowing you are being watched at trade shows, you might find it useful to mislead the competition a bit. But why limit this to just the trade show circuit when you can use denial and deception, the topic of Chapter Six, to throw the competition off your trail all the time?

6

Denial, Deception, and Other Forms of Flattery

My four year old was deathly afraid of bees. She saw another little girl get stung once at preschool and, despite never having been stung herself, was absolutely terrified of them. Just about any variety of flying insect was enough to send her screaming for help. I've explained that bees serve a useful purpose, pollinating flowers and making honey (both of which she loves) and therefore really aren't so bad. They sting as a defense mechanism, and only if you step on them or try to swat them and miss. She got it. She actually accepted the idea they weren't just waiting around all day for her to come outside so they could sting her.

A few days later, one was buzzing around our back porch. She stood her ground, albeit nervously, her eyes squeezed shut and lips pursed, prepared to scream. But she held it together. I was impressed. Giving in to my parental impulses, I walked over and sat down next to her. I figured the little guy might prefer a larger target to buzz around, and she could relax a little.

When he inexplicably landed on my hand, I similarly froze—not from some machismo superman dad complex as much as not wanting to undo the progress she'd made. I didn't want to negate her improvement by running around screaming like a four year old myself. So I braced for it. I sat there and waited for the plunging proboscis to tear into my flesh. But nothing happened.

I unsquinted my eyes and took a closer look at him. Yellow and black stripes. Wings. Fuzzy head. He was now stumbling through the forest of hair on my hand. I prodded him with a pencil but he didn't fly away or hit me. I tried again.

Nothing.

Once more.

Nothing again.

On closer examination I realized my winged visitor hadn't had a sudden moment of compassion. He had no stinger. He was a fake. More correctly, he was a fly called a *bee mimic,* known in biological circles as a Batesian mimic.

Batesians appear to look like more dangerous animals—bees, wasps, or other stinging insects—to prevent predators from eating them. A bee sting to the mouth of a small lizard or bird would interfere with its eating habits for quite a while. By adopting the appearance of its more dangerous cousin, this fly exploited the assumptions of its predators. It also exploited the biases of neighboring organisms (like me) who, although not a predator, also assumed it had a stinger and normally gave it a wide berth.

There's a wide variety of mimicry types and purposes behind them. Different species have used it for different reasons at various times through evolution. The mimics use deception based on color, texture, sound, or other distinguishing characteristics. Purposes range from attracting prey, to repelling predators, to confusing resource competitors. The strategies of a tropical jungle are equally relevant in the asphalt jungle.

Denial and deception (D&D) is an area every business leader must think about. If you know you're being watched (remember that 72 percent of competitors admit to it), why not put on a show that distracts your adversaries from your true intentions? Keep them occupied with non-productive collection and analytical efforts. Let them waste time, money, and other resources trying to evaluate a complex bit of theater while you plug away on your real strategy that is safely tucked away from prying eyes. New products and services in the R&D pipeline are better protected, market share is less threatened, and your sunk costs (in dollars and time) for expensive product development are less likely to be wasted.

Who Says Denial Is Such a Bad Thing?

Individuals, companies, and nonprofit groups must do a better job of denying their detractors important information. If it's on a Web site or filed in a government office, the cat may be out of the bag, but there are ways to coax it back in before the neighbors notice it's on the prowl.

Information on the Internet is among the hardest to protect. Spiders—software tools that crawl over Web sites and inhale data to archive elsewhere—are an increasing problem that shows no indication of slowing down. Jeff Welgan proved this point. But it's not simply local competitors. Domestic media have become increasingly invasive, searching for key words to find salacious content. New facial recognition software can find old pictures of people suddenly thrust into the limelight.

So a Daytona Beach spring break photo from five years ago suddenly pops up when someone becomes the new media darling, even if the person's exposure (pardon the pun) was unintentional. If someone runs for public office or enters a beauty contest knowing there are compromising photos of him or her, it's not an immediate deal killer, but it's certainly something that should be addressed and a crisis plan developed. Thinking the pictures "won't come out" is an extreme case of naiveté. They will come out. And even if your name is not attached to the picture, facial recognition can cull through thousands of pictures that other people have put online and pick you out of a crowd. Next thing you know the media are staking out your home.

It's not impossible. Danielle Smith of St. Louis, Missouri, posted her family Christmas card photo on her Facebook account and blog page. When an old friend from the Czech Republic contacted her saying he'd seen the same family photo around town, she was stunned to learn a Prague grocery store had used it in its advertisements.[1] With cut-and-paste technology now commonplace, our faces may be the next intellectual property we need to begin searching for on the Internet.

Offline, things are a little bit easier. In Chapter Four I outlined how I'd gotten a competitor's key formulation data by culling through their air, water, waste disposal, and hazardous materials permits. But recall how the Georgia Department of Environmental Protection's (GDEP) interoffice memos fell off after a certain point. This is an important distinction, not only on open government but also on how companies should follow up, even after they've committed an egregious error, to deny competitors access to critical information.

FOIA requests provide a paper trail, but they also create one. Everyone who files a FOIA request becomes a notation on that file, cross-referenced a couple of different ways. We did not want Meyer Corporation to do a quarterly or biannual file scrub and have them learn we'd examined their regulatory findings. Yes, it's legal, but that's not the point. We didn't want them to know because of our friend Werner Heisenberg and his uncertainty principle: observation changes outcomes. If the competition knew we were watching this plant closely, they would take evasive action (D&D) to throw us off. Using a cutout like Global Information Resources left no audit trail back to our firm.

So with Meyer Corporation's environmental reports, building surveys, and blueprints data, we were able to reverse-engineer every aspect of its production systems with little expense or difficulty. Any company with similar permits should immediately go to every government office that has records on it and see what's there and then file a request to denote those files as containing confidential business or trade secret information. The FOIA exemptions noted in Chapter Four include one for this purpose. If you choose to not patent something (where it is available for review by the public), exemption 4, covering trade secret protection, will keep it from prying eyes.

The formulations for Coca-Cola and KFC's Original Recipe have enjoyed this protection for years by denying access to those without a documented need to see the information and an ironclad nondisclosure agreement filed with each company's general counsel. A couple of people (from inside the two companies) have gone to jail for trying. But it doesn't stop there.

I have noted how GDEP mangers did not file interoffice memos after their meeting with the new (replacement) Meyer Corporation executive. That's a slight mischaracterization on my part. State officials knew their interoffice communications were subject to FOIA requests but didn't want to tip their hand as to what they would do next. FOIA exemption 5 protects intra-agency communications under select legal privilege. It allows them to communicate privately if litigation is anticipated or ongoing.

GDEP did not release Meyer from liability, so the clock was still ticking on financial penalties. They no doubt had numerous back-and-forth notes after this meeting, but recognizing the path Meyer Corporation was initially taking, GDEP exempted its interoffice notes from the master file. Our analysis was that GDEP had no reason to release Meyer from this liability, using it as leverage to light a fire under the new leadership's feet. Exemption 7 allows similar protection if the case is turned over for criminal prosecution.

It's not only your own documentation you must protect. You must also point out to government officials at all levels when *their* correspondence about your firm or organization must be kept confidential. This is why monitoring government offices through FOIA is so important. When quarterly and annual reports contain competitively sensitive information, it is imperative that it be secured before it is archived. Most government clerks won't know your business well enough to know what's sensitive and what's not, so don't leave it up to chance. Now, while many municipalities are still in the hard copy stage, is the time to review and remove sensitive hard copy company records. Once these go digital, it will be impossible to deny access after the fact. Like Pandora's box, once something is available on the Internet, you should just assume it's compromised.

Seeing Through the Wool over Your Eyes

One problem in detecting D&D operations is that the information available is generally quite ambiguous. It could be a D&D effort on the part of the competition. It could simply be bad reporting. It could be the sources you are using aren't good enough. Maybe it's simply too early to make an intelligent decision on the issue. But when leaders need answers immediately (as they often do), it means new techniques must be introduced.

Analysis of competing hypotheses (ACH) is an analytical technique designed to answer this type of problem. Developed by the government years ago, ACH is a simple, reliable, and now proven methodology for sorting through ambiguous information across multiple spectrums and making sense out of it. With the word *hypotheses* in the title, you might guess ACH borrows heavily from the scientific method, and you'd be right.

The scientific method is a process for exploring uncertainty in a wide variety of disciplines by investigating in a very controlled way. Quantifying evidence and measuring the results makes it possible to acquire new knowledge, redouble efforts on previous areas that may yield additional results, or identify hidden patterns of causality that were not recognized before.

The scientific method is straightforward, requires no specialized training, and can be applied across a broad range of business and nonscientific endeavors to explain complex phenomena. ACH's unique insights and reproducibility through collection, observation, and experimentation around a conference room table prove its value over and over. This is one of its most powerful and, for business, most defendable attributes.

Analysis is such a subjective activity (itself a competition, as noted previously) that recreating a leader's thoughts, assertions, and conclusions across town or across time can be a challenge. ACH creates a short but thorough record of how an individual or group came to a conclusion at a particular time. Adding fields to the analysis later makes it possible to show how perspectives can change over time when incorporating new data, refining data previously examined, or discovering and incorporating evidence of deception. This can often point leaders toward a different hypothesis requiring that the technique be repeated again and resulting in a totally new direction, with the added value of being more reliable and having a higher probability of being correct.

The scientific method is simple:

1. Decide what your uncertainty is—in other words, what is the question?
2. Gather evidence related to this question.
3. Form several hypotheses that answer the question. Don't try to answer them; just write them down.
4. Collect data that relate to your evidence.
5. Interpret the results, and tally the analysis.

But let's not forget this is a competitive endeavor—hence, the C of ACH. The hypotheses listed are competing with each other within the analysis. Here's where ACH takes something of a departure from the scientific method on which it is based. Leaders, particularly those working in groups of others unlike themselves, are going to have hypotheses (even guesses) they do not like, disagree with, or even think are stupid. Not only do we not want individual biases interfering with the analysis, we also want to ensure that any reasonable possibility is at least considered so that if stakeholders (or regulators!) later question the conclusion, ACH can show how the cited possibility was considered, evaluated, and ultimately dismissed.

This is the strong point of ACH: documenting, particularly when someone asks in the future, how an analysis came to a particular conclusion. Memories fade after time, and if data sets are exceptionally large, perfect recall of how something was analyzed is difficult, if not outright impossible. The conclusion looks flawed, the leader looks foolish, and the investors wonder if they were misled, driving a wedge between executives and the shareholders they serve. This is not a tenable situation.

Several software programs offer the ACH instrument to analysts. But the myriad security restrictions in corporate computer networks make it difficult to apply such software easily. This is especially true when leaders want to share the project across a large staff by e-mail or when they must share the results externally. So I recreated the ACH methodology in an Excel spreadsheet. Microsoft Office is commonly found on most corporate and government computer networks, making a convenient workaround for this problem. Because Excel spreadsheets are easily e-mailed, recipients outside the local area network can take part in a complicated analysis and provide additional vetting for the issue being examined.

So how does ACH work? Much of the information available to us, particularly from various media sources, can and often does mean more than one thing, and it can exist in several widely different types of scenarios. We'll walk through an example that shows why ACH works and how it can be broadly applied.

Do You Believe in Magic?

Criss Angel is one of America's most popular young entertainers. Blending psychology, illusion, music, and an irreverent attitude that resonates with audiences, Angel has taken magic off the stage and placed it out into the audience itself. One of his most popular illusions is walking through an office window.

His three and a half minute video is a great way to understand ACH and allow readers to interpret the ways they can try this tool for their own purposes. The video is available at http://www.youtube.com/watch ?v=n3f-WPrKnRU. Angel sets up the scene, tapping on a glass window to prove its validity, and solicits help from a small crowd of onlookers. He places a box in front of the window and selects two people to hold a piece of paper against the glass before starting to go inside. But he stops to untie and remove his shoes, the screen filling with a close-up of high-top sneakers, with the video speeding up faster than normal. The speed then returns to normal, and Angel disappears into the office, closing the door.

The two volunteers hold the paper against the glass. The outline of Angel's hand presses on the paper from the other side and a single finger pokes through. Gasps erupt from the remaining onlookers. The finger curls under, carefully tearing a larger hole in the paper. Angel's foot appears, pushing (and tearing) its way through the paper, followed by a leg searching for solid footing on the box. Angel's head and torso follow, his hands sweeping behind him to push the paper back against the windowpane. He jumps down from the box and, with a flourish, rips away the paper to reveal a fully intact window. It's very impressive, particularly for such a short bit.

But *what* do you really see here, and *how* do you see it?

Angel engages in some witty banter with a red-headed gentlemen leaning against the door frame. You assume it's his office based on his posture, demeanor, and the frequency by which he darts in and out of the office. But what do you know about him? Absolutely nothing. Because he's engaged by Criss Angel in a collegial fashion, appears to be responsible for this office, and is the de facto spokesman for this group, we assume he's in charge. But that's an assumption. He's an assumed authority figure, a common deception technique.

If he'd been introduced before the clip, if his name was known and acknowledged as responsible for this area, if he was recognized to speak for this group, that would be a different thing entirely. But after you watch the clip a couple of times, more points like this come out—and not just on the individuals you're seeing, but also on the action itself—for example:

- A clean sheet of paper is recovered from a convenient trash can.
- The office appears to not actually conduct business. There is no appearance of being open other than a cheesy sign with "Open" written on it.
- The office appears industrial, an odd place to select unless controlling the size and makeup of the crowd was important.
- The cameraman is conveniently helpful. Although the shot is uninterrupted, it tightens in on Angel's shoes at a crucial point.
- The camera compresses time, altering the temporal aspect of evaluation.

This is just a sample of the many points that continue to emerge after watching the clip a few times. (Students over the years have come up with fifty pieces of evidence in this exercise.) So is Criss Angel really walking through this glass? Or is it a trick and we are being deceived? This is where ACH starts to shine.

We'll take the five points listed as our initial evidence. We have two hypotheses: what happened was real and Criss Angel somehow dematerialized through the glass, or it was a fake and we were tricked, even if we don't know how. This last point is important. Leaders don't need to know how they were deceived—not at this point in the analysis. Right now we are interested only in determining *if* a deception effort is under way. Let's see how this would help leaders with a similarly ambiguous situation.

The ACH spreadsheet in Figure 6.1 has spaces for three hypotheses, which is about as many as you want to try and analyze at one time. More are certainly possible, but my suggestion is always to limit to three. Otherwise it gets to be too much on the page at once and negatively alters the analysis. You can reuse the same evidence on other pages; just limit your analysis to three at a time.

Once the hypotheses are in place, it's a matter of listing the available evidence in the first column. The columns designated H1 and H2 are where the analyst will evaluate each piece of evidence and give it one of three simple designators as to whether the evidence is consistent with the stated hypothesis: c (consistent with the evidence), i (inconsistent with the evidence), or n (no effect on the hypothesis). The five pieces of evidence for this example will make the evaluation simple and quick.

Evidence piece 1 (E1) is a clean sheet of paper conveniently found in a nearby trash can. Is it consistent with Criss Angel's being able to walk through glass (hypothesis 1)? There is no reason to think it's impossible, so the answer is yes. Is it also consistent with this being a trick (hypothesis 2)? Yes. So it has no effect on either hypothesis. It's effectively neutral for the analysis, so we place the letter n in the columns for hypotheses 1 and 2.

What about the office (E2)? If Angel is real, does the office window he's walking through need to be real? No; the window should have no effect one way or another. It's the same if it's a trick. Maybe the answer on both is neutral again, and n is added to the columns.

E3 initially appears similar to E1 and E2 until observers consider the issue a bit. Would the office location, some sort of industrial area, be needed? Well, yes, but would the reasons be the same? If Angel is for real (hypothesis 1), he'd want to control the size of the crowd. He doesn't want hecklers or people walking up and interfering. So in this instance, a semiremote location is consistent. We place the letter c in the H1 column. If it's a trick (hypothesis 2) Angel would similarly need a controlled environment. He'd

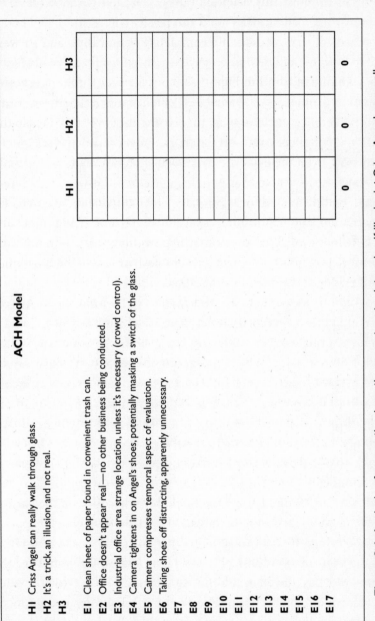

ACH Model

	H1	H2	H3

H1 Criss Angel can really walk through glass.

H2 It's a trick, an illusion, and not real.

H3

E1 Clean sheet of paper found in convenient trash can.

E2 Office doesn't appear real—no other business being conducted.

E3 Industrial office area strange location, unless it's necessary (crowd control).

E4 Camera tightens in on Angel's shoes, potentially masking a switch of the glass.

E5 Camera compresses temporal aspect of evaluation.

E6 Taking shoes off distracting, apparently unnecessary.

E7

E8

E9

E10

E11

E12

E13

E14

E15

E16

E17

Figure 6.1 Analysis of competing hypotheses set up to determine if Illusionist Criss Angel can walk through a plate glass window.

have to prohibit the audience from walking up and potentially spoiling the show. In this circumstance, he'd want the same relative isolation, albeit for different reasons. Column H2 should also receive a *c*.

The two columns thus far are completely identical. E1 and E2 were neutral to both hypotheses, so they were ambiguous pieces of evidence. E3 was a unique fit for both hypotheses but for very different reasons. This is not unusual. Lots of evidence collected across different platforms and from different sources is going to look like this. What ACH helps do is identify which pieces of information are most crucial and which can be dismissed. Even the evidence dismissed should remain on the ACH spreadsheet, however, so that people later can see it was considered, evaluated, and dismissed for legitimate reasons. This can be crucial for documentation and justification, especially much later if additional evidence becomes available, some other hypothesis comes to mind, time reveals more possibilities than are evident now, or one of these previous pieces of evidence is somehow discredited.

Moving on, we come to E4: the camera tightening up on Angel's shoes. Would this be necessary if Angel was real? Probably not. Could it be random, a mistake? Possibly. But because this illusion was set for broadcast on television, which charges by the second, it doesn't make sense. Why pay broadcast time for Angel to take his shoes off? It's inconsistent with the hypothesis that Angel is really magic, so we put an *i* in the H1 column. If the whole thing is a fake, Angel might need that momentary distraction to switch the solid glass with one that has been doctored. That makes the sneaker closeup consistent with hypothesis 2, and column H2 receives a *c*.

E5 is similar. Manipulating time would be unnecessary if the illusion is real; therefore, it's inconsistent. If we need to manipulate time for appearance or subterfuge, then it's consistent. Enter an *i* for H1 and a *c* for H2.

At the bottom of columns H1 and H2 in Figure 6.2, you'll see the numeral count has moved in column H1 from the default 0 to now reading 2. This model makes use of Excel's conditional formatting tool to count the total number of inconsistencies in each column reflected in the *i* entries for each piece of evidence.

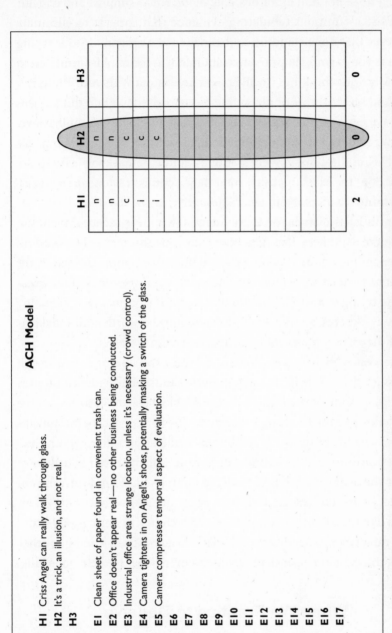

ACH Model

H1 Criss Angel can really walk through glass.
H2 It's a trick, an illusion, and not real.
H3

E1 Clean sheet of paper found in convenient trash can.
E2 Office doesn't appear real—no other business being conducted.
E3 Industrial office area strange location, unless it's necessary (crowd control).
E4 Camera tightens in on Angel's shoes, potentially masking a switch of the glass.
E5 Camera compresses temporal aspect of evaluation.
E6
E7
E8
E9
E10
E11
E12
E13
E14
E15
E16
E17

	H1	H2	H3
E1	n	n	
E2	n	n	
E3	c	c	
E4	i	c	
E5	i	c	
	2	0	0

Figure 6.2 Completed analysis of competing hypotheses model for Criss Angel. Notwithstanding the numerous "consistent" (c) in hypothesis 2, it was the two "inconsistent" (n) points in hypothesis 1 that led students to eliminate that possibility.

ACH does not add up or evaluate evidence to support any conclusion. What it's doing is tabulating evidence that appears to eliminate hypotheses that don't stand up to the evidence. Someone who is trying to deceive you is going to put out an abundant amount of information to try to sway your thinking. It will appear consistent with your thoughts, beliefs, and ideas. The ad or marketing piece might make you think, "This could have been written just for me," because in fact it just might have. Providing evidence to support your conclusion (that you should buy *this* product) is in the company's best interest and is remarkably easy to do. So ACH does the exact opposite, compiling a count of what's *inconsistent*, to determine what's real and what's deceptive.

Our initial assessment on Criss Angel is that the evidence is inconsistent with the hypothesis that Angel can truly walk through a glass window. Now, depending on the expense of additional information, the validity of the evidence displayed, the time available, and the importance of the question we're trying to answer, what should we do? If a business is conducting an analysis like this, an important decision may be worth additional evidence if the answer turns out to be less clear than we see here.

Because the analysis is set up in Microsoft Excel it's simple to e-mail it to others for their evaluation, suggestions for additional evidence, or even alternative hypotheses that will make the problem clearer. Leaders can see the evidence and the resulting conclusion. They either accept the conclusion or restart the analysis with additional evidence or other hypotheses.

At a minimum, it has eliminated some uncertainty regardless of whether the analysis itself is considered completed. It's not uncommon for leaders to restart the analysis with other questions that come off an analysis like this. Because it provides quick clarity in ambiguous situations, it can open the floodgates of decision makers' ideas, leading to other projects, drawing intelligence professionals ever closer to their leadership.

When We Practice to Deceive

One aspect of military strategy that has been repeated for centuries is the need to be ambiguous, immeasurable, a mystery. The late Colonel John Boyd, one of the greatest military strategists of the modern era, characterized it as the need to be unfathomable.[2] The purpose is to increase your opponent's uncertainty by wondering, *What the heck are they doing?* As a result, your opponent will have to dedicate more resources into figuring out what's going on. That will cost money and time and make her question the validity of her conclusions. She won't be quite sure what's happening, and this uncertainty will make her hesitant and noncommittal. Decision making will be stalled by a bad case of analysis paralysis.

They won't know what they don't know, what's really going on, so they cannot react appropriately. Most react by doing nothing at all, which is precisely what a D&D campaign seeks. As Shelton Quarles noted in Chapter Two, the opposing player in a football game tries to make him second-guess, and this hesitation will provide an opening for the ball carrier to run through. Talk about falling into a trap!

When the rival does attempt to react, it is half-hearted and obviously insincere, and the antagonist, having anticipated the inaction due to research and planning, uses D&D that precisely meets what the rival expects to see. Since it is expected, collection and analysis are often cursory or even stop completely because leaders believe there's no point to it or to save money on expenses. Yet when a rival is misdirecting leaders from their true course of action is when it would be most crucial.

Rather than steering their rival onto the rocks, where they might recognize their position and how to react, the antagonist instead steers them in very large circles far away from shore. Never going anywhere, never learning anything, wasting time and resources, they become a ghost ship on an unrelenting sea of uncertainty.

Make no mistake: D&D flatters an opponent as being worthy, not stupid. D&D is expensive, time-consuming, resource intensive, and difficult to do properly. It's applied only to products and projects deemed important or against adversaries known to be good at discerning a rival's strategy.

Trial by Fire and the Cutting Edge

An old expression states, "With time comes perspective." One of the more fascinating intracorporate D&D campaigns of my formative years was the media-centric enmity between Bic and Gillette nearly four decades ago. In 1970 Gillette had purchased a French company that specialized in luxury cigarette lighters but had developed a new disposable lighter called Cricket. Gillette released it in the United States in 1972.

Meanwhile, the Bic Pen Corporation, having the majority share of its core writing market, decided to break into new areas to maintain company growth. *Time* magazine reported that Bic had been test marketing a disposable lighter, and it debuted in 1973.[3]

Gillette's product had come out earlier, and it had a solid customer base over Bic. So Bic turned to what had worked for it in the past, television, and created the famous "Flick My Bic" tagline that became a national catchphrase. Bic also slashed costs so its lighters sold through retail outlets for less than a dollar. Gillette was incensed.

Over several years, Bic ate away at Gillette's dominance, finally taking the lead in 1978. Gillette conceded and in 1984 sold the entire Cricket line to another firm. Bic had around 65 percent of the domestic disposable lighter market at that point.

The animosity between the two firms was not limited to lighters. King C. Gillette had invented the safety razor in 1903, and his company had dominated the market for seventy years. In 1975, as the lighter war raged, Bic's parent company introduced a disposable plastic razor in Europe. Anticipating Bic would push the new technology into the United States, Gillette raced its own disposable, named the "Good News," to market, releasing it in 1976, a year ahead of Bic's razor.

But Gillette's strategy remained too internally focused. Good News had higher costs and lower revenues than its replacement blade products, and the firm had little interest in spending ad money to pirate its own product. This left Bic an opening, which it again exploited through its core strength in television. Blindfolded men were shaved on one side of their face with the (disposable) Bic and on the other side with Gillette's more expensive (reusable) Trac II system. The ads claimed 58 percent of consumers couldn't tell the difference between the two shaves.

Gillette was furious and asked the major television networks not to air Bic's commercials until it provided empirical proof of its claims. But Gillette discounted a fundamental advertising tenet: shows are presented to viewers by advertisers, and viewers are brought to advertisers by shows. The networks, enjoying the buzz and the revenue, continued airing the ads.

At the beginning of 1980, each firm had 50 percent of the U.S. disposable razor market, which accounted for only 20 percent of the total wetshaver business. Gillette eventually stopped advertising disposables completely to concentrate on its primary business in replacement blade shaving systems.

So what are the lessons from a D&D perspective? Gillette always had first-to-market advantage, usually preempting Bic by a year (in lighters and disposable razors). Bic exploited its television ad experience to counter Gillette's advantage. Bic understood the power of this medium in delivering a message to an audience already served by another producer:

The message was concise:	"Flick My Bic"
It was specific to the company:	The name was in the tagline
Told audience what it does:	"Flick" to describe lighter's action
Spoke to value:	Three thousand guaranteed lights for less than a dollar
Differentiated:	Sexual innuendo ("Flick My Bic")

The ad's deception was in the clever innuendo of the on air-talent offering to flick their Bic. It made no reference to the competing products at all, simply suggesting that consumers would meet more of the opposite sex using a Bic lighter. Smoking was swapped with sex as the payoff to buying a Bic.

With the razor campaign, Bic went with a slightly different deception strategy using the same format. Ignoring Gillette's disposables, Bic went after Gillette's cash cow replacement razor business. Gillette exploited a perception that disposables were not as good as razor systems. With ads saying they were not only as good but maybe slightly better, Bic not only trumped Gillette's disposables, it also stole customers from the razor systems as well, a double-edged cut to Gillette's revenue.

By denying any empirical proof of razor performance, Bic put Gillette on the defensive. Gillette couldn't attack disposables outright because it had its own line to protect. But how could it succinctly and legitimately counter Bic's highly effective campaign without increasing its own liability? It couldn't, as the network's responses proved.

Gillette had great insight into its competition's R&D and product development plans, but it should have allowed its competitive analysis team more access to marketing, advertising, and sales to protect its first-mover advantages.

D&D campaigns can be difficult to respond to, and their effectiveness can take years to recover from. With the advent of the Internet, there are many new ways to mislead competitors than ever before.

The Prime Minister's Directive

Winston Churchill famously said, "The truth is so valuable it must be protected with a bodyguard of lies."[4] Any good D&D action is based on the reverse being equally true: effective deception is so valuable that a bodyguard of truth must surround it. This truth must be just off-center enough, just slightly out of the adversary's expectation, that it causes him to pause, to hesitate, to look elsewhere for clues. He becomes uncertain about what he really knows and doesn't know.

Analysis of competing hypotheses can prevent leaders from being tricked through a complex and expensive D&D operation. By creating a proof of record, leaders can adequately defend themselves from those who will later second-guess them with the twenty-twenty advantage of hindsight, but not the foresight to make difficult decisions under uncertain circumstances.

From viral YouTube videos to rumor-debunking sites like Snopes. com, D&D campaigns are as probable in business as death and taxes are to the people who create them. In order to discern the validity of these competing messages, leaders will have to concentrate more than ever before on their antagonists' psyches. In Chapter Seven we'll see that prime-time television forensics pale in comparison to what is available to business leaders today.

Part Three: Back Office Research

7

Psychological Forensics
CSI of the Mind

Why do we make decisions the way we do? Why do we buy the things we buy? What makes us pick one brand over another? Can those decisions be predicted when we ourselves may not even be aware a decision-making opportunity is upon us? Can we influence (dare I say *control*) a leader's decision making without her knowledge?

This is the primary task of advertising and marketing professionals: making us aware of products and encouraging us to purchase only the brands they are selling. Boiled down to the simplest argument, you advertise a *product* and market a *brand*. I *need* a new car but I *want* a BMW: the car is a product while BMW is a brand. How and why people make decisions on products and brands is an important part of business that is more often left to fate than to science—a poor choice.

An enormous amount of psychological science in decision making lends itself to outside examination and evaluation. Once done, it is also possible to influence and sometimes control that decision-making process in a way that favors one side over the other. There are few absolutes, and the human mind is certainly one of the most complex organisms on the planet. But properly examined and evaluated, it's amazing how easily we can all be manipulated.

Our everyday actions, like our language, are quite routine. Much of our individual language use can be boiled down to around fifteen hundred high-repetition words that we use throughout the day. Our actions follow similar patterns. We wake up at preset times (alarm clock) and engage in the same morning ritual (shower, dress, coffee) before getting off to work. Once there, we follow many routine methods for completing whatever it is we do professionally. Even if the tasks we perform are not routine, the manner with which we complete them usually is.

After work, we likely have a small selection of activities we engage in from time to time: golf, picking the kids up, maybe a quick run for exercise if the weather is nice. All of this is fairly routine; anything out of the ordinary is usually predicated by some external trigger. It's rarely something of our own volition because we have a routine. It's our routine, and we like it.

When we return home, we watch television, eat dinner, bathe the kids, and retire for the night—all around the same time every day. We have some variations for the weekends based on (again) external triggers like Saturday soccer games and Sunday morning church, but by and large, it's pretty routine stuff. To detour us from these comfortable routines it is necessary to either manipulate perception or exploit feelings surrounding an event.

Manipulation surrounds us in magazine ads, billboards, radio jingles, television commercials, and every other litany of opportunities that companies have to put their products in front of potential buyers. But how to make those products stand out from the noise of everyday life? How do we make our brand stick with a customer—and not just now but over the long term? How can we sell multiple products or services to a single customer, keeping her so satisfied she won't go anywhere else?

There is also the need to position and protect—positioning a person, product, or campaign to gain favor in the information market. We see it on Wall Street, in boardrooms, and in small businesses where company leaders internally manipulate what's happening around them until it best fits their preferred views of the world. It's why businesses often go under even as the CEO is loudly proclaiming how well the company will do "soon." CEOs simply cannot see the facts for what they are because they're too busy repositioning those facts inside their own minds.

Into the Mind's Eye

Profiling key executives is now a common business practice. It is a popular means for lawyers to profile rival litigators, expert witnesses, judges, and jurors. In doing so, they can delicately influence how case proceedings take place by knowing which critical areas will resonate with their various audiences (opposing counsel, deposed witness, or a jury during a trial). What works in court is equally applicable for mergers, acquisitions, executive recruiting, political campaigns, board recruiting, and other activities where a specific person or a select small group of people can be identified for detailed study.

Executive profiling extrapolates known elements of personality, behavior, and history in order to predict future behavior. There are two types of profiling. A *composite subject profile* is generally a forensic exercise used in investigative applications. It has specific applications in competitive intelligence, generally for finding someone who fits a predetermined personality type. Boards of directors and executive recruiting firms often use this to help screen candidates for a position based on what they know of the recruiting firm's needs, tastes, and culture. A *target subject profile* has much more utility for competitive intelligence work: it focuses on a specific key decision maker or leader and addresses the pertinent parts of his or her personality that can best be targeted for influence purposes.[1] A profile like this has two parts: a comprehensive biographical portrait and a remote personality exam.

A *biographical portrait* is the first step in building a map of future behaviors. Past behavior is the single best predictor of future actions. Biographical elements include fundamental social factors, education and training, key experiences (good and bad), significant influences and mentors, and the target's guiding beliefs. Major milestones factor quite heavily here, incorporating a diagnostic history of the person's decision making, key successes, and significant failures. The focus will always be on how the person "read" the situation and her resulting action.

People repeat their successes and avoid their failures. This is a central tenet of human nature. Changes in beliefs and approaches must be understood in the context of what took place that was different. The context of the conflict becomes paramount; using a scenario analysis, the target's behavior will be similar to previous scenarios.

A *remote personality assessment* means that the subject being profiled remains unaware that a psychological summary is being compiled on her. This is easier than it may seem because so much information is in the public domain and the social nature of business in the United States means it is reasonably easy to find people who know the subject person. They may have worked with or for the subject. Maybe they were a customer or a competitor. Regardless, there is a whole population out there that is happy to answer a few reasonable questions. Individually these people can provide very little data, but combined will provide a full outline of a person's decision-making habits.

Several firms offer specialty services such as this, and leaders should at least understand the differences among them so they can competently judge the qualifications of any forensic professional and ensure the results provided answer the key questions being asked. (The appendix provides a full explanation of various psychological tools.)

The first is the Myers-Briggs Type Indicator (MBTI). This workhorse of the psychology profession has been around for years and is popular because it is easy, accurate, and cost-effective. Numerous companies around the country offer the test in person, online, or by mail. It was the first to be applied forensically for business and is broadly approved, reliable, and easily accessible by laypeople. What must be understood is what the MBTI provides: preferences and broad categories to characterize them:

How does the subject prefer to reenergize?	Introvert (I) versus Extrovert (E)
How does the subject prefer to receive and process data?	Sensory (S) versus Intuitive (N)
How does the subject prefer to make decisions?	Thinking (T) versus Feeling (F)
How does the subject prefer to organize?	Judging (J) versus Perceiving (P)

These broad categories are not designed to predict behavior or what someone will do in a given situation. They indicate what the person's preferences are—how he or she likes things to be. But this kind of information can be invaluable in determining behavior when combined with other tools. Understand the subject's preferences, and you begin to understand his thinking, which is the first step toward predicting behavior.

Introverts need distance between the discussion of a topic and making a decision based on the information gained. They prefer to be alone to think about the issue versus bouncing it around a team of others. They can easily get worn out by team-oriented activities. They generally avoid off-the-cuff engagements and prefer to have prior written notice on topics. By contrast, Extroverts do their best in group environments. They absorb energy in cluster settings and solicit ideas and comments from a trusted set of interlocutors. They need the interaction.

Sensors are detailers: they like facts and figures, historical details and proof. They'll eat up charts and graphs and likely engage in discussion on relevant parts. Intuitives, by contrast, want only the big picture; they avoid details and think forward to the future's impact. Generally these are visual thinkers who conceptualize data (whether that's the intent or not). They are easily irritated by fine points and deeply want to be inspired.

Thinkers are logical, rational decision makers, often pejoratively labeled as "cold-hearted." Feelers are just the opposite: always looking at the human factors in a decision, striving for balance between mercy and justice.

Judgers are orderly types, preferring as much prior planning as can be had. They remain committed to a plan and always, always seek closure. Perceivers are spontaneous, open-minded, flexible people capable of focusing on several things at the same time. They can also be hard to pin down on a specific topic.

The MBTI can be hard to apply for intelligence purposes because of the disconnect between preferences and actions. MBTI doesn't attempt to determine what other factors are at play with a subject's decision making. But a quick look at a couple of famous examples will be instructive in how you can apply this tool to decision makers and use it as a guide to know what specific questions to ask to characterize an individual.

Bill Clinton is one of the most enigmatic presidents in modern U.S. history. Entire books have been written about his candidacy, his presidency, and at times his poor decision making. A remote psychological profile of Bill Clinton shows him to be an ESFP (Extravert, Sensory, Feeling, Perceiving).[2] Extraversion certainly seems to fit the bill (pardon the pun again). He is a consummate showman and in his element on a podium. He is a Sensor, capable of voluminous intake of information, a trait that no doubt served him well in law school. A sense of history is a strong characteristic he is able to exploit at will when speaking to a crowd. He is a Feeler, as the world no doubt remembers with his infamous phrase, "I feel your pain." And he is a Perceiver, voraciously polling the people to get a bead on what the population thinks on any given topic before stating his opinion.

Contrast this with Saddam Hussein. The late dictator of Iraq was likely an ENFJ (Extravert, Intuitive, Thinking, Judging).[3] He was an Extravert like Bill Clinton, but sadistic in his dealings with others. He was Intuitive, caring little for details (like serving his people) and inspired by his own vision of what Iraq's place in the Islamic world should be. He was a Feeler, but that feeling was largely one of "me versus the world," and he lashed out at those around him when his paranoia got the best of him. He was a Judger, reflected in the thousands of people he condemned to death for perceived injustices.

The sixteen combinations of MBTI preferences are just that—preferences. They don't outline future actions or behavior. Every rapist, murderer, and child abuser in history fits into the same sixteen categories alongside Mother Teresa, Martin Scorsese, and Jack Welch. This is a starting point, a launching pad into more specific areas. Like intelligence itself, forensics is a puzzle, and this is simply a first piece.

Special (Psychological) Weapons and (Mental) Tactics

Obviously there are many different avenues for psychological assessment of a competitor. What's best is to identify the problem that needs to be solved through a leadership profile and find a competent forensics professional to conduct and analyze the study. A layperson can offer a few basic judgments, but the truly granular assessments require a professional.

Dr. Marta Weber is a business intelligence scientist. She is a psychology professional who has worked for the intelligence community and federal law enforcement. A few years ago, she decided to apply her skills to more competitive pursuits and formed Applied Behavioral Sciences as a consulting shop.

Her 2004 article, "Profiling for Leadership Analysis," was a lightning rod to the competitive intelligence community.[4] Many people were aware of how government agencies use psychological profiles to determine what a foreign head of state would do in particular situations. Marta was now offering these same methods to boardrooms around the country. What really got attention was her stated purpose of "ensuring the value proposition" in leadership assessments. She wasn't an academic providing esoteric theories. Her products answer real-world questions and produce tangible results.

One of her primary tools is an instrument that she continues to refine and improve: the Weber Behavioral Index (WBI). Motivation is the key piece in determining the future behavior of a decision maker, and her tool helps quantify and qualify motivation.

"Too many people trying this type of work are only making portraits," she told me.

"Portraits?" I asked.

"Yes. Somebody's history: the clubs they're in, what they like to do. It's a snapshot of a person, but that's all. Everybody with a social science degree is jumping on the bandwagon offering these services. But they're not forecasting behavior, and that's the whole point!" she emphasized.

Previous behavior, successes repeated and failures avoided, and identifying the elements behind both are important context to an analysis. If a new opportunity is similar to an old one, behavior is relatively easy to predict. The person will also desperately avoid scenarios with a potential to repeat a prior failure. Her emotional defenses will prevent her intellectual side from making a free choice because it can't risk another embarrassing incident. A rival can exploit this with relative ease.

Forecasting behavior is what sets apart laboratory psychologists who overrely on theory from field personnel like Weber who have applied these tools successfully over and over, as reflected in her high repeat-client rate. As she did in law enforcement, she thinks psychological analysis for competitive intelligence should look backward to locate the requisite data and then forward to forecast behavior.

To give you an idea of what an assessment looks like, Weber provided a sample profile from a previous project. Specific sections have been removed and critical personal details altered to mask the executive's true identity. Although the company and personality names are fictitious, the person, context, and purpose are real. (Many thanks to Dr. Weber for providing this profile.)

Profile: Michael Robin
Senior Vice President, Birdland Products

Contents

I. Summary: Events Surrounding Robin's Appointment to Birdland Post

Confirmed Findings

Birdland announced on December 8, 2003, that Michael Robin had been named senior vice president of Birdland, succeeding Marian Duraney, whose imminent retirement was announced at the same time. Robin reports to Darryl Wolfe, president and chief operating officer, Birdland Group, as did Duraney.

Internal Birdland sources said that it had been "increasingly clear for some time that Duraney was not the person to lead the next charge," despite Duraney's "generally good" track record during her thirty-two-year career at Birdland's parent company. Official statements praised Duraney. "Marian's rare combination of financial expertise and creative business thinking have enabled her to make outstanding contributions in both financial and commercial organizations during her more than thirty years at Birdland Group. Most recently, as president of Birdland, she led the successful initiations of a customer-focused approach to our furniture business," said Stephen Clark, chairman of the board and chief operating officer of parent company Angel Development.

Yet insiders say that despite superior financial expertise and business savvy, Duraney lacked the necessary experience, vision, and drive in precisely the area of customer-focused initiatives Angel Development has in mind for Birdland. This focus was evident in that portion of Clark's December 8 statement pertaining to Robin. "We are very pleased to add an executive of Michael Robin's caliber to our organization. He is a recognized leader in the furniture industry, with a strong track record as a results-oriented leader," said Clark. "His experience will be of great value as we continue to expand Birdland's longstanding leadership in marketing to interior design professionals to deliver leading furniture products directly to consumers. As a member of Angel Development's senior leadership team, Robin's furniture marketing expertise also will provide the broader company with an important new perspective."

Note: Duraney was tapped by Angel Development to run Birdland at the departure of Chris McAllister in 2001. At that time we concluded that Angel Development wanted to (1) fill the position quickly, (2) maintain continuity, and (3) exercise control over Birdland by having an Angel Development insider at the helm. In that context, it is probably the case that Angel Development's vision for Birdland has evolved since and that senior management has determined that a furniture product specialist is needed to move the business division in that direction. Robin's fifteen years of furniture experience fits the bill.

Robin, forty-five years old, joined Angel Development from Dynasty Products, where he held the position of senior vice president for commercial operations. Robin was Dynasty Product's "first Latino in a senior post." Robin is generally credited with leading a highly successful growth strategy for Dynasty's leading brands, delivering both improved market share position and profitability, according to several published and primary sources.

Under an organizational plan announced in September, Robin was to be promoted to the newly created position of senior vice president, Worldwide Commercial Business, with combined responsibility for all geographical business units, effective January 2004. But one week before the Birdland announcement in December, Dynasty Products announced Robin would be leaving immediately to take a leadership position at another company. Business media and Wall Street analysts viewed his departure as sudden, unexpected, and disruptive to the current business strategy articulated by Dynasty Products. One observer noted that "Robin had been recently passed over for promotion to the newly created position of COO, which had been assigned to Dynasty Products' CFO instead."

Unconfirmed Findings

Several rumors have circulated about Robin's recruitment by Birdland. Although unconfirmed, they may provide insights into Angel Development's underlying strategy in hiring him.

A New York business reporter told a senior competitive intelligence consultant that Robin had been fired by Dynasty Products. The same reporter would not confirm the story to us. Other knowledgeable sources close to Dynasty Products indicated that Robin had been paid a "very attractive severance package; Dynasty Products does not want him out there talking." One suggested that Robin had been dismayed by prejudicial attitudes at Dynasty Products, a company known to be conservative and insular. Dynasty had been so cautious that a few years ago, it took some convincing from a major Madison Avenue firm to get the marketer to hire a Latino as the next featured on-air talent for their well-known furniture ads. A reliable internal source said Robin had been appointed to increasingly responsible posts but recently had not been given adequately free rein to "do the job." Still another source with close-in access to Dynasty told us that Robin felt betrayed; he believed Dynasty Products senior executives had broken faith with the agreements made to him. It was suggested that the issue was not personal but revolved around business development strategies.

A source close to Birdland told us there had been an exchange of communication between the two companies after Robin came aboard at Birdland. According to this account, Dynasty sent a letter of dubious wisdom to Birdland, reminding it of Robin's nondisclosure agreement. Birdland officials took offense and fired back at Dynasty that as a top-tier company, Birdland senior management hardly needed reminding of the legal requirements.

Dynasty is viewed as "out of line on this one," informed sources close to both companies have indicated. Internally a Birdland senior official was heard to say that while Birdland didn't "want trouble" with Dynasty, the company felt it had no exposure on the issue and that the latter had "blown it."

One source told us that Dynasty had put out the story (on terminating Robin) in order to counter anticipated "negative press" in the wake of his departure. In this view, Dynasty then had to retreat from that strategy, perhaps due to a warning of some kind from Robin. Another observer said that in the face of the loss represented by Robin's departure, which is considerable, Dynasty did not want to make matters worse; hence, the severance package.

A market analyst who watches the company told us he had heard that Robin "had complaints . . . and when he aired them, things went downhill rapidly. . . There was a mutual recognition that this would not work. . . . Apparently it happened rather quickly, and Dynasty may already regret the process, if not the outcome." "Perhaps the most surprising aspect of a troubling set of events is that it has been kept from the media," one inside source observed.

There is a suggestion in all of this that Robin has knowledge in addition to marketing skills that will help Birdland, even potentially to the disadvantage of Dynasty Products, though the two in no way compete in the same markets. We have been unable to confirm or clarify the issues further. Robin's track record at Dynasty Products may provide clues, however.

This general summary provides a remarkable bit of insight into Michael Robin's hiring that clearly is not widespread in the public domain. It gives decision makers at a competing or secondary firm important insights into what likely happened with Michael at Dynasty Products and what his first orders of business at Birdland are likely to be like.

The overall product Dr. Weber delivered was twenty-three pages of extremely detailed information on Michael Robin and how he'll probably react under certain conditions. One section goes into critical details of how his management style is likely to fit in to Birdland's known and suspected corporate strategies and the changes he'll likely make in the medium term. This in turn was used to design specific collection operations to monitor Birdland's progress under Robin's guiding hand.

Such assessments are widely popular in the mergers and acquisition field, used by leaders in both the acquiring and acquired firms. Bankers and lawyers also use it; they have vested interests in this area and don't want an unforeseen personality issue derailing multimillion-dollar deals. The sections covering previous career trajectory or strengths and weaknesses would obviously be useful. It's also useful for leaders to understand how easily these types of instruments can be written against them—a sobering reminder that in an increasingly complex world, this type of tool can spell the difference between success and failure.

The final section in the profile on Michael Robin is his personality forensics. From this, one could make a number of assessments on how he'll react in a given set of circumstances. By crafting specific scenarios through a guided conversation, it's possible to use an opposing leader's own words, actions, thoughts, and ideas against them.

As the Buccaneers' Shelton Quarles and Dave Levy demonstrated in Chapter Two, it is easier to exploit random chances when you are best prepared. As we'll see in the next chapter, a high level of preparation also allows you to force apparently random events at the precise moment you're ready to take advantage of them.

Labeling People

Psychological assessments are commonly used by governments, special operations forces, Olympic teams, and other organizations that need to understand how and why people think the way they do. A wide array of proven assessment tools are available for this effort.

Having a trained psychology professional is important, but finding one with a strong business background is equally vital. Leaders are not interested in esoteric analysis of a rival leader's feelings. They want to know how the person thinks so they can best use the information in their favor.

One of the most popular applications of forensic psychology is in negotiations. Influencing a rival's decision making can shave millions of dollars off the cost of a new merger or acquisition. And it's not as complicated as you might think, as the next chapter shows.

8

Negotiations
Mastering the Evil Art

A couple of decades back, I was a reasonably good martial artist on my college team. I enjoyed tournament competitions—a far cry from Miyamoto Musashi's sword duels, but a reasonably controlled conflict with authority figures nearby if (and when) things got out of hand. While forms and board breaking were popular in many martial arts programs, what I always enjoyed most was the combat aspect of sparring.

During the 1988 Summer Olympics, tae kwon do was added as a demonstration sport, and the opening ceremony featuring hundreds of martial artists choreographed in unison. The games were in Seoul, Korea, birthplace of tae kwon do, and martial artists of every style around the world were watching.

During one particular match, a commentator referred to tae kwon do as "kinetic chess," a phrase that became wildly popular after the games and to this day remains an affectionate reminder of the sport's Olympic debut. The *kinetic chess* of tae kwon do (like that of football) means that much more is going on than meets the eye. Although spectators see a great deal of action, they rarely have insight into the preparation that precedes the combative exchange of the present. Business can be a lot like this too. One area that can be particularly kinetic and fraught with behind-the-scenes risk is the not-so-gentle art of negotiation.

Despite my years of studying martial arts and the fondness I still have for the mental preparation it requires, I do not enjoy negotiating. Despite my lack of affection for it, negotiation is a necessary skill across multiple dimensions in business. Executives negotiate with boards of directors. Lawyers negotiate with opposing counsel. Sales and marketing staff negotiate with transportation, retail, and wholesale customers to get products into the marketplace at the best possible price.

Competitive intelligence can help foster more productive negotiations through its core purpose of reducing uncertainty. If you're negotiating, there's something in conflict. Boards want higher revenue, opposing counsel want to settle out of court, and customers want lower prices. Everyone has a differing outlook, and they don't want to give up anything.

Sparring has as much to do with negotiation as it does with martial arts. Both symbolize this kinetic chess mentality where preparation is key, mental strategies are paramount, and the confrontation can quickly evolve from stagnant to volatile with little warning. What, then, is the best way to go about it?

First, accept that this is a journey. You want to go from the present condition to a different condition in the future. That difference can be physical or perceptual. It might mean a change in position, activity, responsibility, or a thousand other metrics. It might even be something temporary.

A recent *Wall Street Journal* piece cited numerous midlevel career professionals turning to freelance work and finding out they could make as much as, and sometimes more than, they did as members of a corporate staff.[1] While temp firms often have fees and archaic rules about hiring away staff into permanent assignments, freelancers have a great deal more freedom. As noted in the article, some can afford to choose just "the fun jobs."

There's also a growing market for small firms to provide services as subcontractors for larger firms, particularly those chasing the new federal stimulus dollars.[2] Multinational corporations bidding on government contracts are often required to set aside a certain amount of business specifically for small companies. More and more firms, including solo practitioners, are pitching themselves as subject matter experts on a number of topics to these larger firms. But this also means they are responsible for their entire business infrastructure, from office space and computers to taxes and 401(k) contributions. What many don't want to add to that already growing administrative pile is negotiating for the work in the first place.

But without this crucial skill, you cannot get the contract that pays all those expenses and leaves something to compensate yourself. Negotiation means talking about money, and often other points, in a far more upfront and coldly calculated way than many people are accustomed to. Now that freelancing has moved beyond computer work into other information-based roles such as law, marketing, and accounting, the need for negotiation skills is greater across a larger segment of the workforce. Just keep in mind that this journey requires the interaction of another party: you cannot get there alone.

Some equate negotiation with dancing, a temporary partnership that brings two parties together around an orchestrated event. I find this comparison a little misleading. Dancers aren't competing. Though one may lead the other, they are not taking something from their partner. Both leave the dance floor unchanged. That's not the case in a business negotiation, where there's always some dimension of competition to be overcome.

So anything being negotiated must first pass a basic ABC analysis by both parties:

Attractiveness: Can you articulate what makes this proposal attractive?

Better: Are you better off?

Cost: What is the cost in real dollars?

When these questions have been answered and the decision is made to move forward, it's clear this is not a dance. It's something that must be captured and controlled, because otherwise it can get either party swept off its feet in the worst of ways.

The journey in negotiation has two critical similarities to combat: patience and respect. While I've repeatedly touched on the importance of time, waiting can also be an instrument of analytical competition. Keep in mind the delay tactic discussed in Chapter Six. Time is something that you can leverage or can be leveraged against you.

Then there's respect. Many people approach a negotiation without respecting the person or persons on the other side of the table. This is always a bad idea. Even when you gain what you wanted and the negotiation is considered successful, you can often lose because the frequently adversarial nature of the process creates an enemy where none was necessary. The likelihood of a future negotiation, perhaps for something even better, is reduced, and you remain at a disadvantage over the long term as a result.

So consider for a moment what you stand to gain by approaching a negotiation from a different angle than you've done before. There are three principal aspects to consider when negotiating: the art, the science, and the spreadsheet.

The Art: Establishing Rapport

Leaders must always avoid negotiating blindly. They must know something about the person they are going up against. The more you can know a person before you must negotiate a deal, a change, a purchase, or anything else, the better off you will both be. You've got to find some sort of common ground; otherwise a conversation will be all but impossible. You've got to build *rapport*.

Rapport is part theater, part human nature, and part sincere interest even with an ulterior motive. But without all three in sync, it doesn't work. You're a thinly veiled used car salesman who has missed his quota all month: desperate, clumsy, and with little to lose. So you stumble through a proposal. You look amateurish at best, and that's assuming it's only the opposing team across the table that knows about it. Should word get out about how leadership blew the deal before it could even start, you'll have an altogether different set of problems.

The easiest way to establish rapport (without help) is to consider for a moment the various dimensions of life. What personal dimensions describe someone on an individual level? The descriptions for me in the immediately personal category are father, brother, son, and husband. In religion there's Lutheran, Protestant, or Christian depending on the setting. Ethnically I'm part British, Irish, and Scot. My interests include martial arts, boating, and Southeastern Conference football. I'm an alumnus of the University of Tennessee and Wake Forest, as well as an adjunct professor for Eckerd College. This is a pretty wide range of personal background data, any one of which could easily draw me into a conversation.

And this is what you're trying to do: get a conversation started, a foundation on which to build a proposal you wish to discuss. This is no time for stern-faced rhetoric, preachy dialogue, or stepping up on a political soapbox. Be warm and friendly, smile, and act as if you are really interested in the other person. Listen to what he or she says. If someone gives you a conversational opening, by all means take it. Identify an area of common interest, and talk about it.

Don't hesitate to ask for clarification on something, particularly if it's something you agree on. In this way you establish a pattern of inquiry, a conversational style that will be increasingly less threatening as you get to know each other. You will find this useful later when you need clarification on something you might not agree on. In that instance, you'll be better equipped to mask or misdirect attention from your nonconcurrence until you can find a way around it. In any event, you won't telegraph that it's an area of disagreement until you tell the other person it is.

Patience is hard to overemphasize here. Engage politely but firmly on topics, and let the other person do as much talking as possible. If you're the one talking, you're the one at risk for saying too much—perhaps blowing a strong negotiation position or incidentally revealing a point that could be leveraged against you. Keep the conversation upbeat, end on a good note, and be positive all the way out the door.

Building rapport is not about talking; it's about listening and finding common ground that has nothing to do with the proposal you wish to negotiate. Find something to talk about, and simply converse. Have a few basic ideas of topics (not talking points) in your mental pocket that you can draw from.

The Science: A Remote Psychological Profile

The previous chapter's overview of remote psychological profiling wasn't simply an academic exercise. Here we'll use Michael Robin's personality profile (section 5 in the profile's Contents) from Chapter Seven. The profile laid out how Michael Robins was hired into his current position. Now we'll take a look at how a forensic psychologist can help leverage aspects of his personality during a negotiation.

Following is the executive brief given to a leader to prepare her to negotiate with Michael Robin. Working-level analysts doing preparation work would have access to considerably more data, but everything necessary for a negotiator to position Michael Robin right where they want him is revealed in the brief.

Michael Robin's Personality Profile: MBTI: ENTJ, specifically, Strong E, moderate N, Borderline T-F, Moderate J

Discussion

Not surprisingly, Robin emerges as a strong E, engaged with and reenergized by the external world of people, activities, events, and things. Like most other marketing leaders, he is highly social, interpersonally skilled, and at his best in interactive processes. On the job, he thrives on group projects and analysis, sources say. He runs an orderly but not rigid meeting and prizes assertion on the part of his subordinates. He is approachable and open to anything for which a good case can be made. He likes creativity and, in particular, what he calls "style" or "stylish."

Robin has a lengthy record of dedicated community service and participation in a wide range of social, community, cultural, and athletic activities and is seen by associates as genuine in his commitment to community stewardship. He has always been a popular figure, college alums say. His family is similarly socially engaged and jokes about the complex requirements of family schedules (with three teen and preteen children) and the transportation logistics involved.

Robin has a rating of moderate N preference for Intuitiveness; he looks at the big picture and is fairly intuitive. He likes to ground himself in factual data; however, he is not a "details" person.

While he bases his decisions on information, recognized principles, logic, and rational thought, Robin has a strong bent toward the human factor. He is an individual who will not fearlessly make a "good" business decision whose human cost or fallout is high, and he will expend considerable effort to minimize untoward human outcomes. Associates describe him in the foregoing terms, yet it must be noted that no evidence can be found that Robin has had to preside over significant cutbacks, layoffs, or related business decisions that inevitably lead to human costs, so we do not know the basis for this characterization.

Like most other executives, Robin scores as a J subtype (Judging), with notably comfortable responses to the open-ended, flexible orientation of P (Perceiver) types around him. It may be that he has adapted to the prevailing J preference in the corporate environment while leaning in the P direction himself, much in the way his profile suggests a slight underlying F (Feeler) tendency.

Firo-B

Robin's style and preferences for approaches to himself match; he seeks affiliation and reaches out. He is ambitious but does not have an overbearing drive for power. He seems to want to garner respect for recognizable accomplishments and appears to maintain confidence his influence will be brought to bear in that way. [For information on Firo-B, turn to the appendix.]

EDS—Decision-Making Styles

Robin falls midway between those who wish to gather just enough information to make a decision and those who want everything available on the subject, according to several sources. He will focus on a selected plan of action, but will have some idea of alternatives should that become necessary.

In contrast to his generally high level of communication, however, Robin is described as one who will usually not share plan B. Often colleagues and subordinates are surprised that he has developed, at least sketchily, other options. [For information on EDS, turn to the appendix.]

Motivational Drivers

Robin's priorities are accomplishment, recognition, reward, and contribution, in roughly that order, with very similar emphasis given to each. Moreover, he appears to see these priorities as related; in his worldview, reward and recognition can be expected to come from accomplishment, and contribution is required of those who gain reward. From this perspective on life, we can conclude that his formative years were benign and his environment reinforced his aims and efforts. In essence, he is sound, highly capable, and, no doubt, a substantial asset to Birdland.

Robin has been brought to Birdland to jump-start the changes required for the company to succeed with its consumer initiative. It is a good fit. After the unpleasant chapter at Dynasty Products, he will want to make his mark quickly and dramatically. Competitors might expect to see a rollout within six months.

In an unfamiliar environment, Robin will lead with his strengths. He will position the first of Birdland's expected new furniture designs squarely in consumer products and draw on his proven successes for marketing, promotion, and sales. An early success will give him the time he needs to immerse himself in the new world of consumer marketing at Birdland.

Biographical

On the personal side, Robin and Cleo are living in New York with their three children. Adam, the oldest, is in high school now and looks forward to college. Cleo has a business background as well. She now remains at home raising their children. She is an active alumna of Vanderbilt's Business School, where both received their M.B.A.s.

A Spreadsheet for Negotiations

I'll grant you that a negotiation strategy in a spreadsheet is not the most common thing in the world, but in fact a spreadsheet is simply a series of grids for displaying information. Usually a series of formulas are employed to take that information and manipulate it mathematically. But spreadsheets can also display and manipulate text. Forcing the negotiator to put text on a page helps validate what information is really available versus what is merely *thought* to be available.

The other advantage to using Microsoft Excel is it allows us to put information in once and have the spreadsheet manipulate it for the application phase to follow. As we evaluate the negotiation process, the order of the steps we take is not the same order in which we'll apply the information later. Excel will push it around the spreadsheet and allow you to print out only what you need (analysis or talking points), when you need it.

The steps you'll follow are straightforward:

1. Current status: What the other person has now
2. Proposal: The change you wish to negotiate
3. Object: What the other person wants
4. Risks: What the other person stands to lose
5. Benefits: What can be gained
6. Forces: What pressures oppose the other people

In filling out the spreadsheet, you are crafting an outline. You must appreciate that the emphasis cannot be what's in it for you but rather what's in it for the other party. Don't focus any attention on your benefits, which only pushes the leverage across the table to the other side. Keep things focused on the other party. Don't worry if the person is a competitor, supplier, customer, or colleague. Right now this is the party you are trying to make happy. A successful negotiation is the only thing that will do that.

So begin with the current status. What is it you have that they want, or vice versa? Spell it out. Do they want your custom carpet cleaning business? Then write that down. They want to open a line of widgets for a big-box store? Write that down. Whatever the current state is, or isn't, write it down somewhere in a manner that you can edit until you get the wording exactly right.

Second, what is it you seek to change? Do you wish to sell the carpet business or add a line of widgets in your store? Write it down. Don't skip these initial steps because they seem too simple. They're simple now, but if you try getting through this exercise without doing the initial parts, you'll get lost and hesitate at a crucial time during the negotiation. Do you want to convince your boss of a new detail in the business, or do you want to rip the entire business model apart and start over? Whatever it is, write it down.

Third, and here's where the writing is really important, what's the *so what*? What's the big difference here? This is not where you candidly outline your plan for world domination; just spell out the final objective. What's the payoff, how will it work, when will anyone see it, and how will they know when it arrives? This is not the same as step 2. This refers to the results expected if step 2 is taken. Be specific.

With any change, there is the potential for loss. This is step 4: considering the downside of taking the action. You can begin with a minor or immediate loss, but be sure to build from there. Like the crescendo of an orchestra's finale, you have to arrive at a heart-racing, high-risk damn the torpedoes realization. Losses must be immediate and obvious. Don't gloss them over, and don't worry (now) about aggrandizing. You can tweak the language later.

Step 5 is about the benefits. Don't assume that every change is for the better. Although many benefits might simply be a reverse image of the losses you just outlined, they aren't always like that. Complex situations often have many subtle cascading parts, and the law of unintended circumstances cannot be overlooked. If there are second- and third-order affects, make sure you bring them up here.

Finally, in step 6, point out all the reasons that not accepting the proposal is almost certain to mean the other person's objectives are not going to be met. One of the things you do here is point out the powerful external influences opposing you both: the actions of other people, the nature of things, or international events that remain beyond your conscious control. Depending on the topic, these can be inflation, housing starts, taxes, political activities, the stock market, or any of a thousand other external influencers. Whatever influencer you pick, make sure it results in the same loss you see coming from the rival's current behavior.

After you've identified your six steps, place them in the spreadsheet in the shaded boxes of the sheet entitled "Analysis." For the moment, click on the Talking Points tab of the spreadsheet. This rearranges the steps you've outlined into the proper format for engaging your opponents in negotiations. By reordering the six points for your specific task, the model should keep you in the right lanes, though how you choose to drive through them is up to you. Based on the rapport you've developed and with all the requisite respect for the other person's position in her organization and to this negotiation, you can start out with a very simple opening like, "I know you want to . . ." and immediately hit her with her objective, not yours.

At this point we all know what's going on. There's been at least some lightweight dancing around the possibility of a proposal coming in, if not an outright articulation of the idea. This is not cold calling. The other person knows a pitch of some sort is imminent because this is theater and everyone has a part to play. Perhaps it was just a mention or a passing thought that sparked some attention. Nothing formal or specific was put on the table, but interest was communicated by one party and acknowledged by the other.

What you're doing here is mentally poking the other person with a stick to elicit a reaction. If the objective you've written up is off—if you get oddly raised eyebrows or some other "back-off" body language, then by all means back away. But if you've done your homework, you should know what she wants; now you're just trying to get her to acknowledge it by communicating a positive response to your statement. You want her to do this as much as possible because it is habit forming, so don't be afraid to hit it more than once if you've got the opening.

Once you've got her objective articulated to her satisfaction, it's time to point out why it will not come to pass as things stand now. Ensure that whatever is stopping her, it's nothing she has done (or not done). It cannot be a measure of (her) management competence. It's always an external actor, random chance, or an influential event beyond anyone's control ("could have happened to anyone," "nothing that could be avoided").

You're giving her an honorable out, a psychological gate pass that doesn't hold her responsible for whatever this damnable condition is. It doesn't matter who is to blame (interest rates, oil prices, the Great Pumpkin) as long as you aren't blaming her and the organization she represents. You're opening a door here and encouraging her to walk through it. Having articulated that it's everyone else's fault but hers, now is the time to pile on the losses. Nobody likes losses, especially when it's theirs but (as previously noted) not their fault. You did let her off the hook a moment ago, but the losses are still linked *to* her. So don't be shy; pile on the coal. Don't leave anything on the table.

Once you've stacked the ugliness as high as you can, turn the tables on her: "I think I can help." Your rival can get what she wants in spite of these many adverse conditions. Here you list all the benefits of your plan. This creates a bridge to outline the benefits (to her) in accepting your proposal. Disregard the benefits to you; she doesn't care, and it's not in your best interest to give it more than a cursory mention. Focus with as many details as you can on how she will benefit.

Explain fully what you want her to do, giving as many details as needed for her consideration, while linking those benefits to her objectives outlined earlier. This is the connection. The mental synapse you want firing is how your proposal benefits her in reaching her objective. If you focus only on what you stand to gain, you risk your opponent's getting a bad case of *dollarsignitus,* recognizing the value of what you want.

She may decide she doesn't want to sell. Maybe she'll shop it around. Maybe she has overlooked this asset/item/project and decides to exploit it on her own. If it's a service contract, she may decide the business can do it in-house and doesn't need an outside vendor. You don't want any of this entering her mind. Focus her rather than leave it up to chance. You can focus on your benefits later over a celebratory beverage. Round out the proposal reminding her of the losses the business stands to incur if it continues on its current course. Why am I hitting the loss and risks twice? Because economists have determined people are more likely to act in the face of aggressive loss than aggressive gain.

Dr. Gary Becker at the University of Chicago received the 1992 Nobel Prize in economic sciences for his work on extending the study of economic theory to human behavior. In one of his articles, "The Economic Way of Looking at Behavior," he notes that analysis, rather than being self-motivated, is more often based on a set of assumptions and preferences and on the individual's interpretations of them constrained by income, time, memory, and calculation capability. He wrote: "The analysis assumes that individuals maximize welfare as they conceive it, whether they be selfish, altruistic, loyal, spiteful, or masochistic. Their behavior is forward-looking, and it is also consistent over time. In particular, they try as best they can to anticipate the *uncertain* consequences of their actions."[3]

Once again, uncertainty bares its ugly head. Dr. Becker's research was unique in that it incorporated sociology as much as economics. Other researchers have expanded on his theory and have revealed many subtle nuances of behavior not just in how and why people decide what to buy, but also how they make decisions in politics, jobs, and crime.

So let's apply this to Michael Robin. Let's say we want to pitch a competitive intelligence outsourcing contract to support him in his new position. We're pitching him in character, so to speak, using the information from Dr. Weber's profile as a map to his thinking. In order to develop our positioning based on the profile we have on him, let's lay out the stakes and incorporate his psychological data into the negotiating steps:

1. *Current status.* Michael is the new guy at Birdline. There's no one yet he can genuinely trust: some will have allegiances to his predecessor, and some will likely be reporting to the board behind his back. If he wants a quick success at Birdline, he'll need help.
2. *Alternative.* He doesn't know Birdland's consumer market plans at all. He needs someone whose own success is implicitly tied to his own.

3. *Objective.* He wants to improve the likelihood of success in his new position and minimize uncertainties in new product areas by having an honest broker watching his back.

4. *Risks.* There are two: another contentious departure and career stagnation.

5. *Benefits.* He has no attachment to the former senior vice president or his former company, which provides an easy out to any claims of breaking his nondisclosure agreement.

6. *Forces.* Some allegiances are likely to remain to the former senior vice president and her thirty-two years of service. Robin's lack of finance experience is a liability, Dynasty will be watching him closely, and employees have high expectations.

Fill in the shaded boxes on the Analytics sheet the first time you try this (it is the bottom row in Figure 8.1, filled out for Michael Robin) and then click the tab for the Strategy page to see how it works out. Don't hesitate to go back and forth a few times to customize it to your specific style. Next, incorporate information from the psychological profile (the bottom row in Figure 8.2, which shows the psychological assessment of Michael Robin from Chapter Six) to adapt it for the individual you're negotiating with. Now your strategy is infused with specific intelligence on the target you wish to influence.

You're going to use this to craft a story (within your own head) that will then lead you to craft talking points (to say out loud). But you can see by this example that we have a solid approach to use with Michael Robin. Now this general strategy needs to be tweaked to Robin specifically since we know how he prefers to receive information and have a psychological assessment to determine how he'll react to it.

Customizing the Pitch

We know from his profile that Michael Robin went to Vanderbilt for his M.B.A. If you have an M.B.A., there's a talking point to bring up. Did your alma mater play Vanderbilt in the Big 12 Conference? There's your opener. If not, how about Vandie's last appearance in the NCAA tournament? You get the picture.

2	3	4	5	6
Alternative	Objective	Risk	Benefit	Adversity
What you want done	What they want	What they can lose	What they can gain	What they are up against
New idea, new detail, or using new people—something different from the current status quo	Analysis	Losses that are the logical result of the current status quo. This can be the reverse of the benefits, but that's not necessarily always the case. Second- and third-order effects.	What they gain by accepting your alternative.	Reasons that it will be difficult for them to get what they want, based on the actions of others, the nature of things, or events "beyond our control."
State this positively and in some detail so it's clear		Can start with minor loss and build.	May have to start small and build up.	Adverse conditions will result in the same losses resulting from the current status.
Robin doesn't know Birdland's core markets. He needs someone whose own success is implicitly tied to his own.	He will improve the likelihood of success in his new position and minimize uncertainties in new product areas.	He must avoid another contentious departure and doesn't want any "new guy" failures. Given the economy, that's almost certainly going to lead to personnel losses.	Putting me under retainer gives you top cover from prying eyes, the press, and any goons Dynasty foolishly decides to put on you, hoping you'll trip up.	Some allegiances likely remain to former SVP and her thirty-two years of service. Lack of finance experience a liability. Dynasty will be watching closely; employees have high expectations.

Figure 8.1 A negotiations strategy outline. Filling in the bottom row allows leaders to plan a negotiation and practice their pitch in a timely and cost-effective manner.

| | 3 | 6 | 5 | 2 | 1 | 4 |
| | Objective | Adversity | Benefit | Alternative | Current State | Risk |
	What they want	What they are up against	What they can gain	What you want done	What they are doing now	What they can lose
Reordered Outline	He will improve the likelihood of success in his new position and minimize uncertainties in new product areas.	Some allegiances likely remain to former SVP and her thirty-two years of service; lack of finance experience a liability; Dynasty will be watching closely; employees have high expectations.	Putting me under retainer gives you top cover from prying eyes, the press, and any goons Dynasty foolishly decides to put on you, hoping you'll trip up.	Robin doesn't know Birdland's core markets at all. He needs someone whose own success is implicitly tied to Robin's.	Robin's got no one he can genuinely trust. Some will have allegiances to his predecessor, and some will likely be reporting to the board behind his back. If he wants a quick success at Birdline, he'll need help.	He must avoid another contentious departure and doesn't want any "new guy" failures. Given the economy, that's almost certainly going to lead to personnel losses.
Forensics	MBTI Big picture orientation; grounds himself in factual data; minimizes untoward human outcomes; approachable with anything that makes a good case	Firo-B Seeks affiliation and reaches out; ambitious; not overbearing; confident	Motivation Priorities are accomplishment, recognition, reward, and contribution (in order); interrelated; early success will buy him time	EDS Midway between gathering just enough data and wanting everything; focuses on plan of action, but has ideas of alternatives; doesn't share plan B		Will not sacrifice employees easily; never had to preside over cutbacks or layoffs, will minimize human costs

Figure 8.2 Combining the negotiations outlined with insights from the psychological assessment of Michael Robin in Chapter Six. It customizes a pitch for Robin, using his own motivations, biases, and fears to change his behavior.

Numerous generalities can be made based from someone's MBTI that are useful for communication purposes—both rapport building in general and negotiating specifically. Robin's MBTI profile notes he's an ENTJ. When communicating with extroverts, talk to them face to face whenever feasible. Emphasize the action to be taken. Expect extroverts to toss ideas around and speak up in group situations.

Intuitive types like to talk about big picture issues and the long-term possibilities. Emphasize ideas and broad concepts rather than details. If you must get into specifics of some type, do so using patterns, and emphasize connections among nodes. Give the person a problem that needs to be solved with the latitude to be innovative in a novel and creative way.

Thinking types don't like to waste time, so get to the point of what you're saying. No flowery language. Use logical (not emotional) arguments to appeal to intellect, not feelings. Succinctly lay out the pros and cons of an argument and how the parts might be weighed individually. Thinking types have a strong sense of fairness that can be leveraged against their best interests at times.

Judgers are sticklers for a schedule. Start on time, and end on time. Whatever it is being discussed must be presented in an organized manner. How it's organized is irrelevant, as long as it's not cluttered. Note deadlines, timetables, "goalposts," and other temporal markers. Decisions will be made relatively quickly, but don't plan on surprising them with some last-minute initiative that you haven't already identified.

In broad terms ENTJs are affable people: they make friends easily and have an enthusiasm and confidence that's often described as contagious. They often have the ability to look laid back, but in fact they are maintaining a high level of concentration and mental gear grinding. This personality type is often a good mentor for younger managers.

Robin is likely concerned about his inexperience in finance and technical service. The nuances of new technology in consumer products are unlikely to be a strong area for him too. He might want some help away from prying eyes that might be out to get him.

As noted, rumors persist of some kind of confrontation between Robin and senior management at Dynasty. The uncharacteristic suddenness of his departure in the wake of his being passed over for the chief operating officer position may have resulted from a deep sense of affront. He felt unjustly treated and left.

Figure 8.3 shows how we would tweak a general proposal for competitive intelligence services to Michael Robin. Although the changes may appear minor, the force-multiplying effects of each technique across multiple dimensions of personality cannot be overemphasized. He'll like this proposal, and he'll likely accept it because it has been customized specifically to his preferences, oriented around his needs and objectives.

This type of hybrid method, using a software tool (Excel) and customized data (psychological profile) is widely known as data as a service (DaaS). It's a close relative of software as a service (SaaS) that made the iPhone so wildly popular.[4] The advantage of DaaS is the highly specific data element afforded by the psychological profile. The software becomes a template for future applications. But it is the specific psychological profile of the targeted individual, customizing the application of this method, that makes it successful.

Dr. Weber's client used this profile in a negotiation, and it had a dramatic impact on the outcome. Leaders can now recognize when similar strategies are applied against them. Techniques like this are increasingly popular within large multinationals as the recession forces consolidation across geographical and market segmentation lines. Division and company managers are applying these tools to their own leadership in order to better serve their company's interests. Leaders shouldn't be surprised to recognize these methods being used by their subordinates. Everyone is looking for a competing edge, even within their own organizations.

The Negotiating Trinities

ABC analysis should precede any negotiations. If you cannot fully articulate why a project is attractive, better, and cost-efficient, it isn't worth pursuing at any price.

Build rapport with those you'll negotiate with before you need it. This is not the time to suddenly become chummy. Open doors before

#	Category		Set up / Strategy	Confirm	Personalize
3	Objective		I know you want to		
		Set up	He will improve the likelihood of success in his new position and minimize uncertainties in new product areas	Is that true?	If you take a look at the overall situation, there's an option that might be worth considering if I've read the facts correctly
			Strategy	Confirm	Personalize (MBTI)
6	Adversity		You're following a big name …		
		Set up	Your predecessor had 32 years here, and you don't have her financial experience, which is not your fault but will probably be pointed out to you. She's got some friends here who may view you with unease, especially given the press. It's human nature.	Know what I mean?	That said, I think there's some opportunity to begin building your own inside network, pull folks to your side. They just don't know your skill sets as well as you do.
			Strategy	Confirm	Personalize (FIRO-B)
5	Benefit		I think there are easy gains here		
		Set up	I think if you do something that's a clean break from your Dynasty experiences, nobody could accuse you of anything. You do something completely new in consumer markets, and you've given Birdland something tangible to defend you with. Dynasty can't insinuate.	That's what you want, right? Take Birdland where Dynasty would never let you go?	They want to see what you can do, where you can take them, and they aren't shy about fighting for you. Given the risk, they've clearly shown that the rewards could be substantial.
			Strategy	Confirm	Personalize (Motivations, FIRO-B)
2	Alternative		I think I can help because …		
		Set up	You don't know Birdland's core markets at all. Why don't you let me help you as an outside consultant? You need an outside agent you can trust—someone whose success is directly tied to yours.	Does this make sense?	Birdland fought to get you, so you're going to need some fast results before they start second-guessing themselves. You need someone who can pull in expertise that's not already inside the company. Otherwise why keep you?
			Strategy	Confirm	Personalize (EDS)
1	Current		You know the industry …		
		Set up	Some of the folks here will be back-dooring you—not out to get you, just reporting on you to the board. Watched. The Dynasty folks could aggravate that. You need an early home run.	Know what I mean?	Status quo won't cut it and you don't have time for a good warm-up period, especially after what they're doing to keep you here.
			Strategy	Confirm	Personalize
4	Risk		You want to avoid …		
		Set up	Another contentious departure playing out in the press. Nobody wants one, and they sure don't want it twice in a row! Makes finding another job a lot more difficult; you look like damaged goods.	I'd avoid that at all costs myself.	An early success would reassure that board rallying them around you, as opposed to a "new guy" mistake that could cost people their jobs. Nobody wants job losses tied to their executive tenure. That would really follow you around career-wise.
			Strategy	Confirm	Personalize

Figure 8.3 A finished negotiations outline, complete with setups and confirmation points. Additional notes or comments can be added anywhere on the sheet. As long as negotiators stick to the text in the shaded areas, they should have no troubles achieving their stated goal.

you need to walk through them. Otherwise they can often smack you on the back if you don't move through fast enough.

A spreadsheet can manipulate text as easily as it does numbers. This is one more opportunity to get more done with less effort and time. Exploit it, and don't cut corners in filling it out.

Use a forensic personality assessment to customize a negotiations strategy. Properly applied, it will pay for itself many times over. Understanding the leaders outside your firm is extremely important. As we saw with Michael Robin, that means understanding their communities. As we'll soon see, this is now an art and science of its own.

9

Social Network Analysis and Communities

There is a great exchange between Jodie Foster's FBI agent character Clarice Starling and Anthony Hopkins's sadistic characterization of Dr. Hannibal "The Cannibal" Lecter in the film adaptation of Thomas Harris's *The Silence of the Lambs*. In a pivotal exchange, Lecter asks the young FBI trainee an odd question and then answers it for her: "Do you seek out something to covet?" he asks. "No. You covet what you see every day."

The intense scene is a highlight of the film, and from it we can draw important implications for business. Whom we see and communicate with says a lot about us and the opportunities we'll have in the future. It tells us about the communities we live in. Communities are built on the commonality of ideas.

Ideas are inexpensive to reproduce and spread, and they create communities. Some are philanthropic, like fundraisers for nonprofit firms. Others are criminal—gangs that exploit economies of scale. But what unites the good, the bad, and the ugly alike are ideas. Like a cancer, ideas can metastasize to bridge ethnicity, religion, race, and any other cultural dimension, effectively changing how people identify themselves. Identity politics can redefine who we are.

How many friends do you have? *Real* friends? How many are also colleagues? Are any family? Do you treat family who are friends differently from those who are just friends? How do you separate out what you tell one group of friends from another?

People don't like to admit they do this, yet we all do. If I tell a story to both my mother and my friends, do I use the same language with her that I might use with my buddies over a beer and a game of pool? I'd surely better not! Partly as a result of the different grammar used and partly because my audiences are so radically different in interest, temperament, use of the information, and reaction, the story itself will change depending on whom I'm speaking to. But this is increasingly harder to do than in the past.

New technologies like Twitter, Facebook, and MySpace are increasingly blurring these lines. Rather than customized messages for select audiences, we now find ourselves sending a mass audience the same message. This would appear directly opposite most marketing and public relations strategies that suggest a customized message for select target audiences. But what has changed is the definition of a mass message.

Several years ago, anthropologist Robin Dunbar studied the cognitive power of the brain. She extrapolated studies based on brain size and social networks of apes and determined the number of contacts a person can routinely manage is around 148.[1] Rounded up to 150, this is now widely known in social sciences as the Dunbar number. Although some sociologists have argued this point, a Facebook spokesman told the *Wall Street Journal* the average number of friends in a Facebook network is 120, which appears to follow Dunbar's rule.[2]

What is interesting is the difference in frequency and type of interaction between men and women according to Facebook's own analysis. Just as there were stark differences in the one-way transfer of information versus two-way communication we saw on a professional football team, networks in Facebook follow a similar pattern.

Facebook allows members to post information, songs, pictures, and other content for their invited friends to comment on. An average man with 120 contacts (nodes) in his network responds to only seven friends (on average) by commenting on their posts. The average woman has a slightly higher response of ten. On two-way communication, the average man exchanges information with only four people, while a woman communicates on average with six. Even when members have an unusually large network size (more than three hundred), the approximate ratio of responses remains proportionate.[3]

This suggests that within a large network is a core subnetwork of trusted interlocutors. While seemingly at odds with the entire purpose of social media, this does make a great deal of sense. Within corporate networks, there are many subnetworks, and within these even more granular sub-subnetworks. A corporation (network) will have a finance department (subnetwork) that includes everyone in accounts payable (sub-subnetwork) and on down to the individual level.

Yet it is in these lower-level, highly linked subnets that much of the decision making in social networks takes place. Thought leaders gravitate to each other. Within any social structure there will be friends who are attracted to each other (intellectually, physically, or otherwise), those who are rivals (the big dogs in the network), and those who are friends across multiple network types (work colleagues who also work out together). It is the structure within such networks that makes them as resilient and difficult to analyze as they are.

A social network is like a living organism. It grows, matures, and in many cases eventually dies. But during this time, it is bound together by its communication system. Particularly with social media, the common bond of shared interest forms and maintains the network. People can opt in or out at any time. There are few formal procedures (for the group anyway) and little true authority. The members police themselves, a significant part of the feedback mechanism that binds a group together.

It is these feedback loops that create and maintain a social network. Mike Murphy and Jeff Lumetta spoke to this in Chapter Five: that Consumer Electronics Show attendees' feedback helped them craft new products. If the interaction is simply one way (a linear command-and-control structure), few will participate. But within this construct are multiple overlapping subnetworks that participate, manipulate, alter, and create the ideas sent through these channels.

Note this is not information. We think with ideas, not information, as is commonly thought.[4] These ideas create information as interpreted through experiences, and it is our experiences that are shared through social media technology. The Internet expands our network of friends by minimizing terrestrial limitations and greatly increasing the speed by which we can share. This built networks across a far greater area than had existed before and created a significant amount of content.

Rather than telling the same story four times on four phone calls to four different friends around the neighborhood, it is told one time to fourteen friends around the globe. Taking only 25 percent of the time previously, there's more time available to craft additional content, respond to someone else's post, or communicate with a poster to gather additional data (feedback loop) that will be available for an entire network to see and respond to (multidimensional feedback).

This creates a political structure within a network, even if we don't wish to call it that. Groups form and dissolve online around every contextual idea you can think of. What companies want to do is understand these networks and how they can learn about them, characterize their dynamics, identify leaders versus followers (which every network has), monitor how their company, product, or brand is regarded in these networks, and how they can interrupt competitor's efforts to do the same.

Semantic Arguments

In the previous chapter I used a spreadsheet to manipulate and display text from a psychological profile. There was not any mathematical context to this manipulation, just a relocation of the order of the text. But text does have a mathematical element to it that is extremely useful. Semantics, the analysis of language, is a growing field that is developing new technologies very quickly.

Competitors and customers exist as networks. The connections between customers and the means by which they communicate are extremely important to a firm that is trying to sell a product. Semantics analysis can provide context to information in social media, identifying how information changes due to the movement through these networks while in a constant state of flux.

Statement or contextual analysis generated international attention when Vassar College English professor Don Foster determined that journalist Joe Klein was the author of *Primary Colors,* a tongue-in-cheek satire of Bill Clinton's first presidential campaign. After five years of denials, Klein finally admitted Foster was correct: that he was indeed the anonymous author of the best-selling book. Foster soon found himself consulting on several high-profile civil and criminal projects, including the FBI's pursuit of the Unabomber (whom Foster independently verified as Ted Kaczynski).[5]

But Foster preferred to remain an English professor rather than jump into any full-time consulting work in semantics. He was doing the work by hand, identifying several methods for proving authorship based on grammatical patterns within documents. Although several software programs for semantics analysis existed at the time he was doing this work in the late 1990s, it was his hand-analyzed identification of Joe Klein that fired developers up to create new contextual tools.

Jeff Spivey is the business development director for one such firm. RiskIQ is a semantics software provider with a range of corporate and government clients interested in analysis for identifying and characterizing online content. "Marketing people are interested in online semantics analysis, particularly in near-real time," Spivey said.

Real-time monitoring by RiskIQ of online media like social networks, blogs, and usenet groups allows the firm to provide clients information on what "locations" are working best for their campaigns. These locations can be online communities, geographical locations, or unique demographic segments not identified previously.

"We're seeing a lot of bloggers for hire," Jeff told me, "and clients are concerned not only about how their products are being characterized, they're increasingly concerned with how competitors are mischaracterizing them, spreading disinformation."

"Denial and deception," I noted.

"Precisely," he said. "It can be very difficult to detect some of that without noting the patterns of select individuals that over time are pretty clearly taking a position against a client. While we might not always know exactly why, it eventually becomes apparent what they are doing based on the grammar they use. If clients know this, they can react accordingly while there's still time to do so."

Jeff recommends to clients that they have RiskIQ conduct an assessment before launching a new campaign, giving the company a baseline to compare with. Once the buzz of a new product launch is detected, it gives leaders better insight into what's happening—the "So what?" What's the effect of the new campaign?

"If someone says something negative, what's the sentiment and severity?" Jeff asks. "That's something clients can immediately react to by crafting a specific response."

What RiskIQ does is measure "above the noise," as Jeff describes it, finding the trends, the spikes in conversations to identify locations (Web sites or communities), and content (attacks or strong endorsements) for clients to respond to. Many campaigns are incompletely defined at the start, allowing leaders the flexibility to react based on RiskIQ's data (feedback) from previously or newly identified customer segments to better customize the message going out.

At the same time, the firm also monitors competitors' reactions to the client's new campaign. Like commanders responding to a changing battlefield, leaders can adjust the intensity, duration, and reach of their messages based on real-time competitor reactions—or the lack of reaction. If the competitor takes no action at all, RiskIQ's client saves his or her clients considerable advertising costs by identifying channels where no message is required. Empirical data captured in real time provide this information and free decision makers to reinvest those dollars elsewhere or save them for a follow-on campaign.

Who's Who in the Zoo?

Although RiskIQ can detail the sentiments being shared online, the structure of the network itself is also of interest to companies. Characterizing networks and their dynamic, changing nature is a science in and of itself. Fortunately, some very smart scientists are working in this area and have made their tools available to anyone who wants them.

Dr. Kathleen Carley is a professor in the Institute for Software Research and the director of the Center for Computational Analysis of

Social and Organizational Systems (CASOS) at Carnegie Mellon University in Pittsburgh, Pennsylvania. She is one of the preeminent researchers in social network science and one of the key developers of the Organizational Risk Analyzer (ORA), a tool for locating individuals or groups based on social, factual, spatial, and task-specific information and changes in their status over time. ORA finds and characterizes individuals within a network and characterizes key relationships among them. For instance, in evaluating a large company, ORA might identify a researcher instrumental to a key R&D project. A rival firm may choose to hire such a person outright for its own purposes or encourage a non-competing entity to hire him, crippling the rival's research efforts in the near to midterm. Dr. Carley's colleagues, staff, and students have used ORA for a number of commercial and government projects to isolate and identify key individuals and network groups.

This social network analysis (SNA) can also reveal how a network evolves over time. Members come and go, dropping in and out at their own discretion. What triggers these changes? Can reasons that specific members leave be characterized? What is the timing of this evolution in the network? As people depart, they leave virtual trails that can also be analyzed. Where did they go? Why did they choose to go there versus somewhere else? Was a competing network more attractive? If so, why? What role will the person have in this new network? Will he have the same attitudes, ideas, and biases? How will he function within the leadership structure of the new network versus the old one? Will anyone from the old network follow him to the new one?

Social network analysis has a number of forensic applications. When Enron Corporation collapsed, prosecutors planning the criminal case seized the company's e-mails. These same e-mails were also used in numerous civil cases—but how can a lawyer quickly and thoroughly go through literally thousands of e-mails in a manner without missing the context of key exchanges?

Dr. Carley and the team at CASOS analyzed the Enron e-mails, combining SNA and semantics analysis at the same time. They identified key subgroups within Enron based on specific topics discussed over e-mail.

Standard SNA analysis reveals only contacts among individuals. Dr. Carley's team added the who, what, when, where, and how to the activities taking place *within* the firm. SNA didn't accuse anyone of anything; it merely identified which e-mails were most relevant, allowing investigators to concentrate on those most likely to be important in the case.

"Semantics analysis merged with SNA tools can reveal the heartbeat of a company," Dr. Carley told me. "After the Enron bankruptcy, employees started talking about match.com, a reference to finding a new job, not dating."

SNA can similarly identify opinion leaders within a firm based on specific topics being discussed. This would be useful to minimize panic during crisis management efforts, and it has broad human resource applications to identify who is overloaded with work and who is isolated. Who represents a security risk to the corporation?

Dr. Carley suggests that companies conduct their own audits to preclude problems before they boil over, though some clients are stifled by privacy concerns. But as Enron's case shows, once a company enters the public domain of the courts, e-mails are usually a matter of record. It would be far better to prevent the company from entering civil or criminal proceedings through the use of SNA than try to litigate its way out of it after the fact. To facilitate this, individuals' names can be anonymized prior to analysis.

Nobody Ever Says, "It's Just a Game," When They're Winning

A unique SNA application is the identification of emergent leaders within a population. Characterizing connections is one thing; identifying those who task other people to do things is another. Although these people are not formally in positions of authority, they become underground leaders and successfully get things done.

SNA can also identify individuals most similar to each other—people who could be tapped to backfill a position during temporary surges in work or when a key employee must be out for medical or other reasons. Although many people might volunteer for such a role, leaders may not know who can best fulfill the position. SNA can do this with hard data to back up the assertion. Alternatively, it can also identify which leaders should be quietly removed from their positions to minimize company risks and the optimal composition of key teams for a particular task.

Even if they're just playing around.

One of the Internet's most popular activities is massive multiplayer online games (MMOGs), online computer games played through a computer or popular gaming consoles. MMOGs involve hundreds, even thousands, of online gamers who simultaneously play a game despite being thousands of miles apart. *World of Warcraft, America's Army,* and *Final Fantasy* are popular MMOGs with large followings worldwide.

Dr. Carley's lab has analyzed MMOG teams across entire game spheres. Who had the best kill ratio? Who passed key information to team members the best? Who played against whom, what weapons did they use, and how much experience do they really have?

She found networks of "co-play" by analyzing the structure of the game through its network organization. Providing feedback to players lets them pick better partners for certain games or particular strategies. For MMOGs like *America's Army,* SNA reveals the optimal communications sequence for specific players in a linear format versus everyone trying to contact everyone else. By avoiding gaps in communication structures, the team's optimal strategy can be determined.

As MMOGs become more and more popular, this type of analysis will be increasingly valuable not only to players but also to developers who will use it to improve the experience of the game. Most games, however, have no way to visualize or reason about the networks that form as they are played.

Usability and Relational Data

ORA has one of the best interfaces in the SNA field. However, ORA and all SNA tools may take some getting used to for mass audiences.

"It comes down to ease of science or ease of software," Dr. Carley said. "Today's packages are designed for the researcher. They make analysis easy. Many people think that since it is easy to understand that 'a person is important because they talk to a lot of people,' it should be easy to understand network science. In actuality network science is like statistics: some ideas are easier, but many have subtle nuances that require expertise for full understanding." In other words, SNA can be thought of as statistics for relationships.

Relationships are about the connections among things. In contrast, standard statistics is about attribute data, focusing on the properties of things. The difference is that relational data look at who talks to whom, while attribute data look at contextual dimensions (how tall each person is, for instance).

Many SNA packages can handle only simple networks—single mode/ single link data—for example, a network of who works with whom. In contrast, ORA is a multimode/multilink/multilevel analytical tool. It lets you handle a meta-network of who, what, where, how, why, and when. Rather than simply displaying a link between entities, it fully characterizes those links. Friendships, rivalries, abilities, preferences, limitations, and other distinctive qualities are captured in the analysis. These relationship dynamics provide the critical value to SNA analysis.

Message Masterminds

Information like this is invaluable for strategic influence purposes by identifying the best way to insert a message into a network and discretely swaying members. As noted previously, disinformation is a real concern for marketers. Is a person who moves from one network to the next taking her disinformation efforts with her to an easier audience? Social network analysis can help determine this.

One useful function would be resegmenting a particular market for a new product. SNA tools could identify a competitor's network across multiple demographic strata. Knowing which key nodes to target could lead to specific interruptions breaking the network apart, improving the new product's acceptance in this customer base. Establishing a baseline before a product is released makes it possible to focus specific messages that will lower the rejection of a new product by a core group.

If a network is reparsed, targeting each subgroup may be the most efficient means of establishing a new network around the newly released product. The resiliency of the old network is overcome by knowing which node to target in a particular way (Figure 9.1).

This analysis to deconstruct the network followed by synthesis to rejoin selected parts into a new second network is key to applying this technology. Determining the path of least resistance, a perennial problem in new product development, lowers the cost of a market launch. As a new product's network evolves and grows, SNA tools help leaders keep the competition on the defensive by continually learning what new opportunities are emerging in a given market segment community. By modeling these network dynamics ahead of time, it may also be possible to simulate a competitor's reaction in order to preplan a response. Like the NFL coaches described in Chapter Two, it provides a series of potential responses already designed, approved by leadership, communicated to key personnel, and available at a moment's notice when the opportunity arises.

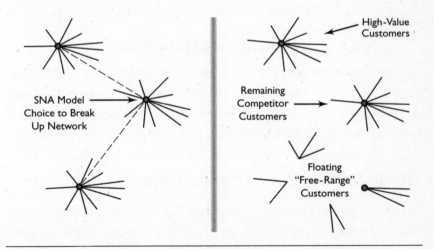

Figure 9.1 Social network analysis identifies the correct node to break a network apart in a distinct way for a competitor to take only the highest-value customers, leaving less profitable customers for the competition.

SNA tools can also identify key influencers, who may actually be more important than key leaders. While leaders may be the most vocal in formal media channels, it is not unusual to find key influencers quietly toiling away with a product or service in the background. They may not have much of a public voice (preferably or not), but their judgment is privately respected by enough people that whatever opinion they give is enough to move a large cadre of like-minded souls.

Knowing who or what shapes this key influencer is another application that can pay big dividends. Reaching the key influencer may mean putting a message out two or three links away. Knowing which links to use, which to avoid, and how to parse the message so it moves through the chain to the key influencer the way you want it to is crucial. SNA can also detect when a competitor does the same. It's called change detection.

What happens when an established customer suddenly moves away from a company's product? The worldwide distribution of messages means that disinformation, deception campaigns, or just plain incorrect information can permeate a market segment and have a dramatic impact on sales with little warning. Change detection captures this in the early stages, giving leaders time to counter through direct intervention or by subtle back channels before revenue is affected.

Geospatial referencing provides leaders the option of reaching a target audience in the offline world as well. If SNA shows that a particular subset of a competitor's customer network is located in Atlanta, Georgia, and likes music from the 1980s, radio stations may be the most efficient way of selectively targeting this demographic with an offsetting offer.

Trade Shows: Social Network Victims or Victors?

The Earth Sciences Research Institute (ESRI) annually turns San Diego, California, into the center of the geospatial world. Anyone making, reading, or even thinking about maps, geospatial analysis, or cartography attends the national conference and trade show. I attended it in 2007 and found it to be part conference, part trade show, and part spiritual event. There are public sessions on how environmental groups can innovatively clean up the earth and classified sessions on how military units can blow it apart.

A colleague of mine returned from the 2009 conference and told me I should contact James Fee. He'd met James in the convention center, and it changed the entire outcome of the conference for him and a number of other people. He did so without the knowledge or control of ESRI and the firm operating the conference.

James works for WeoGeo, a file management and consulting firm serving the geospatial industry. It makes perfect sense for him to be at ESRI, particularly if he works in marketing or operations. But James didn't share with me the area he worked in or any kind of job description, which I certainly should have asked for after I learned his job title: evangelist. It's not a common designation, even among those who proselytize professionally. It's no misnomer to call James a social kind of guy. He's very social. In fact, he's out on the edge, sometimes in your face, sometimes out of sight completely. James has a modern, high-tech interpretation of the stately art of preaching: he's a writer, a blogger, and now a Tweeter.

Twitter is a social networking tool that allows users (called Tweeters) to send out 140-character (maximum) messages, called "Tweets," of whatever they are doing to people who sign up to receive them. These short messages can reach thousands of followers simultaneously (hence the preaching reference) and motivate them to action with little formal urging. Tweeting has gotten so big, so dominant, that actor Ashton Kutcher famously challenged CNN's Larry King over which of them would be the first to sign up 1 million Twitter followers. Kutcher won.

When I asked James Fee what competitive advantage Tweeting offered over his more typical blogging posts, he jumped to his pulpit. "Blog posts feature more content and let you hyperlink among topics," he told me. "I generally have more time to research the topic I'm writing about on a blog. I'll Twitter a title and blog a report. Twitter is better for quick posts, where you state something and move on."

An observation that factored heavily into James's ESRI experience also was part of the experience of hundreds who followed him. Some followers were readers of his popular blog (spatiallyadjusted.com), but many signed up at the ESRI conference itself. Some were referred by current readers, while others learned of James for the first time at the conference. But all of them followed his Tweets on the ESRI conference *while they were attending it.*

Some of the followers then begin following each other using Twitter. What began with a few early adopters in the opening hours of the conference grew to a hundred, then five hundred, and before long, James Fee was a thought leader in a conference he was simply attending. He had no official duties at all.

As James walked around the trade show floor, he dropped Tweets about booths that intrigued him, moved him, or bored him, and crowds shifted around based on his recommendations. When he Tweeted about a speaker he thought was especially dull, crowds thinned at the man's next two sessions. The power of this type of influence has made it a target for marketers.

"I've been offered all sorts of free stuff," James told me, "as long as I would write favorable reviews of the technology or the item's value through my Tweets. I get pitched with offers fifteen or twenty times a week."

Marketers paying for message placement are hardly new. As noted previously, shows are presented to viewers by advertisers, and viewers are brought to advertisers by shows. Trade shows similarly bring potential customers and suppliers together. But what's new is placing such material through an informal channel like a trade show attendee's Tweets. It is more evidence that traditional mass marketing is dying and customized messaging will become more common. As people sign up for media streams based solely on their interests, individuals like James Fee are increasingly important. But they can also be a mechanism for misdirection (D&D).

"I see sock puppets all the time," James told me.

Sock puppets?

"Registering a persona on Twitter that's not real," he explained.

I pointed out that a lot of people have e-mail addresses that don't reflect who they are. Many consider it a safety issue: they don't want personal information going out that could be exploited by another party.

"I'm not talking about that. I'm talking about a guise for the purpose of driving traffic to something. It's covert marketing. People think they're getting information when instead they're getting a product pitch. It's fraud. And it's insulting. People aren't so stupid they are going to drop what they're doing just to watch a 140-character commercial. That's not what Tweeting is about."

James says people drop in and out of Tweet feeds regularly. Although that can be chaotic, it is also indicative of how interests tend to shift. Sometimes market conditions force a change. Other times it's competition over resources, time, or money. Sometimes people just lose interest and move on. But this constant movement is what is so attractive to marketers.

"Remember a couple of years back when the CEO of Whole Foods was posting derogatory stuff on Yahoo Finance about Wild Oats?" James asked me. "Same type of thing. That was a company CEO! It tells you how freaked out firms are about this stuff, realizing it can make a significant impact on their business, but how incredibly uncertain they are in how to use it effectively."

Whole Foods CEO John Mackey had used an anagram of his wife Deborah's name to post over a thousand entries on Yahoo Finance's investor site for over five years. In addition to glowing about his own company, he took numerous shots at archrival Wild Oats. Although many readers were highly suspicious of the posts at the time, it took lawyers for the Federal Trade Commission (FTC) to cite Mackey's actions in a report before the story became widely known in 2007. The FTC sought to block Whole Foods's $560 million acquisition of Wild Oats because it would limit competition within the organic food market. One message board poster euphemistically noted that the vegan CEO was suffering from a bad case of "foot-in-mouth" disease.[6]

Tweeters like James Fee tend to be thought leaders among their real-world peer groups and can quickly turn markets in favor of one product over another. Just as James's Tweets moved segments of attendees from one booth to another and shunned a particular speaker, their chaotic evolution means they tend to remain the high-value early adopters whom companies crave. As a result, there are more and more of these attempts at hidden messages like John Mackey's to sway them.

Unless companies are keeping a cautious eye on their brands, disruptive forces like James Fee are going to sneak up on them every time, even if they have no malicious intent.

Rescue Me

Corporate and nonprofit boards are an important aspect of many executive relationships. Although the socializing aspect has waned over the past few years (many boards were nothing more than CEO rubber-stamp clubs), they are an important part of many executives' education, training, and leadership experience. Some leaders cut their teeth in industries they otherwise know little about, and others use it as a springboard to new opportunities. Although board membership has more accountability now than in the past, it remains an important part of the executive experience.

Yahoo! is one of the oldest search sites in the digital world. Started by Jerry Yang and David Filo the company has grown with the Internet explosion into one of its most regularly visited sites. Microsoft has long sought to level the competitive field with Google in the online search engine business, but with little success. At the time of this writing, Microsoft has a paltry 8 percent market share, less than half of Yahoo!'s 20 percent. Both firms are eating the dust of Google's 64 percent market share, its highest on record. The most expeditious way for Microsoft to increase its position is to buy a rival, so it did. Well, it tried.

Microsoft offered to buy Yahoo!'s search business in summer 2008. Although this is the publicly acknowledged position, it's not unreasonable that Microsoft wanted to acquire the entire firm. Companies are hard enough to absorb as a whole; having to cleave off parts to assimilate into another is even harder. Better to purchase an entire firm unless there's a compelling reason not to. For Microsoft, a full purchase of Yahoo! would appear to be the stockholders' (and most stakeholders') best interests. What's interesting is analyzing the many past relationships that were key to the deal, and it's apparent unraveling. Ultimately the two firms agreed to a unique partnership in July 2009.

Susan Decker, president of Yahoo! joined the firm in 2000 after Wall Street equity firm Donaldson Lufkin and Jenrette (DLJ) was acquired by Credit Suisse. Decker had spent fourteen years at DLJ in equity research, befriending coworkers Jill Greenthal, Tony James, and Kenneth Moelis. Greenthal went on to join the Blackstone Group as a banker, becoming a key advisor to Microsoft in its takeover attempt at Yahoo! Moelis started his own firm and was advising Yahoo during the same negotiations.[7]

Moelis is reportedly close to Yahoo! board members Ron Burkle and Gary Wilson. He is also a close advisor to Yahoo! investor Carl Icahn. Icahn has little tolerance for board members he deems not to be working in his best shareholder interests, and who can blame him? Moelis had advised Icahn on his prior takeover of TWA and a protracted proxy fight with RJR Nabisco several years ago. Icahn wanted a Microsoft deal for Yahoo! and was considering a similar proxy fight against Yahoo!'s board.[8]

As I stated in Chapter Eight, it's quite useful to know something about the people with whom you're negotiating. Decker, Greenthal, and Moelis all knew each other from their DLJ days, giving them a sizable advantage over others who might not know each other as well. But theirs were not the only relationships at play during this time.

In November 2008 Jerry Yang was foundering in his management of Microsoft's bid for Yahoo! Nothing he did made everyone happy. Some wanted to remain a separate entity, while others wanted to cash out with Microsoft. After considerable wrangling, Yahoo!'s board decided Yang had to step down and let someone else take over the strategic leadership role.

Yang approached former Autodesk CEO Carol Bartz to gauge her interest in the top job after both finished a CISCO Systems board meeting.[9] She initially rebuffed the overture but later accepted an invitation to Yang's home, where he described Yahoo!'s strategic decision-making process. Bartz is also a board member of Intel Corp with Yahoo! president Sue Decker, who'd been promoted from chief financial officer in 2007.[10]

Although Decker lobbied for the role, she was passed over for the CEO position at Yahoo! which was instead offered to Bartz. Decker tenured her resignation the day Bartz took over.[11] She's now borrowing office space at Blackstone Group from pals Jill Greenthal and Blackstone president Tony James (another DLJ alum). She's likely not bored, though, still serving on the Intel's board, as well as that of Berkshire Hathaway with Microsoft CEO Bill Gates.

In June 2009 Bartz was still fielding questions about a Microsoft purchase of Yahoo! Her comments to the media vacillate from selling Yahoo! "only for boatloads of money,"[12] to (Microsoft's new Bing search engine) "interesting, but not over the top interesting,"[13] to (a Microsoft-Yahoo! merger) "wouldn't get past DOJ approval."[14] If that sounds like a D&D campaign, it's likely because the two companies were still trying to work out an agreement, as indicated by the July 2009 announcement The two were likely hurried by the pursuit of yet another rival: Time Warner's AOL.[15] Any publicly traded company will have its board members listed in its annual reports, as will virtually all nonprofit boards. By examining board memberships over time it's possible to tease out relationships that, when properly analyzed, can reveal who might be tapped to fill a future board seat, become a new CEO, or offer to purchase a rival firm—and who might block it.

Products of Our Environment

People exist in multiple terrains: information, geographical, and human. Each of these dimensions interrelates to each other in many ways. As a result, mapping them can be challenging, but also quite revealing.

Just as a fingerprint can discern us from an otherwise masking crowd, the language we use can do the same. Semantics analysis can identify individuals, indicate potential threats, and reveal leaks within an organization.

Social network analysis can reveal influential players who may be better approached than officially recognized community leaders. Knowing whom leaders listen to, formally or informally, provides opportunities to influence their decision making.

Twitter, Facebook, and other tools require sales and marketing leaders to equally consider tactical, operational, and strategic aims. Understanding the differences among these three is crucial to leveraging social media.

Part Four:
Three Stages
of Conflict

10

Tactical Advantage
The Who

My wife loves to shop and she loves to haggle. One of her favorite places to do this is around Times Square in New York City. One of the more fascinating examples of field information collection is on the side streets off Broadway, from Tenth Avenue to Park, and Fifty-Seventh Street to Forty-Second. There are roving teams of vendors selling high-end sunglasses, electronics, purses, clothing, and jewelry. Inventory is mobile—taped or wired into various foldable linens, tarps, or other rapidly deployed contraptions limited only by weight and imagination.

But unlike the popular image of young men aggressively chasing potential customers, these men and women have learned something about competition. They've learned to mirror the customer's actions: if the customers are tentative, the sellers are tentative back. Joke with them, and they'll open up with a string of one-liners. Mirroring is an oft-taught tactic in sales organizations. Match the person's mannerisms and actions, even his breathing, if you can do so without being caught, and he'll relax despite the fact that he's dealing with a stranger.

But if you watch closely, as street vendors are talking and mirroring, they're also looking behind you—and behind themselves. They're looking uptown and downtown. Their eyes are in constant motion watching for the police or armies of private security around large office buildings employed to keep them away from the entrances. And if you look even closer, you'll notice the wires.

The typical New York street vendor is as wired as a Secret Service agent. Forget the walkie-talkies of our youth—the garbled, stringless tin can radios that connected kids across backyard fences. The transmitters on the belts of these street jockeys are state of the art. These are hands-free, multiband devices sporting military-grade encryption, set up for one-on-one communication or spread broadcasts to the entire network simultaneously.

These roving showrooms of networked entrepreneurs show their wares while remaining alert to everything going on around them. Any patrolling officer or security guard stepping outside for a smoke break is instantly noted for everyone in the network. It's very formal—no stray comments, no joking around—just the pertinent information on the location or direction of a cited person. And it's not just uniform personnel.

Street vendors know that luxury brands are increasingly hiring private investigators to search the streets for counterfeit goods. While firms like Versace, Kate Spade, and Rolex may apprehend the occasional foot soldier on a sidewalk, what they really want are the big guys—the distributors. That means following the street vendors back to their inventories, usually buttoned up in a van or car trunk not far away. Following the vehicles leads to warehouses, which lead to distributors, manufacturers, and the money men. It reveals every member of the network. That's what they're after.

Without a network, the street vendor has no product to sell. If they get a reputation for being sloppy, for getting caught and the goods confiscated by authorities, suppliers cut them off. The only way to protect the network is to ensure that prying eyes can't see anything they're not supposed to. That means vendors must communicate to each other quickly and succinctly without interfering with face-to-face customer marketing.

The radios allow them to track large groups of tourists spending money, the locations of competing vendor networks, traffic and weather conditions, and where supply vehicles are parked. It gives them a unique advantage that suggests law enforcement and luxury brands have few available options to stop them.

Creating competitive advantage meant taking their business strategy and breaking it down into a series of specific tasks. Some tasks conflicted with each other; that had to be corrected. Others required a precise order of events, and assigned roles were doled out. But once in place and operating, it was as robust an operating design as anything built by the finest technology companies. And the common denominator for any firm's tactical advantage is identifying and characterizing the *who*.

Like many companies, these networks face a dynamic set of evolving problems and limitations that evolve over the course of every day. They are in conflict with many entities simultaneously—police, guards, and private investigators—all of whom are hiding within the population of potential customers the vendors are selling to. It's similar to the insurgents' strategy I mentioned in Chapter One: a high degree of uncertainty because it's impossible to distinguish good guys from bad guys. Any one of the customers could, without warning, pull out a set of handcuffs and say, "You're under arrest."

This level of uncertainty means vendors are largely on their own. Yes, they're part of a network, but if they are caught and arrested, they go downtown alone. The rest of the network will continue on as before, lamenting the loss of the individual's merchandise but acknowledging that stopping is not an option. The suppliers, manufacturers, and fellow hawkers across the street will not mourn for long.

They must move more quickly than their competition. They must adapt to the environment, even using the environment as a shield sometimes, while interfering with the competition's ability to do the same. They will deny police and guards access to their inventory. They will delay putting their wares on display if they sense the environment is not right. To confuse competitors, they may act as if police or security guards are imminent, prodding competitors to pack up and move to another area when they didn't actually need to.

They are shaping, and on occasion manipulating, the competitive environment. In return, the environment also shapes the vendors: What products will they sell today? To whom? How? The environment (weather, economy, time of year) is the backdrop (some would say the back wall) that all competitive pressures eventually assimilate around.

Like Professor Hu Soung's fish, it is communication among individual network members at the tactical level that provides them a sustainable business model. Law enforcement is exhausted trying to arrest and convict them. Security guards are constrained by their limited authorities. Private investigators remain paralyzed when savvy vendors don't lead them to the golden goose. Vendors follow classic guerrilla warfare doctrine: small, autonomous teams using hit-and-run tactics, blending into a well-understood population within a limited geographical range.

At the same time, customer focus is essential. Sharing information in real time has established street vendors as a legitimate part of the New York City business community. They are popular with tourists and even many native New Yorkers who could otherwise not afford a Rolex Submariner or the latest Hermès scarf. Vendors help tourists with directions and hail cabs. They've secured medical assistance and participated in neighborhood watch programs. These helpful roles they play undermine public support for police, guards, and private investigators to shut these operations down.

Understanding the Terrains

If the street vendors demonstrate nothing else, businesses should at least acknowledge the importance of knowing who's who. This is what the sales organization, customer service staff, and call center operators do: interact with customers, competitors, and regulators every minute of every business day. They are at the pointy end of the spear with regard to competition. They live and die by it—the first line of defense and the first collectors on offense.

In Chapter One I outlined the intelligence cycle and what a misnomer it is. Now I'll describe what I've found to be a much more realistic and robust interpretation of that model. I refer to it as the *CARP model* (Figure 10.1). The first two sections are somewhat similar with collection, using methods such as FOIA or trade shows, feeding into an analytical function. Often collectors cannot interact with customers, watch the competition, and analyze everything going on around them. Complicated analysis is often a function for a separate support element whose job is to ensure these frontline operators have what they need.

The public faces and voices of a firm should reach back into the network for assistance as needed, but otherwise they need autonomy to work independently. The network enterprise cannot survive without them. Without these folks interacting with customers and gathering information, the entire company grinds to a halt.

But that also means the analysts can and will shape the collection effort. Rather than simply accepting what they're given, analysts often reject pieces of information. This feedback loop is vital. Far from a linear "we'll take whatever we can get" orientation, the analyst function will reject many information sources. Other times it requires additional information from current sources. It can also insist that new sources of information be developed because what frontline collectors have provided is simply unclear (Figure 10.2).

This puts the collectors on notice that what they're doing is of interest to the firm. The previously provided data didn't answer the mail, so

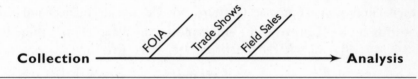

Figure 10.1 CARP model collection leading to analysis.

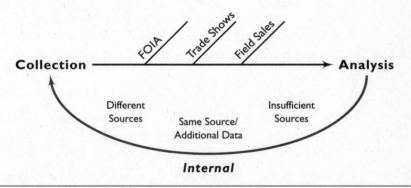

Figure 10.2 The initial analysis disavows collected information, requiring collectors to find additional sources, acquire additional information from existing sources, or seek out new sources of information.

now they're on the lookout for new data or new sources. When they find what they are looking for, they put them into the same original communication channels to the analytical function. These new data, enhancing or refuting the previously collected information, will amend the original analysis, expand on it, or change it completely (Figure 10.3).

It creates independent feedback loops within the collection effort itself, in addition to the feedback loop that now exists between analysts and collectors (see Figure 10.4). There's little senior leadership involvement here. The collectors keep digging for data until the analysts have gotten what they need. Like the old joke about pornography, they may not be able to describe it; sometimes they don't know what it looks like until they see it.

What did Meyer Corporation do to keep Georgia's Department of Environmental Protection happy? They sent a senior executive from headquarters to the Meyer facility on a long-term assignment. Would a senior corporate executive normally move across the country for a temporary capital improvement project? Of course not. He's not an engineer and had little direct authority over the employees or the plant. He was there to

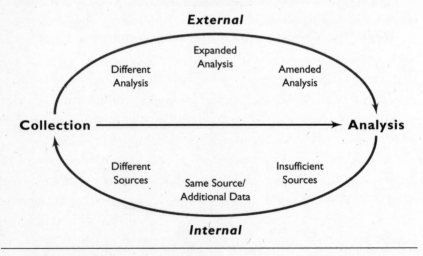

Figure 10.3 With new sources or new information, the analysis is adjusted, revealing different results, an expanded viewpoint, or amendment of the original conclusions.

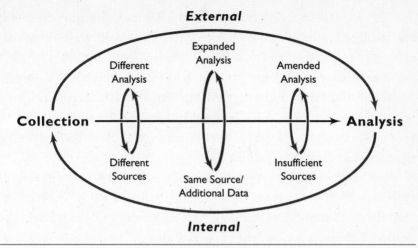

Figure 10.4 The feedback loop from analysis, back to collection, and returning to analysis, comprising smaller feedback loops within the collection effort, depending on the new or additional data gathered.

provide a new face for Georgia regulators, demonstrating that senior-level officials were taking the problem seriously. This strategy to tactics orientation is not unusual. In fact, it should be the norm for all companies.

Competitive intelligence is about shaping the environment and allowing business strategy to be shaped by it. The company must understand its terrains—physical, human, and information. All three are important, though the effect of each on a business varies by industry and changes over time. It's a balancing act in the dark; sometimes it is impossible to know how out of kilter something is until it is almost crashing down.

After a while, field personnel get a "feel" that's hard to explain to those who've never worked it. Salesmen just *feel* when a client has a big order in mind. Retail clerks *feel* when someone's about to shoplift. Reporters *feel* when a story is going to knock the editor's socks off. But in order to get this feel, they have to interact with customers in good times and bad. It can't be a one-way street. Business is a form of communication, which means it has to be two way. If you're going to communicate with someone, you'd better know who that person is.

This is personality driven, as any good sales techniques class will teach, and it's not at all unusual for a change in salesperson to have an extremely negative impact on a client's orders. Clients can end up ordering more from a new salesperson, but that's far less common. Customers go into a sort of mourning period if their trusted sales rep is suddenly promoted, relocates, or takes a position with another firm. Some customers even go through a variant of the five stages of grief. It's the bargaining stage that can be most troubling.

Advantage is about preparing for random, unexpected chances. If there is ever a time for the competition to pounce, this is it. The haphazard way most companies manage customer hand-offs is precisely the random opportunity competitors need to drive a wedge between a rival and its customer. There has been no reason to change to another vendor until their favorite sales representative was suddenly taken away. So why shouldn't they consider another source now?

The relationship is no longer built on personal rapport. Now it's simply a transaction—a cold, heartless, and bloodless exchange. This is the perfect time to force price concessions on the supplier or let the competition know that if they can provide more value, the customer will consider changing suppliers. Competitors will fall all over themselves getting a proposal in front of the potential new customer.

This is why frontline representatives must watch the customer and the competition. The new incoming rep will need as much information about the competitor who is pouncing on her account as she can get. What has the customer shared with the firm in the past about what he likes about the company and dislikes about the competition? Why did he pick the firm to begin with? How had the previous rep leveraged rapport with the customer to create and maintain such a high level of goodwill?

For the competition, the same questions apply. What did the current suppliers do to land that account? Can we match it? If not, can we articulate how we provide a better value? Can we update our pitch to reflect new revenues, new values, or new opportunities the current vendor cannot (or has not) supplied? How would we go about making a pitch without sounding desperate?

Finding a way to solve the customer's problem is usually the best strategy, and frontline employees are in the best position to do so. They often know the customer personally even if it is not their account. They will also benefit from having spoken with other customers who've likely had similar experiences and can share what worked or didn't. By providing this type of help, particularly when a customer's vulnerability could elicit a persuasive proposal from an otherwise silent competitor, the relationship will temporarily be returned from the company to the salesperson again.

It's natural that customers tend to bond with the face and name of the company representative. During every transaction, that salesperson's likes and dislikes are, for the customer, the company's likes and dislikes. The customer makes no distinction between the individual and the firm. It's not something intentional; it's just how we're wired.

Transactions take place across all three terrains. Physically a good is delivered or a service is provided. Information, starting from invoice and payment, then moving on to company and competitive data, is exchanged in the information terrain. The human terrain is the vector for both. Although they can be done without the firm's human interlocutor, that's not what most customers want. They want the interaction, and they want the partnership with a trusted agent with whom they've forged a relationship despite their best efforts to avoid it.

Who Are You?

Jeff Lumetta's scouting at CES is classic tactical *who* activity. As Jabil's R&D chief, he is not after a specific person so much as examining all the people who are there: customers, competitors, and new companies showing off their wares. At forums like this, Jabil and other large firms are less interested in the technology and more interested in the person responsible for it.

Who is this entrepreneur? What is he or she like? Would he fit well with the company? Is this someone the company could partner with? At the show, is the entrepreneur courteous to others or rude, seeking out only big-name firms who could buy or license his technology? How the entrepreneur acts around those who cannot help him tells a lot about how he'll act around those who can when he isn't looking.

That's the real value of trade show work: the face-to-face time with a wide array of people. Jeff Lumetta and other senior corporate leaders will review and consider the technology when they get home. Right now they want to know the man or woman behind the idea. It's one facet of how intelligence is moved throughout a large organization.

Whom do we meet at a trade show (tactical), how does the company choose to follow up (operations), and what opportunities might we pursue together (strategic)? Each dimension refers to the others, uses the other's products, and generates requirements for the others. It's an organized chaos that evolves based on the environment in which the intelligence staff and the leadership work.

Shelton Quarles and other Buccaneers scouts write specific products against each player's opposite week to week (tactical). They also work with line coaches and staff on how those players are used in specific plays and styles (operations) and offensive and defensive coordinators working on Buccaneers' play designs (strategic). Less importance is placed on collecting the information and more on recognizing the value of the information once it is available.

But most large organizations are not set up to manage such an unwieldy and chaotic function. As more companies realize they don't have a lock on innovation and that plenty occurs outside their organizations that passes them by, the competitive intelligence function is increasingly serving research and product development—and not just by looking outside the company.

Google recently revamped how it defines and develops new projects from its own in-house workforce. Google is famous for allowing its employees to spend a full day a week on pet projects (as 3M did twenty years ago), but it has failed to turn enough of those projects into products to sell. Google has acknowledged it failed to get employees' projects in front of senior managers in a timely manner.

As the company's hiring paralleled its wild growth, the perceptual distance between working-level engineers and senior managers grew. It became increasingly difficult for innovative ideas to get proper consideration from the company, and frustrated employees, recognizing an opportunity, started leaving to start their own firms. Former Google employees started Twitter after they couldn't get any traction in house.

This is a serious hazard to Google. Twitter would have been a crown jewel for the firm as it expands beyond search engines, yet it slipped right through the company's fingers. Other firms, recognizing Google employees' passionate work ethic and creativity, are only too happy to provide funding, work space, and engineering assistance to product developers looking to depart the Mountain View, California, firm. For Google, it's the worst of all possible worlds.

New products are imperative to corporate growth. Without them, Google stagnates, as so many of its former competitors have. Realizing it was heading down a similar path, Google CEO Eric Schmidt forced company leaders (notably including himself) to set aside time to hear new ideas from company employees. Some of the early results of this new orientation are seeing beta-testing fruition, including a potential new application that syncs with Microsoft Outlook e-mail and a facial recognition imaging project.[1]

Competitors are similarly interested in Google employees' ideas and have the same issue: How can they identify the employees with the best ideas? Recognizing that sharks are circling, Google has applied its statistical rigor to mathematically determine which employees are most likely to leave.[2] Identifying them may be the easy part. Getting them to stay could be a challenge.

Jabil Circuit is similarly looking at technology opportunities. Jabil has provided the electronic circuitry for PakBots, a military robot that can search rooms, sniff out bombs, and explore caves while soldiers remain a safe distance away. Made by the same firm that builds the popular room vacuum robot Rumba, Jabil won a competitive bidding process that put it in partnership with iRobot.[3] It's a partnership that has benefited both firms. Jabil was looking to expand its defense aerospace business, and iRobot needed a partner with more experience in large-scale manufacturing. They've delivered thirteen hundred iRobots over the past six years. Diversification benefits Jabil, whose manufacturing expertise and technology consulting benefits iRobot. In December 2008, the U.S. Army awarded iRobot a multimillion-dollar contract for three thousand more PakBots. But Jabil is not alone in collaborating with a much smaller partner.

In 2004, Crane and Company, the sole producer of U.S. currency since 1879, began a partnership with tiny Nanoventions Corp., a 2000 start-up of anticounterfeiting technology. The pair created the exclusive passes for President Obama's inauguration and are scheduled to debut a newly designed hundred-dollar bill as soon as Treasury Secretary Timothy F. Geithner approves it and his signature is added to the design.[4] In this case the *who* was engineered by Crane and Company's client, the U.S. Bureau of Engraving and Printing, which had received a demonstration of Nanovention's anticounterfeiting technology and thought there'd be a fit between the two firms.

In 2006 Kraft launched an initiative seeking inventors and entrepreneurs to partner with on product development. Its vice president for innovation, Steve Goers, told the *Wall Street Journal,* "We realize there's a very large body of innovators outside of Kraft." Kraft receives forty to fifty pitches a month in writing, by phone, or through a Web site set up specifically for the program. Gary Schwartzberg had developed a tube-shaped bagel filled with cream cheese for hungry patrons on the go, even getting it into local retail stores. But after partnering with Kraft, he saw his idea go national as Bagel-Fuls, filled with Kraft's own Philadelphia Cream Cheese.[5]

The Innovations Café at Memorial Hospital in South Bend, Indiana, doesn't serve food at all. It's a teaching laboratory and the brainchild of Memorial CEO Philip Newbold, who turned a failed restaurant space into a place for employees and outsiders to pitch ideas that would give the hospital a competitive edge. It's not just the successful ideas that get attention. He invites presenters to tell his senior managers the lessons learned from projects that didn't work out.[6]

These are the kinds of relationships every company wants, and it starts when one company identifies the right person, the right *who,* to make it happen. But it requires senior leaders to take the time to listen to these frontline initiatives before their competitors do it for them.

A Laser-Like Focus

Guy Ontai and Ed Dottery are situational entrepreneurs. Both men are building unique R&D companies when many with their experience are retired, kicking back after long and illustrious careers of faithfully serving their country. But Guy and Ed aren't the puttering-around type. *Tinkering* around, well now that's another story.

Guy and Ed are graduates of the U.S. Military Academy at West Point who went on to become instructors. Both are retired U.S. Army officers with impressive credentials. Guy received his master's in physics from MIT, and Ed did the same at Stanford. Both were on the physics faculty at West Point and wouldn't have guessed they would use that experience to more directly support troops in harm's way.

Improvised explosive devices (IEDs) were killing and maiming many young men and women in Iraq. IEDs are homemade bombs using ordinary materials available throughout the Middle East, tied to a remote control trigger, often an ordinary cell phone. The devices can be masked as bricks, buried in the center of dirt roads, even hidden in animals that have died along the highways. However they are placed, militants wait until a U.S. military vehicle comes by and selectively pick out what they think is the most vulnerable one. Newer IED devices are specifically designed to penetrate armor plate, substantially increasing the lethality of the devices.

Neither Guy nor Ed is the type to sit around and wait for someone else to fix it, particularly when they've got skin in the game. Guy has a son in the Army serving overseas, and both have many friends and colleagues still in the fight. They decided to apply their considerable technical acumen to the problem. Guy had served in the Corp of Engineers. Ed was in Special Forces Infantry and Army Acquisitions. Surely two scary-smart physicists with field experience could come up with a solution.

The result is a small engineering firm called Alaka'i. As IEDs evolved throughout the Iraq conflict, Guy and Ed thought they could make a significant contribution at the most local level, identifying the "who" of enemy insurgents, where soldiers are the most vulnerable. Working out of locations in Hawaii and Florida, they evaluated current remote-sensing technology and designed a new stand-off detection protocol.

In examining the steps necessary to build, emplace, and detonate a vehicle-based improvised explosive device (VBIED), where a car is used to deliver an explosive payload to the target, the pair created an interruptive method to identify and isolate high-risk vehicles before they can get inside a U.S. military compound or a crowded market full of civilians. What they developed looks like something out of Star Wars. Their prototype device took a standard piece of analytical equipment off the laboratory bench and supersized it to sit on a small trailer or atop a Humvee.

Many IEDs are low-signature environment weapons, where there's no apparent behavior pattern to warn of an impending attack. Other firms are working to stop the explosives in transit or interfere with the electronic signals of detonating devices. But those solutions will take months, perhaps years, to perfect and deploy. Soldiers need a more immediate solution, even if it is at the most lethal point—just before a device explodes. But having been soldiers, Ed and Guy are perfectly attuned to what is operationally feasible. And that's where their device is unique: it operates at the last interdiction point before a device can injure a soldier (Figure 10.5).

They use a laser to detect the threat. If the laser does detect a threat, troops can search for or neutralize it from a safe distance. If the threat is a person who opts not to comply, other more kinetic options are available to soldiers, who will be fully alert and prepared for possible hostilities.

While technologies such as up-armoring a Humvee or deploying the mine-resistant ambush-protected vehicle are fine for convoys, soldiers at checkpoints to military facilities, Western hotels, or U.S. embassies are still at great risk. Segregating an insurgent from the general population is extremely important in humanitarian assistance, noncombatant rescue, or national security operations. Soldiers must maintain a strict defensive posture yet still be accessible to the people they are trying to protect and assist. The insurgents have every advantage here. They know who everyone is, but the soldiers do not; farmers, insurgents, merchants, and militants all look alike to them.

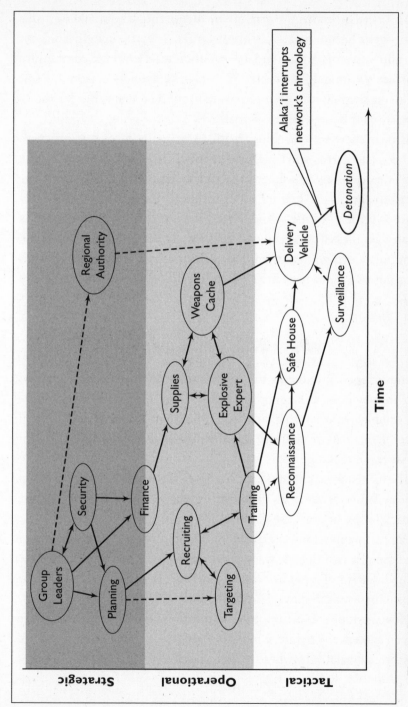

Figure 10.5 Alaka'i interrupts the IED network (identifying the "who") at the most tactical, time-critical point: as the weapon is being delivered, potentially seconds from detonation.

Alaka'i reduces this uncertainty by identifying who might be a suicide bomber before he arrives at his target. They reduce the soldier's uncertainty in working around a population with a hidden community of hostiles within it. Like the NFL players in Chapter Two, frontline soldiers make the majority of decisions in ground conflicts, but for them, the penalty for being wrong is lethal.

This counter-IED technology is still in its infant stages, but early tests have been successful, and the Department of Defense is field-testing the Alaka'i devices. Giving soldiers a tactical solution for determining the most likely threats and crafting new procedures for reacting to this information is critical. While soldiers need a fast tactical solution, speed is immaterial unless it accurately answers the all-important *who* question. But because it challenges the high-speed method of the insurgents, it gives soldiers a fighting chance. Alaka'i's solution may be the last line of defense.

Who's Who in the Zoo?

The importance of knowing the relevant players in any conflict should be obvious by now. These are relationships, and although they don't have to be established on mutual affection, they should at least have mutual respect. Don't hate your rivals; the intensity of your emotion throws off your decision making.

The feedback loops within the CARP model are essential to its effectiveness. Without them it's just another management theory. Use the feedback loops, or don't use CARP at all.

Big companies, long criticized for being impersonal, are beginning to see the error of their ways and are developing the means to know customers and potential innovation partners at a personal level. Their early successes mean other firms will follow suit.

How firms operationalize their innovations can make the difference between success and failure. Operations are where competitive advantage is born or, alternatively, where it dies, as we'll see in Chapter Eleven.

Operational Advantage
The How

Ticketmaster, the world's largest concert and sporting events ticket broker, has been the industry leader for many years based in part on the long-term contracts it has with event venues such as forums, amphitheaters, and municipal stadiums around the country. Ticketmaster has always leveraged these contracts as its primary competitive advantage, and it is a powerful one.[1] Without a venue with seats, staff, food, and bathroom facilities, there is nowhere to set up stages for performers.

Concert promoter Live Nation was one of Ticketmaster's largest customers, accounting for 17 percent of its $1.24 billion 2007 revenue. But Live Nation developed a plan to sell tickets itself, allowing its contract with Ticketmaster to expire in January 2009.[2] Live Nation, rather than try to beat Ticketmaster at its own game, chose to change the rules, exploiting its close relationship with performers. Live Nation is the preferred concert promoter for the largest venues, but rather than leveraging locations, it chose to leverage the artists, such as U2 and Madonna, to distinguish itself from Ticketmaster.

Live Nation signed a five-year deal with SMG, a firm that manages two hundred major properties around the country, from the Los Angeles Forum to Soldier Field in Chicago. For the duration of the deal, Live Nation will sell the lion's share of tickets for SMG venues, a revenue stream estimated to be \$50 to \$60 million. SMG was Ticketmaster's second largest client.

Media mogul Barry Diller's InterActive Corp (IAC) divested Ticketmaster along with Lending Tree and Home Shopping Network (HSN) in mid-2008, so Live Nation's stomach punch couldn't have come at a worse time. Whether Ticketmaster could have or should have known what Live Nation and SMG were doing is at this point irrelevant. The competitive environment has radically changed, and Ticketmaster's key business revenue is at risk.

Live Nation's research into its main supplier/competitor and the overall competitive marketplace led it to conclude that the only way to increase its business was to take this radical step. But rather than compete head-to-head with Ticketmaster, which had a competitive advantage Live Nation could not directly counter, it chose to work around that advantage. What was extraordinary was the speed with which they made these decisions and took action, radically changing the routine of their business.

As analysts report their findings to leaders, it can be a quick process, particularly when they know their leaders' preferences about how they like the analysis structured and presented. But even with that, leaders might not like the manner in which it is provided, perhaps they think something has been left out, or they might think there is a particular context that could affect the efficacy of the decisions to be made. Having analysts reconsider their evaluation could result in the crafting of a new story, examining adjacent perspectives, or finding a new dimension to the conflict. Analysts might even trigger the previous feedback loop to collectors for more data. These feedback loops are similar to what we saw between collection and analysis. (See Figures 11.1 and 11.2.)

Understanding the *how* dimension is important because operations are the critical connections between corporate strategy and the leading-edge activity at the street (tactical) level. How should a firm implement the senior executive's strategy? How should it leverage the information being gathered by frontline employees? What competitive advantages

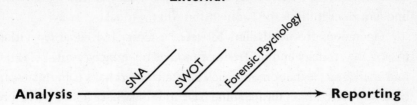

External

Internal

Figure 11.1 CARP model, analysis to reporting. Analytical methods vary depending on the dimension of conflict, time available, resources, and nature of the uncertainty.

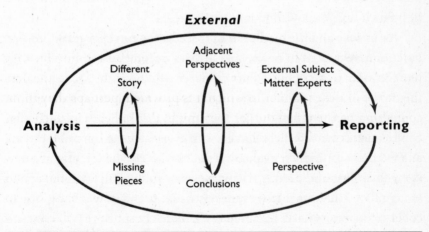

Figure 11.2 CARP model, analysis to reporting. Like analysis, reporting can often reinitiate the analytical sequence, requesting additional data or expertise.

does the firm have now, what does it anticipate requiring in the future, and *how* does it think the competition will try to take it away?

Operations provide the link between customer and leader: operationalizing the strategy and delivering products or services while collecting and analyzing feedback from frontline staff. Operations is both a reachback knowledge base for frontline staff and the wise sages who interpret data and advise senior leaders. Operations has characteristics of both tactics and strategy yet is itself a separate dimension of competition.

But it is a critical dimension. Operations makes or breaks a company. Strategy is important, but not if midrange managers cannot do what a firm has promised. Frontline employees can collect all the information in the world, but if operations cannot act on it, the company will wither and die. Sometimes acting on information is harder than it first appears.

Puppet Master

Bob Finch wasn't allowed to talk to the media.

It was 1989 and the medical trade association he represented refused to let him be quoted in newspaper articles or interviewed by television reporters. He was a public affairs manager with no authority to speak to the public or the press. Unflattering articles went unanswered, with no countermessage to refute the lies, half-truths, and rampant misdirection.

He maintained cordial relations with even the most spiteful reporters and fed them off-industry stories. He'd done his opposition research and knew their likes and dislikes. He knew what would drag them out of bed at night. He knew what their supervisors liked and how certain stories could get reporters raises and bonuses. It wasn't long before Bob arranged for individual doctors to speak with reporters. He prepared them, coached them, even provided talking points based on the industry association's prepared strategy. Yet media bosses, and his own bosses, remained blissfully unaware of his hand in the stories.

Ironically those draconian working conditions prepared him for the firm he would start some two decades later. The R. E. Finch Company fills a specialized niche in business today, and any ambiguity about its role is clear in Bob's job title: covert media specialist. Just as physicians can specialize in precise areas of medicine, Bob has surgically carved out a unique position in advertising and promotion.

He has moved on from spokesman to puppet master. Pulling the strings behind the scenes, Bob has adapted the techniques used over three decades to turn media, market segmentation, and audience analysis on its head.

"Social media are so new, and evolving so quickly, most firms can't get their arms around it," he told me. When I asked why, he pointed out where most senior executives get their advice.

"They're talking to the CFO, the VP of marketing, or the head of corporate communications. Most of these older professionals—(men *and* women)—went to business school over twenty years ago. They understand classic market segmentation and channel analysis. When the lines blur, when markets overlap, when each cannot be carved into individual pots, they lose their way. When segments aren't easily parsed, they shun them."

"They're *uncertain*," I suggested, offering my often-used point.

"Absolutely. But more important," he corrected, "they don't know what to tell their bosses: the big cheese—the president, CEO, or the board. They're reading about Facebook and Twitter in the *Wall Street Journal,* but senior staff have no idea what these social media tools are or how to use them."

"Why can't they learn it like anyone else?" I asked, already anticipating the answer.

"Because that's not professional," he laughed and told me in a huff-and-puff parody of ill-mannered bluster what these professionals are thinking to themselves: *I'm an executive vice president! The last thing I'm going to do is admit to my boss, my staff, or myself that I don't know something about marketing or public relations. I've been doing this for over twenty years . . .* I felt like I was rereading Jerome Groopman's book on how doctors misdiagnose by steering clear of uncertainty and miscommunicating with their patients. Groopman cited researcher Renee Fox, who had identified three types of uncertainty: imperfect mastery of the topic by an individual, an incomplete knowledge of the topic as a subject, and the inability to distinguish between the two.[3] This seems dangerously on the mark.

Communication, the central purpose of marketing, is failing to adapt to a changing environment. Some businesses know their target markets and what they want to sell to them. But they've lost *how* to reach them through the new channels of social media. The days of simply buying broadcast time on premium television networks and creating a snappy jingle are over.

The power of social media is how customers can self-organize. Unlike television media planning, where the program is brought to you by the sponsor and you are brought to the sponsor by the program, social media self-organize continually, evolving with only the most valuable (dedicated) consumers remaining involved. This "free" aspect is what is so offputting to senior leaders. Market forces are the basis of capitalism. But leaders are accustomed to companies, not customers, running the show. Company leaders can exert little real control and it's driving them crazy.

How firms get a message to their audience, that is, the operational aspects of putting a message in front of a buying audience, has only started to change. To borrow the evolutionary explanation again, we're clawing our way out of the slime and crawling up on land. Tomorrow we'll walk upright, and by Friday we'll see people soaring through the skies on their own wings. It's changing, adopting, and adapting at such breathtaking speeds that many companies fail to realize that even with a product that perfectly fits their identified customers' needs, they have no idea how to reach that customer anymore, and it scares the hell out of them.

"You haven't seen anything yet," Bob tells me. "Wait until they realize their HR department is an overhead expense that future competitors won't bother with."

"We have to be able to hire people," I pointed out.

"Sure. But *how* we'll hire them is changing. Employee handbooks, medical and dental policies, direct deposit and 401(k) applications: they're all commodities. It's out-of-the-box boilerplate anyone can buy at a half-dozen supply houses. Why maintain a staff for that? Hiring is the last bastion of the old business model and it's going to be radically redesigned in the next five years."

"How's that?" I asked, with no idea where this was going.

"Are you on LinkedIn?" he inquired, simultaneously looking me up on the site.

LinkedIn is a social networking site specifically for business. People can find each other based on industry types, profession types, or for the purposes of proposing new business, asking and answering questions, keeping constantly updated on the stream of information about their peer connections' careers.

"LinkedIn is evolving," he said, clicking through the site as we spoke. "It's evolving into a structure with groups and new software plug-ins designed by both users and companies that see opportunity in group exposures. This thing is taking new technologies developed for other purposes and adapting them [his words] to LinkedIn's audiences and purposes. And the main attraction is altruistic; you *give* information [advice, criticism, and support] to friends and new acquaintances with the faith that your return will come."

I was a little slow on the uptake here and didn't mind saying so, so Bob explained further: "It's a business *learning* environment. It will surpass Monster.com for corporate hiring functions. You've got résumés, recommendations, and evidence of how people defend a position, how they make decisions. It's all there. Why do you need interviews? Just ping the community they are part of with some well-worded questions, and you'll know in fifteen minutes if you have a legitimate final candidate."

I was still missing his point.

"*Groups* are the future," Bob continued, slightly frustrated with my lumbering appreciation of his point. "*Communities.* Look at how many chambers of commerce are financially struggling right now. They'll continue to struggle. It's faster, easier, and less costly to achieve the same outcome through LinkedIn, and you can limit your interaction to only those you've got an interest in speaking with. Time, despite all our efforts, is still a restraining factor for everyone."

Bob's interpretation of the necessity of managing time required a bit more explanation. He told me that Twitter, for all its frivolous uses (and he cited several), is also one of the more efficient means for monitoring a firm's competitors. He monitors Twitter feeds to follow rivals for several clients—listening to what is being said about their product or service, brand, or the company itself.

"Social media will force companies to reread their old Dale Carnegie materials," Bob said.

"What does that mean?" I asked.

"*Listen* to the customer," he implored. "Don't walk into a conversation and start pitching something."

When my response (correctly) suggested I thought he meant interrupting a random conversation between two people, Bob politely rebuffed me by e-mailing a link to the *ClueTrain Manifesto* (http://www.cluetrain.com/). Written in 1999, the book (now available for free online) argues that future markets are conversations. Human voices, the users of a product or service, are the best promoters of that product or service because their voices are real. Unlike the typical general counsel–vetted, marketing department–approved, public relations–screened formulaic language, real voices communicate with people rather than simply talk at them. He directs me to the manifesto's list of signatories, fourth from the bottom.

Bob Finch.

He's been at this podium for a decade.

"Social media has surpassed porn on the internet," Finch inculcates his naive writer-student. "Companies have to relearn marketing and PR. The staff must set up a social presence for the company, then write something about themselves, the individual. When that's established, when it's an animate person rather than an inanimate corporation, markets will converse with you. If they like you, they'll buy what you're selling. If you touch them the right way, they'll even evangelize for you."

Evangelize? James Fee's title might become more common.

Marketing in the future will consist of which customers to vet, block, follow, support, or flag (or tag) based on the nature of the relationship they bring. "That's what scares companies," Bob said.

The marketing staff and product managers will make important decisions on their own. Despite multimillion-dollar capital expenditures on information technology, there will not be time enough for them to capture information from social media and direct it to a central corporate office for decision making. It's too inefficient.

There will not be time for general counsel, marketing, public relations, and finance to make sequential decisions one to another. There won't be time for them to make a single evaluation simultaneously either. By the time the group has made a decision, another issue will come up, or the previous opportunity will have passed. Many of the most resistant to this change will still be out there for a while, managing their social media like Don Quixote tilting at windmills.

Like the NFL teams discussed in Chapter Two, companies must study as individuals, plan within specialized units, and articulate strategy across entire organizations under the rubric of extraordinary time pressure. Raheem Morris and other head coaches have to contend with only seventeen high-pressure weeks. Most companies have all fifty-two to deal with.

"They've no idea how to compete in it," Bob finishes, our conversation now running in excess of two hours late into the night. "All the methods used by competitors in the past exist in social media, but they operate in faster, more complete, and more convincing ways, even when they aren't real."

He cited a Twitter feed he'd recently followed from Chick-Fil-A, only to learn it was a fraud. The stream used similar verbiage and had successfully fooled many people for several days. The information appeared real, even to an experienced professional like Bob, and it took several days before it was revealed to be a complete fabrication.

How much had the real Chick-Fil-A been damaged? How will it reach out to customers who'd been duped? It wasn't the company's fault, but it was *their* customers who'd been targeted. The company will respond, Bob assured me, but it's a problem that's hard to define. The company had been defrauded, yet there were few metrics to measure the damage. Nothing was stolen, nobody was hurt, and the brand remains one of the strongest and most admired in the industry. Yet damage had been done. What to do about it?

Companies can't just watch the competition. They must also watch themselves, using the tools available to find out when and how their names are being bandied about through social media. Catch them early, exploiting the new media that customers are using to communicate about your brand. Analyze patterns to determine the genesis of problems with enough time to respond before they grow into a crisis that creates measurable impacts on revenue and profits.

Cancelled Czechs

Pratt and Whitney, a unit of United Technologies, began making spare parts for General Electric's best-selling engines a couple of years ago. P&W makes turboprops, and GE generally concentrates on jet engines, so the pair weren't exactly direct competitors. P&W's decision to enter GE's lucrative spare parts business rubbed GE leaders the wrong way, so when an opportunity came to return the favor, GE jumped.[4]

They bought Czechoslovakian-based Walter Engines, an eighty-five-year-old firm with a sizable niche market in agriculture and cargo planes. It filled a hole in GE's aviation portfolio, but the main reason GE took the plunge was the price. To develop a new turboprop would cost GE in the neighborhood of $350 million, but it bought Walter for less than $70 million. Real estate, equipment, and a flight-certified engine was simply too good an opportunity to pass by. The company's owners wanted to turn the Prague real estate into something more profitable, so GE had to agree to move the plant to another location.[5]

For operational decisions, when the parameters and the competing entities' characteristics can be specified numerically, it's possible to mathematically model decisions to help managers position and price a proposal in the most attractive way. Known as multiobjective value analysis (MOVA) it's a simple, yet powerful means for empirically characterizing the complex dynamics of competitive decision making.[6]

MOVA allows managers to analyze a given selection of choices while also providing the flexibility to determine the sensitivity of their assumptions. As noted previously, analysis and synthesis are a cornerstone of operational intelligence, and MOVA is a shining example. By analyzing the decisions of leaders or competitors, it is possible to determine a range of options for company managers to select from.

MOVA runs quite well in a Microsoft Excel spreadsheet, with straightforward graphics that can quickly be copied into PowerPoint for briefing purposes.[7] MOVA provides a means for ranking alternatives to a decision and selecting the best one. By running the analysis in reverse, it's possible to determine what a competing firm might do under select circumstances.

MOVA's use is predicated on quantifying strategic values—combining multiple evaluation metrics into one measure of the overall value of each weighted alternative. There's the subjectivity of the analysis—the weights. What numerical value to assign to the weights is the dilemma, but that's where the sensitivity analysis can come in handy.

The MOVA spreadsheet template is quickly filled with the required information. The options are keyed in, as are the criteria for evaluation. Press the F9 button, and the calculation shows which alternative is the most attractive (Figure 11.3). In this case, it is readily apparent GE should spend the $70 million to acquire Walter Engines. Operational unit managers can easily explain to senior leadership how spending $70 million for a plant they have to move is a good idea.

The sensitivity analysis in Figure 11.4 shows it's not just a good idea; it's an outstanding one. (A sensitivity analysis measures the robustness of

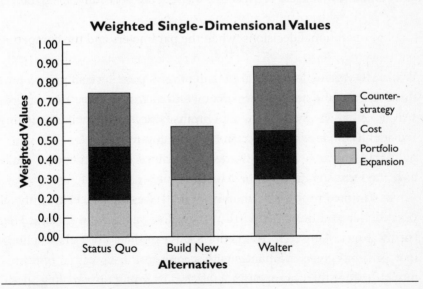

Figure 11.3 Multiobjective value analysis.

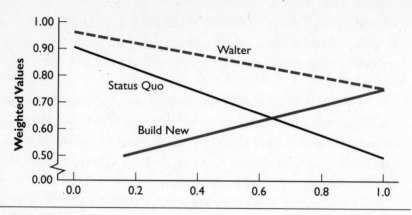

Figure 11.4 Sensitivity analysis of the multiobjective value analysis.

a model by quantifying the uncertainty of the variables being considered.) GE has wanted to counter P&W for some time, partly to cover the portfolio gap and partly to offset P&W's poaching its parts business. That the opportunity presented itself at such an extremely low price put the analysis over the top. At higher costs, the choices are far less distinct. While GE must still move the plant, real estate will not be a significant cost factor, and company managers can feel confident in the decision they made.

Shopping Wars

While MOVA's use for internal consumption is clear, it can also look into the unknown and help discern a competitor's moves as well. It requires a realistic knowledge of the competitor's strategy and plans, but it also provides a couple of useful action items for future evaluation. The sensitivity analysis can help identify areas for additional collection that would have the most significant impact on the analysis.

In summer 2009 Dell Computer's stock was half the value it was a year earlier and down 65 percent from five years before. But it was hardly alone. Many tech companies have seen their stock prices plummet. This has given companies with strong cash balances an opportunity to bolster their competitive position by going on a buying spree.

It's an opportune time to leverage mergers and acquisitions to expand into new business areas.

In April 2009 Oracle announced it was buying Sun Microsystems for $5.6 billion, and Cisco announced an entry into the server business. Cisco is sitting on over $30 billion in cash. With Dell's market capitalization dropping to $21 billion, Cisco could buy it outright for cash. Dell is sitting on $10 billion in cash itself, making it an attractive acquisitions target or providing the funds necessary to purchase a few rivals of its own. But Michael Dell appears to still enjoy the computer business, and his hiring IBM's vice president of corporate development, David Johnson, in late May 2009 underscores this point. Johnson is widely known as IBM's dealmaker and his importance to Big Blue is evident in the lawsuit it filed against him, asserting he was violating his noncompete agreement by taking the job at Dell.[8] He'd spent twenty-seven years at IBM, the last ten in acquisitions, overseeing several lucrative deals.

Although Dell purchased storage vendor EqualLogic in January 2008 for $1.4 billion, most of its deals were substantially smaller than Hewlett Packard's 2002 purchase of Compaq ($19 billion) and 2008 acquisition of EDS ($13 billion). Rather than a select few big-ticket purchases, IBM has steadily picked up smaller firms, a strategy Dell apparently likes, leading to its interest in David Johnson.

Assuming he can get past the legal predicament, what is Johnson likely to do? The rapid consolidation among major computer technology firms means they are encroaching on each other's markets now far more than they have in the past. Will Dell remain a consumer-oriented player (its historical strength), or will it throw its hat into the enterprise technology market for corporate and government systems against IBM, HP, and Oracle?

Dell purchased Microsoft's consulting business and Allin Corp.'s solutions business in an all-stock deal ($12 million). So for the consumer/enterprise computer question, the most recent purchases support the enterprise option. But there are interesting possibilities as to what each firm might bring to Dell. The order of acquisitions could be important too.

Dell is a network company. As noted earlier, a network's three criteria finish with the order in which they do things. If Dell goes on a buying streak, order could have a sizable impact on acquisition prices. A first purchase or two could be telling as to what Dell's strategy is: staying on the consumer side or gearing up to be in the enterprise business. If it purchases Palm or Motorola, it supports a consumer strategy. Buying NetApp or Emulex would suggest a more enterprise-focused strategy.

But regardless of any first or second purchased firms, any remaining suitors in those segments are going to be bid up by investors. A purchase of Motorola would likely drive up the cost of Palm. The purchase of both would signal a serious commitment to the consumer market and be a negative price influence on enterprise firms while driving up the costs for other consumer firms. So if a follow-on company has a higher market capitalization, it might be better to purchase it first rather than last, before the price is bid up by external investors looking to ride Dell's coattails on a fast stock escalation. Either way, the consumer–versus-enterprise question will likely no longer be a question.

These types of questions lend themselves to multiobjective value analysis precisely because multiple objectives need to be considered and the value of the firms under consideration will drive part of the decision making. If NetApp decides it doesn't want to be part of Dell, it must be able to move on before a competitor jumps in. Cisco's $34 billion in cash is a considerable competitive threat in the acquisition space; it could easily outbid firms up to a point where it's no longer economically feasible for Dell to purchase them.

Other companies might mask their true interests, applying denial and deception to force Dell into committing to a strategy that's not in its best interests. Apple, the reigning king of consumers retail, has $25 billion in cash and could gobble up a few companies it doesn't want Dell to have, essentially forcing the company into the enterprise business whether it likes it or not.

Dell has several options, all of which require far more explanation and description of assumptions than can be easily done here. The bottom line is that if Dell can hold on to David Johnson, if its competitors don't scoop up several of these smaller firms before Dell has a chance, and if Dell seriously commits to one strategic direction, there will be several new purchases in its future. Evaluating Dell's next series of moves should make it clearer what its long-term strategy will be.

If Michael Dell, no stranger to unconventional thinking, should decide to purchase several firms in both the consumer and enterprise markets (and with certain assumptions, this could be the most profitable option), it could easily see itself as a larger firm's strategic acquisition target in the medium term, giving an Apple or Oracle a number of new options and market segments they currently don't have. It's all a question of how decision makers operate their firms.

Spreading the Wealth

Apple has had quite a run. The iPhone became a runaway cultural phenomenon, with 17 million units sold since the 2007 debut. But how can Apple keep consumers spending in a recession? The product and the service are unquestionably hits, but can the firm sustain its current level of success with the competition breathing down their necks?

Apple's new 3GS iPhone features a video camera, voice controls, a built-in compass, and a push notification service that operates independent of the user's text messaging system. The operating system includes a highly anticipated copy-and-paste feature and an unexpected external accessories system. At one event, Apple demonstrated a diabetes application that turned the phone into an insulin meter for diabetes patients to check their glucose level, a feature that has many product development firms very excited.

The new phone's software signifies a new direction for Apple in that it allows iPhone users to make purchases within third-party applications. The previous application suites would link users to Web sites where they could make purchases. The new software allows application developers to conduct the transaction within the application itself, a benefit that sent software developers into a tailspin.

Developers previously made money only when someone bought an application through the Apple Store or by selling advertising within the application itself—something not always popular with consumers who could (and often did) drop applications they felt weren't delivering value. With this new direction, application developers can charge for increasing levels of difficulty on a video game, higher levels of customization on a design, or a hundred other new ideas that are only now being discussed.

Apple's new operating system is not restricted to the new hardware. Current iPhone users can download the system and enjoy the new applications for free. It will turn iPhones into a storefront for hundreds of companies whose programmers have already developed applications on the previous Apple system. This will render them unavailable to deliver applications for competing handheld devices. Apple will own this space for the short to medium term as developers push a new generation of applications into the hands of millions of excited consumers.

The strategy Apple chose, as impressive as it is, is perhaps less important than *how* it chose to implement it, particularly the timing. The new 3GS iPhone was launched less than a week after rival Palm released its new Pre smartphone for the Sprint network. Research in Motion (RIM) has just debuted a new BlackBerry for the Sprint and Verizon networks.

Apple's timing of the 3GS release means its competitors are already committed to hardware and software capabilities based on the *old* iPhone model. While it's possible someone could have learned about specific hardware upgrades (like the faster new processor or the video camera), the new operating system means the current customer base of 17 million users can access these new tools for free.

Apple released the phone in the United States, Canada, Britain, France, Germany, Italy, Spain, and Switzerland—a sweeping cross-section of the high-end cell phone market. Unlike the last iPhone upgrade, lines have been shorter, sign-ups faster, and customers considerably happier with this release.

Apple's operations and market research couldn't have been better. While their competition crafted products based on the original iPhone design, Apple created a new product (3GS) and a new service (operating system) that not only changed the competitive landscape completely but incorporated the more than 17 million current Apple customers, preventing RIM or Palm from persuading consumers to try a competing product, much less purchase one.

It is another instance of a company leveraging its current customer base as a barrier to competition. While competitors might have learned about the new video camera function or the cut-and-paste software feature, nobody seemed to know about the new applications strategy Apple had taken. The operational timing involved in the 3GS release is indicative of how competitive intelligence activities such as reverse engineering, technology surveillance, and network analysis are changing the ways companies compete, especially at the operational level.

Time is now a weapon and communities are the objective.

How We Do Our Voodoo

Without diligent monitoring, customers can become competitors, as Ticketmaster learned with Live Nation. Now the two will merge (pending FTC approval), with Ticketmaster effectively buying its own customers back. Companies cannot afford to make this a habit.

The CARP model's feedback loops continue, further distinguishing it from the better-known government intelligence cycle. These feedback loops resist any formalized standard operating procedures, and that's the way they work best.

Covert media will continue to grow, particularly through external professionals like Bob Finch who specialize in this area. His competitive advantage is the in-depth knowledge of social media that he can immediately leverage for his customers. We'll see much more of this in the future, particularly among highly successful firms.

GE jumped at a (random) chance to purchase a firm it knew would give it a powerful weapon against Pratt & Whitney. By having the money and the responsive leadership available, GE was able to close the deal before any other suitor could interfere.

Methodologies such as MOVA allow leaders to make big decisions quickly in ambiguous situations. When opportunities that fit company strategic plans arise, prepared firms are ready to exploit them.

12

Strategic Advantage
The What

Best-selling author Malcolm Gladwell worked his way up through the *Washington Post* starting as a science writer who ultimately became the New York City bureau chief. Gladwell's unique mix of experiences in science, sociology, and history (his undergraduate major) give him a rather powerful set of skills for competitive analysis and explaining complex information to a broad audience.

Gladwell recently wrote an article for *The New Yorker* comparing the competitive strategy of a Redwood City, California, middle school girl's basketball team to David versus Goliath.[1] He noted that the Redwood City team coach, a Mumbai, India, native who'd never played basketball himself, led his seventh- and eighth-grade girls to soundly defeat better teams.

Coach Vivek Ranadivé could not understand why basketball teams raced down court after scoring to get in place for the opposing team to return with the ball, giving up half of the game's time and competitive field. *Why concede that?* he thought. *Why not interfere with the opposition from the moment the ball is returned to the court? Why give away that time and territory?*

Bucking conventional wisdom, he coached his girls to exploit the distance from the goal at every available moment of the game. Applying a full court press strategy, his lesser-skilled team consistently and regularly beat nearly every team they played, all the way to the National Junior Basketball Championships.

Playing to their own strengths rather than those of the opponents, Ranadivé's team expertly delayed their opponent's ability to get the ball back into play in under the required five seconds. They also often prevented the opponents from moving the ball past midcourt within the required ten seconds, using the ninety-four-foot length of the court to their full advantage. It sent competing team coaches into tantrums.

Ranadivé's strategy changed basketball from a periodic process of moving down the court after each successful offensive-defensive switch to one where his young charges operated in near real time beginning with the inbound pass. This meant a continual reevaluation of the entire competitive chronology, not simply changing a single part of it. By changing the competition to a continual process rather than a periodic one, Ranadivé's team forestalled virtually any strategy the competition brought to the court.

Ranadivé's appreciation for periodic versus real-time processes was not born on the basketball court. Instead, basketball borrowed heavily from his full-time occupation as founder of a company called TIBCO. Ranadivé had noted how Wall Street traders compiled information from disparate databases that all operated on their own schedule—each a periodic process. There was no one-stop shop for information that could be accessed in real time as needed. TIBCO changed that by consolidating all of these data streams so traders had a single access point to data that could be harvested and used in near real time. The intervals affecting trader decision making were radically altered by the advent of real-time information availability. TIBCO's software now runs most of the trading floors on Wall Street.

Wall Street itself lives and dies by the periodic processes of quarterly and annual reports from publicly traded companies. These reports are often quite complex, even for those with solid financial training. Uncertainties about a competitor's financial state often confound senior leaders, particularly those who do not have a background in finance, creating the very uncertainty Ranadivé directed his players to inflict on their competition.

Fortunately, there is a tool that doesn't require a CPA to analyze a competitor's publicly accessible, periodic financial information. More important, it allows a nonfinancial analyst to brief a nonfinancial decision maker in a way they both can understand because it applies visual analytics to complex financial information. It's called the DuPont chart.

DuPont: Better Analysis from Uncertainty

The DuPont chart method is a means of charting out complicated financial data in an easy-to-understand form. It is named for the DuPont Chemical Company, which began using the method in 1919. The company's purpose was to find a way to visually display financial information in a way that nonfinancial company officials and managers could easily understand.[2]

The DuPont system is predicated on several key points. Among these are a need to keep everyone focused on the point of discussion at any one time. Prior to using the charts, company managers would find any number of reasons to move their briefs onto a variety of external topics, diverting time and attention away from any negative information their financial statements might hold. The charts prevent that from happening, keeping all the managers clearly focused on the question at hand.

But the charts themselves do not require a great deal of explanation. *It is what it is,* as the saying goes, and personnel who might not understand corporate finance are more than capable of understanding a simple network diagram. That's what the DuPont chart ultimately is: charting the financial network within a company. How does money move from one point to another? What are the subnetworks within the larger corporate structure, and what has happened in that area over the past year?

Displayed with all of the network's interrelated subcomponents laid out in an orderly fashion, it is harder for a manager to hide when his numbers, revenue, or expenses are significantly off. The charts don't require a lot of repeated updating because they're based on annual reporting. Once those numbers are in, there's little chance of their changing until the following year unless something is quite wrong in a firm's accounting department.

But one fundamental benefit of the DuPont chart is that it displays a company's arcane financial data in an engaging manner. Beginning with the uncomplicated return on equity (ROE), the DuPont chart's cornerstone metric, the charts look backward, as all financial data do, to deconstruct where and how a company made (or lost) money over the preceding twelve months. Each component used to derive ROE is similarly charted to reflect its network orientation among the other parts of the annual report. (See Figures 12.1 and 12.2.)

By reducing ROE to its component parts and then deconstructing each one into its basic network sequences, it is possible to figure out how well a company's leadership is managing the company. Where are they spending money? Where are they investing it? How much are they borrowing, and at what terms? What are they doing well? What are they doing not quite as well?

Any publicly traded company whose stock is sold on the major exchanges is required to file quarterly and annual financial reports—SEC

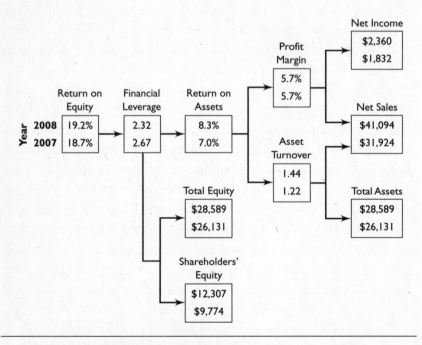

Figure 12.1 DuPont chart comparing Hess Corporation's 2008 financial information to 2007 results.

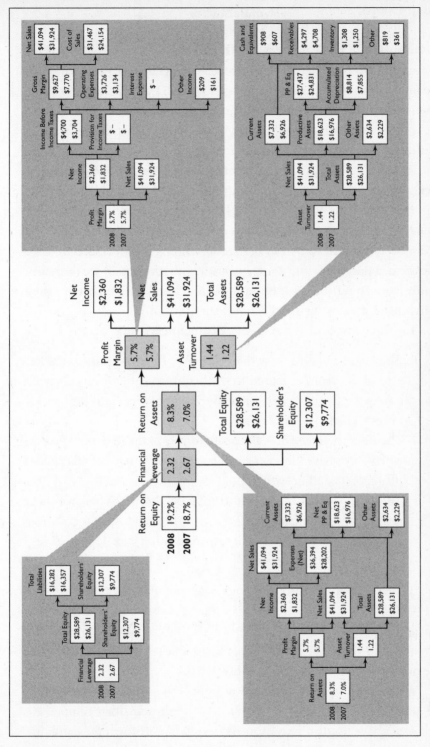

Figure 12.2 Each of the return on equity's main nodes can be further expanded to reveal more about the company's (financial network) performance.

Forms 10-Q and 10-K, respectively. There are three financial instruments in the annual report that contribute to a DuPont chart: the balance sheet, income statement, and statement of cash flows. Each has a different purpose. What the chart does is take the columns and rows of numbers from these three reports and display them in an aesthetically pleasing manner while also handling some basic calculations.

Until a few years ago, annual reports were generally public relations pieces to attract new investors. With most firms now publishing their reports electronically, investors ignore the fancy rhetoric and focus on financials. An annual report contains financial statements, notes on those financial statements, a summary of the accounting methods used to compile them, a narrative from company leaders about the past year's results, a note from an outside auditor on the validity of the information, and a couple of past years' financial data for comparison.

The three financial sections have distinct purposes:

- The *balance sheet* shows the company's financial position at the end of the year compared to the beginning of it. It reveals what assets the firm has and what the stockholders' liabilities are. It reflects efficiency and leverage.
- The *income statement* is the profit or loss of the firm for the year; essentially sales minus expenses equals profit. That's what it shows: profitability and growth.
- The *statement of cash flows* integrates data from the balance sheet and income statement to show how the firm managed its cash over the year. Is the profitability or growth coming from increased revenue or decreasing expenses?

If you think of a balance sheet as a snapshot of the firm at the end of the year and the income statement as a film of how it made or lost money, you get an idea of each statement's purpose. The cash flows combines the two into something of a hybrid designed to reflect how management ran the firm's sales, investments, and borrowing.

While an accounting lesson is way out of our scope here, a nonfinancial professional can use a DuPont chart to supplement other competitive analysis. I have used an Excel spreadsheet to handle the inputs and displays of the DuPont chart method. It accepts the balance sheet and income statement data of any firm and automates all of the mathematics, ratios, and charting. A firm can be analyzed by simply keying in the information down to its component parts or compared with other companies to determine investing options for the future.[3]

Another useful aspect of the DuPont system is the ease by which the charts are copied from Excel and dropped into PowerPoint for briefings or into Word documents for specific profiles. It takes what was a complicated and time-consuming function of competitive analysis and reduces it to a few mouse clicks.

By comparing the company's numbers over time (Figure 12.3), it is relatively easy to determine how the firm is performing in general. It's

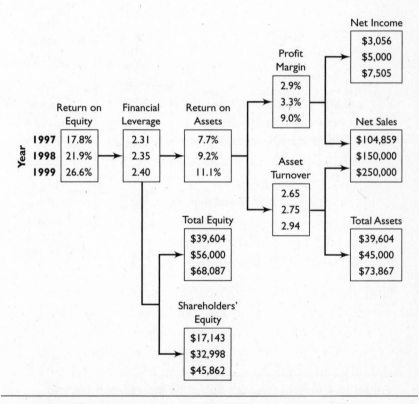

Figure 12.3 DuPont chart of a single company showing a three-year comparison of how management is running the company.

not a guarantee, of course, but the DuPont chart has been used for nearly a century because it satisfies a primary need: displaying financial data where they can be discussed and analyzed by a broad cross-section of leaders.

Even when leaders don't have a finance background, they can speak astutely about competitor's financial statements in an abbreviated time span. When a CFO explains the firm's own financial position, a non-financial leader can provide the same level of granularity about each competitor, displaying the data at the same time in chart format (Figure 12.4).

The DuPont chart is also an excellent tool for nonprofit groups that want to better understand the mechanics of their business and compare

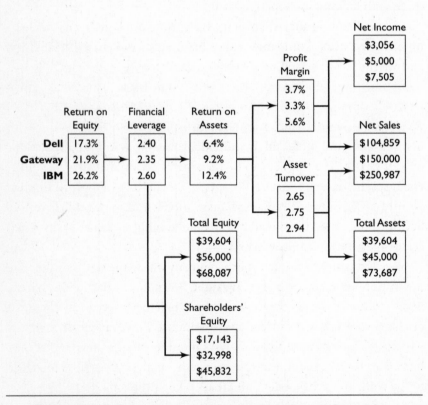

Figure 12.4 DuPont chart comparing the annual report financial statements of three companies in the same industry.

their financial data with those of competitors. Because much of the mathematics is based on ratios, it tends to normalize the numbers to better compare companies of different sizes and revenues. It is a powerful tool that is easy to use and share across geographically dispersed organizations by using a spreadsheet.

Enron: If Only Someone Had Bothered to Look

Investment analysis isn't what it used to be. Before the recession, Wall Street analysts embodied the subjectivity of analysis in how they read the same reports but came up with often radically different perspectives of what the reports meant. But the recession has taken its toll on the analyst trade with far-ranging repercussions.[4]

Firms that lose analyst coverage have more difficulty reaching institutional investors. Companies count on analysts to help tell their story, and when that story-telling service suddenly ends, leaders must spend more time spreading the word themselves. When Scholastic lost coverage from Goldman Sachs, J. P. Morgan, and Citigroup, only three analysts were left to cover the stock. Leaders must spend more time meeting with institutional (and increasingly individual) investors to get their company's story out. The impact can be far greater on smaller firms. In mid-2008, seven brokerage firms followed California technology firm Intevac. By mid-2009, only one remained. Institutional and some retail investors became concerned they wouldn't be able to build or sell as easily when companies start losing coverage.[5]

Analysts can direct interest in a company due to the way they describe it, write about it, and, to a certain extent, promote it. Like fiction writers, many stock analysts develop a following. When they move to another firm or change portfolios, it can lead to cross-industry investing from investors who have come to trust their analyst's opinion even in an area that may be new to both of them. But sometimes the analysts get a little too close to the companies they follow, and that's when problems start.

Before joining Barclay's Global Investors as director of accounting research in 2004, Charles Lee was a Cornell University professor who taught an advanced class in financial statement analysis. The course prepared students for pressure-cooker Wall Street jobs by teaching them to use a wide variety of advanced statistical tools. One of his students, who had interned at Enron, chose the firm for a class project in 1998. The student's analysis, posted on Cornell's Web site for the world to see, clearly stated that Enron's business model appeared seriously flawed and that "Enron may be manipulating earnings."[6]

Malcolm Gladwell, writing about Lee's class, makes some intuitive observations about the important differences between puzzles and mysteries. While puzzles can quickly be solved when missing data are suddenly revealed, mysteries can remain mysterious for long periods of time due in part to the overload of information that often masks important pieces of data. One of his key points was that "*mysteries require judgments and the assessment of uncertainty*" (emphasis added).[7]

Students learned that to analyze a firm, they had to assess the situation, understand the changing environment, and make a recommendation on what decision makers (potential investors) should do. In the Enron case, their recommendation was clearly printed on page 1: *sell.*

Everything needed to discern Enron's problems was published in its annual report, but few people had bothered to read it. That is not at all unusual. Most people, including professional investors, neglect to read the reports of the companies in which they invest. Had anyone bothered to analyze Enron's financial structure, they would have seen the same red flags Charles Lee's students had found.

Enron inadvertently proved one of Thomas Friedman's central tenets in *The Lexus and the Olive Tree*: changing a structure changes how a system works.[8] Just as DuPont charts display how the networked parts of a company's financial structure are interrelated, changing the structure of a network ultimately affects the output. What Enron was trying desperately to hide was that there was no output. Cash flow is the lifeblood of a company, and Enron had bled itself dry.

The lessons learned from Enron have filled academic journals, business magazines, and management textbooks. Capitalism, which is competition allowed to follow its natural evolution, is often called *destructive chaos.* This is a fair indictment. Allowing new thinking, new technology, and new market dynamics to tear down old systems and reconfigure them into new ones on a constant basis is what creates investor value—the whole point behind adopt and adapt.

Sony's Walkman paved the road for Apple's iPod; both firms relied less on classic market research than on simply listening to what customers wanted (recall Bob Finch's Dale Carnegie reference in Chapter Eleven), noting how competitors weren't meeting that demand and inventing technology customers could never have imagined on their own. Demand fosters innovation, which fosters growth, and evolution (survival) depends on growth.

Intel(ligence) Inside

In his autobiography and elsewhere, Andy Grove has spoken eloquently about his initial resistance to the innovation-growth dynamic when Intel Corporation was a victim of its own success.[9] Personal computers were growing in popularity with the advent of new programs that delivered additional graphics, sound, and advanced computing power that would dominate anything currently available. In order for them to do so, these chips had to process ever-larger amounts of data.

As a component manufacturer, Intel realized that companies like Compaq and Gateway would soon apply extreme pressure on it to cut prices. Personal computers are modular, known as plug-and-play technology, where a broken or defective hard drive or modem can be quickly pulled out and replaced with another from any manufacturer. Lower prices meant lower profits for computer parts companies like Intel. There was no competitive advantage among the standardized suppliers.

Grove was pleased with Intel's research and development, but it had gotten a little too good. The company's new Pentium chips could process information faster than the computer's bus systems could handle. The bus would soon be a chokepoint: the Pentium's incomparable performance stymied by the small pipes that transfer the chip's calculations to the rest of the computer. His people told him Intel would have to design a new bus to accommodate the Pentium's growing capacity to process information.

Grove was incensed, arguing for weeks that Intel was in the processor business, not the bus business, and it was overfocusing on its particular node in a computer rather than on the entire system's *network*. But Intel soon realized that this problem was actually an opportunity. It was in a heated competition with Advanced Micro Devices and Cyrix Technologies for the high-end computer chip market. What if Intel could leverage against cost-conscious procurement managers while distancing itself from the competition?

Intel's new strategy became a watershed event in computing. It created demand for its high-end chips by influencing consumer decisions on when to buy new computers. Intel designed the new bus architecture so it used only Intel chips. This strategic lock-in eliminated the option of using a competitor's chips unless the customer designed an all-new bus system or forced the other component manufacturers to do it for them.

This conceptual distance tactic meant competitors had to catch up with the new technology. While the delay increased their costs, Intel's new Pentium chips were available immediately. Lock-in as a lone strategy was suicide if computer companies chose AMD or Cyrix, which would also create proprietary bus systems to lock out Intel. That wouldn't be good for anyone because it would fragment the market into individual fiefdoms that would similarly drive down prices.

So Intel marketed to its customers' customers, the retail consumers, making the processor brand, instead of the computer brand, the decision point. The *Intel Inside* campaign was a stroke of genius, turning a computer into nothing more than the packaging that the latest Intel Pentium chip was shipped in. Going right to the source of the market, Intel altered consumers' perceptions of computers.

Intel provided early prototypes of new chips to developers, ensuring new software was concurrently developed featuring video, animation, CD-ROMs, and high-bandwidth modems. By the time new chips were released, new applications were available as well, justifying the consumer's purchase at a premium price point. Rather than responding to the market, Intel chose to lead it, encouraging demand through the creation of applications that didn't previously exist. (Sound like Apple's 3GS iPhone?)

This cobranding is a particularly powerful strategy for influencing end user perceptions and has been widely copied by other firms facing cost-cutting pressures. Realizing the utility of cobranding, Apple positioned iTunes as a conduit for a multitude of new third-party software applications. DuPont positioned Teflon as a component brand and went on to internally cobrand with other innovations like Corian. Nutrasweet placed its brand on soda labels to appeal to weight-conscious consumers.

Decisions like this are not made in a vacuum; they are the result of solid intelligence work and bold leadership. Nutrasweet's intelligence program was started at the suggestion of Peter Drucker, who noted the company's single product line would soon face overwhelming international competition, particularly as aspartame's patent expired. Nutrasweet CEO Bob Flynn famously told attendees at a conference that "competitive intelligence was worth up to $50,000,000 a year to the company."[10]

Strategic decisions like these are irreversible in the short run. But as the pace of business accelerates, it can be increasingly difficult to differentiate between strategies and tactics. Most strategic decisions are made in periods of great uncertainty. The firms in the examples chose to handle the uncertainty by creating new markets in one of four ways:

1. Choice of bets: Increasing the probability of success by providing options
2. Choice of robustness: Exploiting the network advantage in some capacity of the business (customers, production, service, or suppliers)
3. Choice of pace: Using delay or distance to push decisions back until the last possible moment
4. Changing industry structure (the rules of the game)

Having options through a choice of bets provides decision makers with the flexibility to adjust their strategy as the competition, market, and economy react. Like a football coach whose staff and players have practiced together, these small adjustments are quickly decided and communicated to the field before competitors have time to react.

A robust strategy works under a variety of conditions by engineering flexibility into the approach. Mazda can build five different models on a single production line, while GM can typically build only one. In recent years, GM had to close its highest-quality production line because the model was not selling well. The employees' conscientious attention to quality brought them not reward but layoffs.

As noted, delay is a viable strategy if decision makers understand the potential consequences. Will more time to gather information reduce their uncertainty? Does more time to generate options (bets, per above) allow them to delay a commitment but not the decision? It's okay for firms to delay a decision to the last minute, but they must do so consciously. (Do you call the weather service after you decide to take an umbrella with you?) Like any network, there is a proper order to decision making.

Finally, companies can change the industry structure by forcing competitors to play their game, as Vivek Ranadivé and Andy Grove did. Federal Express did the same when it guaranteed delivery by 10:00 A.M. Customers had to decide if the premium they paid was worth the price. Most did. The U.S. Postal Service never regained the lost market share because it could not change its business model fast enough to counter FedEx's unexpected move.

CARP Fishing

So now the CARP model has come full circle: collection to analysis to reporting to production, the taking of some action. If no action is taken, it's not intelligence. That action then elicits additional collection. Superficially it doesn't appear that much different from the normal intelligence cycle. But the feedback loops inherited throughout the model are important; they are the reason some leaders are successful when others aren't. These feedback loops catch mistakes that otherwise get into the system: biases, overlooked collection, flawed analysis, and a host of other problems that are inherent in subjective professions. The process of intelligence is a complex endeavor. (See Figures 12.5 to 12.7.)

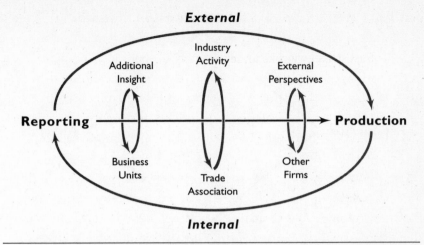

Figure 12.5 CARP model: Reporting to production. Feedback loops also take place at the leadership level. What is produced (an action, decision, or policy, for example) based on the intelligence effort?

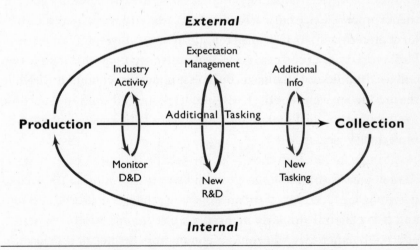

Figure 12.6 CARP model. The leadership, in taking action, generates new tasking for collection and analysis.

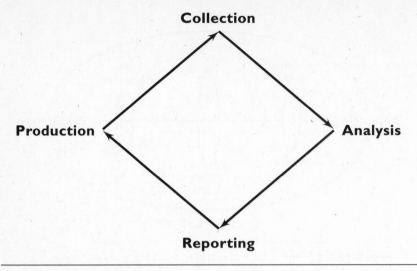

Figure 12.7 Completed CARP model without feedback loops. This is similar to the intelligence cycle, but only superficially.

But the CARP model has another facet missing from the government's process. Once businesses decide to take an action, it must be better at protecting it. As I've noted repeatedly, protecting information must be the first order of business leaders take after deciding what their action will be. Competition that can deduce that action can counter it. So while the production aspect of the CARP model remains the primary purpose for the effort, it must remain hidden in order to be effective. It must be protected (Figure 12.8).

Protection lies atop the CARP model's production node, masking the company's real intentions through two primary means. Denial and deception are directed toward an adversary's collection efforts. Distance and delay should similarly be used against a competitor's analytical efforts. Together they will confuse competitors despite all appearances that their intelligence activity has been successful (Figure 12.9).

Leaders must evaluate the best way to protect their actions based on the type and use of the intelligence they've been given. How can denial, deception, distance, and delay be applied in a measured, methodical way? The addition of protection strategies to mislead competitors gives the

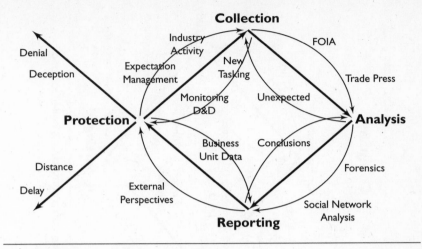

Figure 12.8 Finished CARP model.

CARP model its resemblance to the fish of the same name and makes a final and distinct disconnect from government intelligence methodologies. But protection is not easy, it's not cheap, and it's not for anyone other than senior decision makers to employ.

Leaders should continually update their assessment of the competition's leadership staff, management, company capabilities, specific tools, individual techniques, and customer relations. Knowing how they do what they do is integral to interfering with it. Like Shelton Quarles and the other NFL scouts, experience goes a long way toward pulling a fast one on someone.

Denial and deception are either trying to deny the competitor's ability to gather accurate information or deceive them with false information specifically positioned for them to collect. Knowing what sources they read and what opinion leaders they follow or consult with is critical. Without it, you are just guessing. Since your competition has just as much access to you, it's imperative you take measures to protect your competitive advantage.

Deny public access to new projects for as long as possible. Slap nondisclosure agreements on everyone involved; suppliers, advertisers, manufacturing, and marketing and PR firms. If that's not possible, consider using a cutout for project management purposes. Just as I used

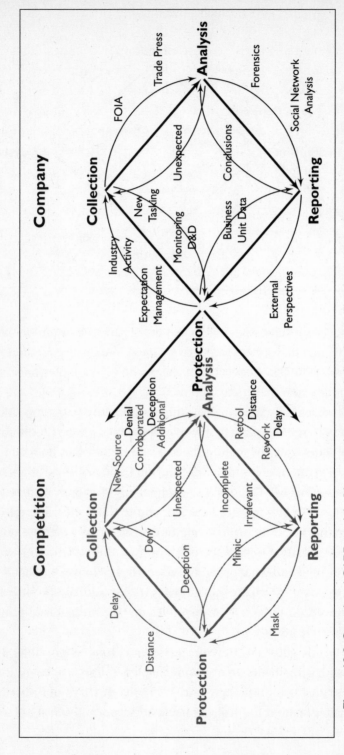

Figure 12.9 Completed CARP model with protection methods lined up to interfere with a competitor's collection and analysis structure.

Global Information Research and Retrieval for FOIA filings, a firm can similarly use one to purchase land, order equipment, screen potential hires, and scores of other low-signature activity that together tip competitors a new project is under way.

Alternatively, you can deceive the prying eyes. If former employees or current suppliers can reliably tell you about a source the competition depends on, you might plant disinformation in a news article, suggesting a story that your firm is "considering investing in Cleveland." If your company's name suddenly shows up in the Cleveland press, even if it's completely benign, the competition is going to suspect something. Just be cautious of overselling it; you want an easily dismissed hint, not a binding declaration. Make them spend time and money looking in the wrong areas. A competitor could spend weeks and thousands of dollars chasing their tail.

Delay and distance are directed at the competitor's analytical functions. Coach Vivek Ranadivé's players confused their competition by not allowing them time to think. From the moment the ball changed hands, the pressure increased exponentially. With each subsequent turnover, the player's analysis of the time available to put the ball in play continued to shrink. In fact it hadn't changed at all, of course: it was the exact five seconds it had always been, and the same five seconds afforded to the Redwood City team. But the competition's perception of time was affected by Redwood City's relentless pressure. The delay confounded all their other talents and efforts.

Ranadivé's use of the entire competitive space was another factor. Rather than localized to a contained area around the basket, the team used the entire length of the court (distance). Knowing his team didn't have the superior skills of other teams (preparation) who'd played together longer (implicit communication), Ranadivé stretched the competitive distance beyond what the rivals had prepared for. This affected their timing and communication—and generally exhausted them. Like an invading army that cannot sustain its supply lines, opposing teams couldn't keep up with Ranadivé's superior athletes. They ran the competition ragged, increasing their agitation, and negatively affecting their fine motor skills so they missed more shots.

Any competitor can do the same. Delay the competition's ability to take action, no matter how trivial. Stop, cajole, disrupt, and interfere with decision making to the fullest legal limit, and most will have no idea how to respond. Having never encountered the problem before, they will be flustered. Gladwell's article cited opposing coaches screaming at players and one being physically thrown out by a referee.

When a competitor goes outside the expected norms, the unprepared foe is frequently unable to deal with it. The foe's unproductive rage sets the entire team back because they're not prepared to adapt in the face of uncertainty. Applying denial, deception, delay, and distance at the tactical, operational, and strategic levels means competitors will never be completely certain what's going on.

Evolution of the CARP

Hyperformance is replete with biological metaphors for reasons that should now be self-evident. We could all take lessons on adaptability from the myriad organisms evolving around us every day. One or two strategies from the least of microorganisms would put many companies on a far more stable road than they now travel. Adaptive leaders must acknowledge uncertainty exists; they do not have all the answers. Embrace uncertainty if possible; hold it closer, and give it more attention than your competitors do. In this way, leaders can more quickly adjust their strategies because this chapter should at least make clear that the days of standard procedures are as dead as the one-way command-and-control paradigm that created them. Leadership as a top-down construct remains unchanged, but it means leaders actually lead and direct their charges with a degree of trust and confidence not taught in graduate schools.

The new competitive strategies thrive on the edge of turmoil, feeding on daily intelligence, and kept warm through feedback from employees, suppliers, customers, and stakeholders. *Management by walking around* has been replaced by *leadership by mandated adaptation*. Understanding what is happening outside the walls of a company has far more of an impact on operations, revenue, and profit than ever before. While minding the shop will always be important, the priority will increasingly be watching the external environment in all its complexity.

Leadership and decision making will be two distinct skill sets that must be cultivated throughout an organization. Leaders will be nurtured internally where possible to maximize the investment placed into executive employees. But decision making will be pushed further down the food chain than has ever been known before. Employees must not just be trusted to make the decisions; they must be rewarded even when their decision making turns out wrong.

When there is no support for incorrect decisions, there is no incentive to take risk. This is not the same as accepting bad decisions. When employees make decisions based on imperfect information, they will invariably be wrong some of the time. But leaders must never condemn or berate those employees. Instead they should figure out what could have been done better and then fix the problem rather than hand out blame.

If employees are truly following a leader, they will make the same decisions the leader would have made given the same information: they are in effect acting on the leader's behalf—based on the guidance, training, and direction they've been given. When they have been given that guidance, their decision is the leader's decision in all but name only. Leaders must support them just as they want support under the same conditions. Fail to do this, and the trickle of decisions that had been pushed down the hierarchy will become a flood racing back to leaders' desks.

Other employees, having witnessed the condemnation heaped on those who made a wrong decision, will avoid making the same mistake— not in the decision itself but rather the act of making a decision at all. It will be pushed right back up what is once again an ivory tower of management rather than leadership. Employees will shy away and never put themselves in the jeopardy of trusting the leader again.

What began as an evolution will digress to a vicious cycle, a stagnation, where nothing improves and the competition overtakes the firm's competitive advantage. The leader once again is staring into the cold, dark recesses of uncertainty with nowhere to turn. It has occurred repeatedly throughout history, increasing a rival's uncertainty over dwindling natural, financial, or personnel resources.[11]

This information superiority, giving leading-edge staff the knowledge and freedom to make independent decisions while pushing their information into the network, is an affront to most leaders' self-image of what being an executive means. It's also risky because we've not eliminated the threat that something can't or won't go wrong. But the pace of business now far exceeds even the most intuitive leader's ability to do it all. Shortening the distance from collection to analysis to action leads to what one respected military analyst calls the "survival of the best informed."

Risk is part of life, part of business, and a large part of leadership. But it can be minimized and managed as long as leaders are willing to adopt and adapt their decision making processes. As President John F. Kennedy wrote, "There will always be the dark and tangled stretches in the decision-making process—mysterious even to those who may be the most intimately involved."[12]

Game Changing

If a man who had never played basketball can coach a team to national championships, there's something to be said for not playing your adversary's game. Do something your rival doesn't expect; then exploit that uncertainty over your actions.

The DuPont chart is an excellent way for nonfinancial managers to understand what annual reports offer. Accounting is the language of business; consider the Dupont chart a Berlitz course in corporate financial reporting.

The CARP model finishes with a twist: protecting company information through denial, deception, distance, and delay. Use them all to keep the competition on the defensive.

Peter Drucker's advice to start up a competitive intelligence operation at Nutrasweet has been a $50 million a year success that every company should emulate. His sage advice is wise counsel to any company looking to keep a competitive advantage long term.

The DNA-like linkage of intelligence and strategy means leaders are as prepared as time, resources, and technology can make them. What happens now is entirely up to them. You can make a difference in your company. Keep your rivals uncertain and hesitant as you carve that wooden sword.

Epilogue:
A Look Back at the
Next Twenty Years

In Chapter Two I made reference to a tenet that is close to my heart: "Tools don't create analysis. Analysts create analysis." It's part of a sign I have over my desk—a reminder that all the technology in the world cannot replace the creativity, intuition, and curiosity of the human mind. But there's a limit to what our minds can absorb, use, and apply with any real degree of expertise.

This book is primarily oriented to the leaders of American businesses—the people who create these firms, sometimes through nothing more than the sheer force of their will. What I hope is that having built it, they will use this book to maintain and strengthen it in ways they would not have done before. So what does that mean for those who want to help leaders do this?

I believe there is a fundamental reform under way in the professional community of competitive intelligence. The industry is separating into distinct specialties. If it copies the path the medical community did a hundred years ago, this will be ideal, as it encourages everyone to focus on their strengths and minimize the negative impacts of their weaknesses.

I believe intelligence professionals will increasingly be general contractors of sorts, responsible for building the specific intelligence structure leaders need to be successful. As a building contractor does with framers, electricians, and plumbers, these general practitioners will bring their professional network of subject matter intelligence experts to customize a solution for leaders' needs.

The costs associated with expensive subscription services, complex visualization software, and the ongoing development of skilled analysts are best spread across a flexible organization for whom these are the core products and services. Some will concentrate on specialty areas like forensic accounting, behavioral science, or laboratory services. Each will be employed on an ad hoc basis by the general practitioner, taking on additional roles and responsibilities as leaders' needs change. The competitive intelligence consultant's greatest contribution will be telling an integrated story assembled from all these external subject matter experts.

Storytelling is a skill that has culturally ebbed and flowed over the centuries. From ancient Greek oratory to Hollywood blockbusters, it is the ability to open, describe, and close a narrative that remains the highest pinnacle of a storyteller, a skill every intelligence professional must have. Nothing can replace it and nothing ever should.

Retired Colonel Robert Killebrew, former deputy director of the Army's Training and Doctrine Command, said it best: "The story you're trying to tell in future conflicts is the strategy by which the [conflict] will be fought."[1] He's absolutely correct. Whatever the evidence, however the facts have played out in the far, dusty corners of the world, the analyst's responsibility is to tell the story of those events in a manner that most closely engages his or her leader. Without this requisite skill, all the analytical tools and methods in the world will have no effect on decision making.

And that makes all the difference.

It strikes me that the intelligence profession today is much like the information technology (IT) profession was twenty-five years ago. It took a number of missteps and failures before everyone learned how IT was supposed to work. Eventually companies got the idea and established technology departments to manage their internal information. Competitive intelligence provides a similar service for a company's external information needs.

Companies are now regularly outsourcing their IT departments, overburdened by the costs of maintaining the tools and expertise necessary to manage information. We've seen similar efforts in human resources, benefits management, janitorial services, and even corporate legal departments. Intelligence will similarly be outsourced, and everyone involved will see considerable improvements to service and stability.

Analysts, like the companies they serve, are in a competition of their own. Those who can do the work will be employed by intelligence boutiques that are firmly embedded in a small, select pool of client firms. These entrenched analysts will benefit from group learning across industries; analysts working in a product firm will save time and money by leveraging new techniques from their boutique colleagues in a service firm. They will have opportunities for advancement, specializing in select disciplines, and with the freedom to live virtually anywhere while remaining with the same company.

Leaders will have greater options with intelligence capabilities at a much lower cost. Many will start out as part-time customers, eventually hosting a small cadre of outsourced analysts in client offices or at the outsourcing firm's site. Some analysts will telecommute.

From basic services, leaders will expand into specialty areas as they realize the financial savings of this business model and are comfortable in having an outsider with a chair at their boardroom table. Intelligence professionals will be viewed as trusted partners, routinely consulted on significant projects, with direct access to senior C-level company officers.

Some intelligence professionals will work directly under the umbrella of the corporate general counsel. Working by, with, and through counsel provides an unprecedented level of privacy and trade secrecy protection. Attorney-client privilege is revered in the United States, offering the discretion, legitimacy, and assurances many corporate leaders crave when they see the word *intelligence.* By integrating legal counsel into the equation, company leaders are confident everything will be done legally and ethically. I believe it is the future of competitive intelligence.

It's an exciting time for this profession, long overdue in taking its place at the top of the corporate hierarchy. I invite you to be part of it.

Appendix: Psychological Assessment Tools

With the Myers-Briggs Type Indicator (MBTI) to set a baseline for how a person prefers information, several tools are available for gaining insight on how leaders will react in various situations. Specific instruments explore different areas depending on the type of insight needed, the time available, the experience of the psychology professional, and the habits, motivations, and individual styles of the person being studied.

The *Firo-B* is a psychological assessment tool with powerful application to competitive strategy planning. It measures the extent to which a subject will attempt to satisfy three basic social needs:

- Inclusion—belonging to a group, participation with others
- Control—the ability to influence, project power, and exert authority
- Affection—the degree of closeness to others, often called "warmth"

The Firo-B captures motivators that, combined with the MBTI's preferences, start to color a fairly specific picture of how individuals accept leadership roles and position themselves within their work environments.

The *16PF (Cattell)* measures and predicts consistent behavioral responses based on sixteen primary causes clustered into the five global factors of extraversion, anxiety, tough-mindedness, independence, and self-control. It provides a perspective on leadership behavior over time and is excellent for cross-cultural assessments, particularly when a merger or acquisition takes place between firms of disparate cultures.

The *DiSC* measures four dimensions of behavioral response: dominance, influence, steadiness, and conscientiousness. It is an outstanding tool for crafting an approach for target marketing, sales, and negotiation.

The *People Map* characterizes motivating factors among six major leadership categories and identifies strengths and weaknesses and quality-of-life needs. Like the MBTI the People Map is relatively simple to apply remotely, uses very few questions, requires no special training, and has a fast turnaround time.

The *Berkman* test is the best instrument for predicting negative response behaviors. It has been very popular for negotiating team analysis for several years. It can also be used to reverse-engineer observed stress behaviors to determine specific triggers. This can then be applied to tweak overall strategies to increase these stresses, putting an individual or opposing team at a greater disadvantage.

The *Team Management Index* measures stylistic preferences and matches them against eight major management tasks. It evaluates role preferences and learning styles. This is a preferred method for evaluating the strengths and weaknesses of executive-level teams for war gaming, mergers and acquisitions, and red cell exercises.

The *Attentional and Interpersonal Style* (TAIS) inventory is a 144-item self-report questionnaire that measures twenty concentration skills and personal and interpersonal attributes. Those specific skills and characteristics are the building blocks on which more complex human behaviors depend. TAIS is widely used in selecting Olympic athletes and in the Special Operations Forces (SOF) community.

Executive Decision Style (EDS) identifies key decision-making processes—essentially how a decision maker evaluates alternative solutions to a problem and why he or she rejects some. It is the best instrument for understanding a decision maker's behavior.

Notes

Introduction

1. Anderson, S. "In Defense of Distraction." *New York Magazine*, May 17, 2009. http://nymag.com/news/features/56793/.

2. Toffler, A., and Toffler, H. *War and Anti-War*. New York: Little, Brown, 1993.

Chapter One

1. Watson, J., and Crick, F. "Molecular Structure of Nucleic Acids: A Structure for Deoxyribose Nucleic Acid." *Nature*, 1953, *171*, 737–738.

2. Zweig, J. "Is Your Investing Personality in Your DNA?" *Wall Street Journal*, Apr. 4, 2009, p. B1.

Chapter Two

1. Deming, W. E. *Out of the Crisis*. Cambridge, Mass.: MIT Press, 1986.

2. Chambers, I. "Teachings from Dr. Deming Apropos for Today." Munro & Associates Case Study. http://www.leandesign.com/pdf/Teachings_of_Deming_Today.pdf.

3. Deming, pp. 23–24.

4. Berke, J. "Deaf Sports: As Much Cultural as Athletic." Nov. 11, 2005. http://deafness.about.com/od/sports/a/deafsports.htm.

5. Lewis, M. *The Blind Side: Evolution of a Game*. New York: Norton, 2006.

6. Futterman, M. "Behind the NFL's Touchdown Binge." *Wall Street Journal*, Sept. 9, 2009.

7. Baden-Powell, R. *Scouting for Boys*. London: Horace Cox Publishing, 1908.

8. Deming, p. x.

Chapter Three

1. Dell'Amore, C. "Robot Fish to Detect Water Pollution." *National Geographic News*, Mar. 20, 2009. http://news.nationalgeographic.com/news/2009/03/090320-robot-fish-video.html.

2. Smith, E. "As CDs Decline, Walmart Spins Its Strategy." *Wall Street Journal*, June 9, 2008, p. B1.

Chapter Four

1. Groopman, J. *How Doctors Think*. Boston: Houghton Mifflin, 2007, p. 152.

Chapter Five

1. Hill, J. *Tips and Tales from the Booth: Avoiding Trade Show Mistakes*. New York: Legwork Team Publishing, 2008.

2. Hill, J. "From the March 2007 Exhibitor Magazine." Cited from *Exhibitor Magazine*, Mar. 2007.

3. National Counterintelligence Executive. *Annual Report to Congress on Economic Espionage*. Washington, D.C.: Government Printing Office, 2004.

4. Sorkin, A. R., and Kouwe, Z. "Sirius XM Prepares for Possible Bankruptcy." *New York Times*, Feb. 10, 2009, http://www.nytimes.com/2009/02/11/technology/companies/11radio.html?ref=technology.

Chapter Six

1. Detman, G. "Missouri Family Photo Becomes Ad in Czech Republic." *First Coast News*, June 12, 2009, http://www.firstcoastnews.com/news/spotlight/news-article.aspx?storyid=139758.

2. Boyd, J. "Destruction and Creation." Sept. 3, 1976. This was an essay that accompanied a several-hundred-slide briefing, "Discourse on Winning and Losing," that Boyd frequently gave inside the Pentagon and has been widely disseminated since his death.

3. "Entrepreneurs: Going Bananas over Bic." *Time*, Dec. 18, 1972.

4. Brown, A. C. *Bodyguard of Lies*. Guilford, Conn.: Lyons Press, 2001.

Chapter Seven

1. Weber, M. "Profiling for Leadership Analysis." *Competitive Intelligence Magazine,* July 2004, pp. 6–13.

2. Post, J. *The Psychological Assessment of Political Leaders.* Ann Arbor: University of Michigan Press, 2003.

3. Ibid.

4. Weber.

Chapter Eight

1. Needleman, S. "Negotiating the Freelance Economy." *Wall Street Journal,* May 6, 2009, p. D1.

2. Knight, V. E. "Subcontracting to Snare Stimulus Dollars." *Wall Street Journal,* Sept. 3, 2009.

3. Becker, G. "Nobel Lecture: The Economic Way of Looking at Behavior." *Journal of Political Economy,* 1990, *101*(3), 385–386.

4. Machan, D. "The New Information Goldmine." *Wall Street Journal,* Aug. 19, 2009.

Chapter Nine

1. Dunbar, R. *Grooming, Gossip, and the Evolution of Language.* Cambridge, Mass.: Harvard University Press, 1997.

2. "The Size of Social Networks: Primates on Facebook," *Economist,* Feb. 26, 2009.

3. Ibid.

4. Osinga, F.P.B. *Science, Strategy and War.* New York: Routledge, 2007.

5. Anonymous. *Primary Colors.* New York: Grand Central Publishing, 1996. Foster, D. W. *Author Unknown.* New York: Holt, 2000.

6. Martin, A. "Whole Foods Executive Used Alias." *New York Times,* July 12, 2007. http://www.nytimes.com/2007/07/12/business/12foods.html.

7. Swisher, K. "From the Desk of Yahoo President Sue Decker." May 19, 2009. http://kara.allthingsd.com/20090519/from-the-desk-of-former-yahoo-president-sue-decker/.

8. Karnitschnig, M. "Yahoo, Microsoft, and the Ties That Bind." *Wall Street Journal,* May 23, 2008, p. C1.

9. Packzkowski, J. "Yahoo CEO Carol Bartz: We're a Different Company Than Google." D7—All Things Digital Conference June 4, 2009. http://d7.allthingsd.com/media/.

10. Peers, M. "No Yahoo for Tech Company's New Chief." *Wall Street Journal,* Jan. 14, 2009, p. C14.

11. Swisher.

12. D7—All Things Digital Conference, June 4, 2009. Interview (video). http://d7.allthingsd.com/media/.

13. Weisenthal, J. "Yahoo's Bartz Still Not Interested in Microsoft Deal, Trashes Bing." June 3, 2009. http://www.businessinsider.com/yahoos -bartz-says-no-to-microsoft-deal-trashes-bing-2009-6.

14. "Yahoo CEO: Merger with Microsoft Won't Get Past DOJ." *Marketwatch,* June 3, 2009. http://www.marketwatch.com/story/yahoo-ceo-merger -with-microsoft-wont-get-by-doj.

15. Morrison, S. "Yahoo CEO Keeps Microsoft Deal Door Open, Shuts Out AOL." *Wall Street Journal,* June 8, 2009.

Chapter Ten

1. Vascellaro, J. E. "Google Searches for Ways to Keep Big Ideas at Home." *Wall Street Journal,* June 18, 2009, p. B1.

2. Ibid.

3. Bora, M. "Jabil Digs In on Defense." *St. Petersburg Times,* Mar. 10, 2008, p. D1.

4. Lublin, J. "Bringing a New Business into Fold." *Wall Street Journal,* Apr. 20, 2009.

5. Corel, S. "My Brain, Your Brawn." *Wall Street Journal,* Oct. 13, 2008, p. R12.

6. Lublin, J. "A CEO's Recipe for New Ideas." *Wall Street Journal,* Sept. 2, 2008.

Chapter Eleven

1. Smith, E. "Ticket Wars Heat Up." *Wall Street Journal,* Sept. 11, 2008, p. B8.

2. Ibid.

3. Groopman, J. *How Doctors Think.* Boston: Houghton Mifflin, 2007, p. 152.

4. Lunsford, J. L. "GE Takes On Jet-Engine Rival." *Wall Street Journal,* July 3, 2008, p. B2.

5. Ibid.

6. Kirkwood, C. W. *Strategic Decision Making.* Belmont, Calif.: Wadsworth, 1997.

7. Ibid.

8. Caulfield, B. "Dell Could Hit Acquisition Trail." *Forbes,* May 28, 2008.

Chapter Twelve

1. Gladwell, M. "How David Beats Goliath." *New Yorker,* May 11, 2009. All other references to this team and its coach come from this article.

2. Jablonsky, S., and Barsky, N. *The Manager's Guide to Financial Statement Analysis.* Hoboken, N.J.: Wiley, 2001.

3. Ibid.

4. Opdyke, J. D., and Lobb, A. "MIA Analysts Give Companies Worries." *Wall Street Journal,* May 26, 2009.

5. Ibid.

6. Gladwell, M. "The Formula." *New Yorker,* Jan. 8, 2007. http://www.newyorker.com/reporting/2007/01/08/070108fa_fact.

7. Ibid.

8. Friedman, T. *The Lexus and the Olive Tree.* New York: Anchor Books, 2002.

9. Grove, A. *Only the Paranoid Survive.* New York: Doubleday, 1996.

10. Herring, J. P. "World Class Intelligence Programs." *Competitive Intelligence Magazine,* 2006, 9(3), 20–25. http://www.academyci.com/Resource-Center/JH060601.pdf.

11. Osinga, F.P.B. *Science, Strategy and War.* New York: Routledge, 2007.

12. Kleindorfer, P., Kunreuther, H., and Schoemaker, P. *Decision Sciences: An Integrative Perspective.* Cambridge: Cambridge University Press, 1993, p. 67.

Epilogue

1. "Killebrew: Developing Narrative Crucial to Winning Wars." *C4ISR Journal,* Jan. 4, 2008, p. 8.

Acknowledgments

"No man is an island." John Donne's oft-quoted closing phrase has endured for nearly four centuries. More remarkable was his opening: "All mankind is of one author, and is one volume; when one man dies, one chapter is not torn out of the book, but translated into a better language; and every chapter must be so translated."

This book is far from the work of one man. Its genesis was a simple backyard conversation with my friend and neighbor Eric Vance, then a free safety for the Tampa Bay Buccaneers, who first suggested that a book like this might even be possible. The idea germinated in the back of my mind, finally taking root a decade later.

That seedling found a willing gardener in literary agent extraordinaire Bob Diforio, a former president/publisher of New American Library. He liked it and tended it, and he found just the right editor to champion it.

Susan Williams embraced and encouraged me at a time when it could easily be argued that wise men (and women) should fear to tread. Fearless in attitude and tireless in patience, she coached, counseled, and cajoled in all the right ways. Any accolades are clearly hers. Any inaccuracies or omissions are entirely mine.

I also thank my principal reviewer, collaborator, and muse: my wife, Cathy. She is the first to see my hieroglyphic prose and gently guides me back when my storyline ship sails a bit too far from shore—a lighthouse of sanity to a gratefully insane writer.

The Author

T. J. WATERS has twenty years of private sector and government service experience in research, strategy, and intelligence. He is currently a senior analyst (contractor) adapting business intelligence methods to irregular warfare for the Department of Defense. He previously worked in counter-intelligence for U.S. Central Command and as an intelligence officer for the Central Intelligence Agency. Prior to his government service, he was vice president for an intelligence consulting firm serving Fortune 500 corporations, law firms, and military intelligence units. He held several positions in corporate America, including with BASF, Lexis Nexis, and Celotex Corporation.

Waters has an M.B.A. from Wake Forest University and a B.A. from the University of Tennessee at Chattanooga. For the past four years, he has been an adjunct professor in the intelligence management and analysis program of Eckerd College in St. Petersburg, Florida.

He has been interviewed by the *New York Law Journal,* the *Wall Street Journal,* and *Government Executive Magazine.* He has published over twenty articles on intelligence and strategy, and his memoir, *Class 11: Inside the CIA's First Post 9/11 Spy Class,* was optioned for television by ABC.

He currently serves on the board of directors for the Ronald McDonald House Charities of Tampa Bay and volunteers at the STARTEC Technology Enterprise Center in Largo, Florida.

Index

Page reference followed by *fig* indicates an illustrated figure.